THE CELTIC SPIRIT AND LITERATURE

Grace Clunie & Tess Maginess

The
Celtic Spirit
and Literature

the columba press

First published in 2015 by

the columba press

55A Spruce Avenue,
Stillorgan Industrial Park,
Blackrock, Co. Dublin

Cover design by Helene Pertl / The Columba Press
Origination by The Columba Press
Printed by ScandBook AB, Sweden

ISBN 978 1 78218 2375

We dedicate this book to the memory of our mothers, Ella Hutchinson, for sharing her gifts of wisdom and creativity, and Bridget Hurson, for her courage and vision; to our spouses, Bruce and Ian, for their faith and grace and to the memory of Terry Maginess, Iona voyager, who, in his own inimitable way, brought us together.

Foreword

To read this book is to undertake a journey, as we are led in the following pages across a wide and fertile territory, the 'rough field' of Celtic literature in all of its expressions. So much of Irish life was governed, in the period before writing, by light and shade and the journey of the sun across the sky, as a visit to Newgrange will attest, but the journey metaphor is more than apt for a book that surveys the literature of Ireland. We have described, in all senses, many journeys in our words down the ages: there are outward *immrama* and forays across uncharted lands and seas with the attendant encounters with the exotic and the fantastic. We read of the Fianna marauding across heath and moor as they follow their champion-hounds in pursuit of their quarry; there are visitations from and to the realm of the Sidhe, and the natural world that surrounds us – on our journey we can almost hear the song of the blackbird as it travels over Belfast Lough, while Aogán Ó Rathaille and others, as they travel on dark eighteenth-century roads, dramatically and evocatively describe mystical encounters with the beautiful fairy-entity who perhaps, for them, represents the Gaelic essence of Ireland.

These 'journeys' I have spoken of thus far have taken place within the great body of works in the Gaelic language, which is of immense significance to European culture, as it is its oldest vernacular literature. To an extent, that literary culture, as travellers through this book will learn, influenced the tradition of English writing which came to find a uniquely valuable expression in Ireland – this contact which brought about the expression of a new set of journeys, as the expression of each literary culture was enriched and enlivened by the multivalent modes of interaction that followed. W. B. Yeats perhaps exemplifies best the Anglo-Irish writer who journeyed to discover a rich seam of inspiration within the 'waters and the wild' of the folklore of rural Ireland – as he sought refuge, it has been suggested, from the increasingly utilitarian culture of the period in which he found himself. We should not, however, read this contact as a one-way street or as some act of harvesting; the Irish literary tradition also gained from contact with literary cultures from across the water, as this book convincingly shows.

Throughout the long and varied history of literary production in Ireland, one constant has remained: the creative spirit that resides strongly in a resilient and enduring caste among us, which has been varyingly known through the ages as *saoi* (Druid), *file*, bard (in either language!), poet, rhymer, writer, singer – and the list goes on. The dominant characteristic of these personae is that they have been, and are, gatekeepers who stand at the portal between our reality and our imagination; they can deftly express for us what we can only glimpse – they can, with their acuity of thought, present to us what without them we can only grasp at. In the later period, as cultural and political bifurcation became entrenched, we must add translators to that list, as there are plenty among their number who have evinced the same creative impact as they build bridges across the linguistic divide, and who, in so doing, allow original works to strut forth anew in their new clothes, parading themselves in front of a new audience. Without these acts of translation, a wealth of literary culture would have remained obscure, and while the relationship between Irish and English will always have its fault lines, their acquaintance is now surely on a firmer footing, and the transaction of translation has had much to do with that.

The huge value of the links that literature, and its practitioners, forge for us with our land and culture, with ourselves, are what strike me most when reading this book and it is that which has made me keen to revisit and reread works, as well as inspired to explore further the territory mapped here. Not to engage with our literature, with how we have expressed, in the past and in the present, our attitude to our existence, is to cut ourselves off from ways of feeling at home and to allow a cultural amnesia to take hold. In the hands of the present authors, any such amnesia will not stand long, as they skilfully interpret the myriad forms of expression that have emanated from our Celtic Spirit. The Open Learning Programme at Queen's has performed a huge service to many individuals but also to our society generally as it seeks to deepen and enrich perspectives and understandings of its students. The present work is a fitting example of such a contribution, and to those who follow the course steered by these following pages, I wish a good journey.

DR CHARLES DILLON
Irish and Celtic Studies, Queen's University Belfast

Acknowledgements

We wish to thank the very many people who helped us in making this book: Rita Duffy for the special series of drawings she made for this book; Ian Maginess for the photographs; Trinity College Library for kind permission to reproduce the image of the Virgin Mary and Child from the *Book of Kells*; The Nerve Centre, Derry, for kind permission to reproduce the logo for the Digital Book of Kells; St Patrick's Cathedral Chapter, Armagh, for kind permission to photograph The Tandragee Man; Mrs Julia Maginess for loaning us her copy of *Joyful Pilgrimage*; Rev. Canon Jonathan Barry for kind permission to reproduce a photograph and a drawing from *Joyful Pilgrimage*; Norma Menabney, Librarian, Queen's University Belfast for her unstinting help with referencing; to Patrick, Helene and all at The Columba Press for all their patience and guidance. The inevitable sins of commission and omission in this book must be laid at our own threshold and forgiveness sought.

Table of Contents

List of Illustrations

Page 107   COLUMBA VOYAGE TO IONA
          The booklet, *A Joyful Pilgrimage*, was kindly loaned to us
          by Julia Maginess, widow of Terence Maginess, who was
          one of the crew members. The photograph is by kind
          permission of Canon Jonathan Barry, who, with his father,
          Canon John Barry, was a member of the crew. The
          photograph has been reproduced by Ian Maginess, son of
          Terence.

Page 120   DROMBEG STONE CIRCLE
          Office of Public Works. Photograph by Ian Maginess.

Page 151   SWEENEY
          Drawing by Rita Duffy.

Page 163   NESTING SWAN
          Photograph by Ian Maginess.

Page 200   THE POETS' GLEN, PLAQUE TO ART MAC CUMHAIGH
          Photograph by Ian Maginess.

Page 204   NEW FORMS
          Drawing by Rita Duffy.

Page 210   DRISHANE HOUSE, CASTLETOWNSHEND, CO. CORK
          By kind permission of Tom and Jane Somerville. Edith
          Somerville was the great-aunt of Tom Somerville, the
          present owner. Photograph by Ian Maginess.

Page 228   THE LAKE ISLE OF INNISFREE
          Photograph by Ian Maginess.

Page 250   BRONZE STATUE OF SWEENEY
          Sculpture by Holger C. Lönze, with kind permission of
          the artist. Photograph by Ian Maginess.

Page 256   CELTIC SPIRIT IN THE TWENTIETH CENTURY
          Drawing by Rita Duffy.

Page 266   COLMCILLE DIGITAL, NERVE CENTRE
          Reproduced by kind permission of the Nerve Centre,
          Derry.

Introduction
Grace Clunie and Tess Maginess

This book arose from a series of lectures we developed on the Celtic Spirit and Literature for Queen's University's Continuing Education Open Learning Programme. The students in the programme are mature learners and the aim of the lectures was not to offer a highly academic, detailed study of every aspect of so massive a subject, but rather to provide a set of glimpses into the Celtic world and its literature. We tried to use an approach that was accessible and encouraged participants to ask questions and to see how the Celtic Spirit and literature might resonate with them in today's world. We are only too conscious of the very many scholarly studies of all things Celtic and we are indebted to the great authorities in the field. Our own modest work is, we can only hope, a small, very personal response to what the Celtic Spirit and literature means to us and could mean to the interested reader who is not approaching the topic as an academic. In this way we hope that the book may gain a broader readership for this complex and rich subject.

We have chosen to focus mainly upon the relationship between the Celtic Spirit and literature. We do so not because that spirit does not manifest itself in a myriad of other creative forms, but because it seemed to us that an examination of the literature across many different periods right up to the present day was especially illuminating in enabling the tenacity of the Celtic Spirit to be apprehended in a very tangible way. And, while we are aware of the vast scholarship on matters Celtic far beyond Ireland, we have restricted our study to a focus on Ireland.

But what do we mean by the Celtic Spirit? What is the essence of the Celtic Spirit? For us, qualities such as a deep connection with nature, and with otherworlds, which seem to be only across the threshold of the world of nature; an appreciation of the other, for they who are different and for difference and otherness in ourselves, and thus an hospitable and generous welcome for the stranger. That is, in every sense, quite a compact. We are suggesting that the Celtic Spirit is intimately in sympathy with and responsive to nature in the physical sense, but at the same time, is open to the immanence of nature, its sacral or metaphysical dimension. So, the Celtic Spirit is less about a hierarchical relationship between nature and supernature – represented, for example, in the Elizabethan concept of the Great Chain of Being (Tillyard, 1960) – but rather about a kind of contiguity. There appears to be a sort of neighbourly relationship between the physical, natural world and the otherworld of the spiritual, whether it be pagan or Christian, and between the pagan and the Christian. But, at the same time, there is a juxtapositional relationship enacted also; for, as we learn, for example, from immram literature, the Celts voyaged out to terra incognita, to places and spaces that were distinctly other, that were vastly different from their native Doric. These voyages of discovery were both physical and spiritual, as they are in all great literatures. So this sets up a different sort of relationship; one that is not neighbourly, the crossing of a threshold that is not natural or organic, but an entry into, a being in, a world that is alien and not infrequently hostile. It was once thought that the Celts themselves came to Ireland from very far away, though some recent scholarship suggests that Celtic civilisation may have spread from the insular Celtic Nations to the Continent (Cunliffe and Koch, 2012). But perhaps it may be too that they supplanted a people who were already here. Or, perhaps, it is only in more recent centuries that we have developed the concept of 'us' and 'them', the idea that the relationship between peoples must be oppositional and based on the politics of conquest and defence.

Inevitably, our thinking is conditioned by our own historical time.

What seems to be universal is that in the nexus of voyaging what is familiar, what is known, is challenged, tested. In later eras, when both the concept of the self and ideas of nations have been developed, we find the Celtic Spirit finds itself responding not just to self-imposed exiles, voyages into strange lands, but, over the centuries also to successive waves of invasion beneath which it becomes, at times, submerged. If Ireland is the most mapped country in Europe, perhaps it might lay claim, as a logical cause, to being the most invaded. But, of course, that too depends upon your point of view. 'Invaded' is a very emotive word; some would say, 'settled'. At any rate, our history on this island seems to suggest a complex engagement between natives and settlers, planters and Gaels, which involves on the one hand a recognition of neighbourliness, of how smooth and well worn the threshold is between self and other, one community and another, one religion and another, one political dream and another, this world and the otherworld, or some of the above. And at the same time, we have, again and again dramatised a gallant or frigid polar opposition between one culture and another, one way of being and another; a fight to the death. Within such a state, a word like 'Celtic' has been used and abused, hurled for and against. There is no end to its appropriation from every quarter. But then, there is also no end to its resilience and variety, either. For, while we speak of the Celtic Spirit as an essence, we are only too well aware that an essence is both organically experienced and also the result of a chemical, artificial process (art, religion, culture). It is not for us, in this postmodern, relativised world to plead for some instantly recognisable, absolute markers of a natural or authentic Celtic Spirit. Rather, each age redefines, recycles the Celtic Spirit through the art forms that best reflect or critique the values of that age: Elizabethan, Classical, Romantic, Modernist and Post-modernist.

It is this sense of connection with the past, balanced with the imperative that we must live in and for our own time, that is perhaps one of the most salient attractions of the Celtic Spirit. Perhaps a part of the essence of the Celtic Spirit is in the term 'Gael' itself, said to derive from the Brittonic word which means 'wild'. And the connotations of this word, 'wild', as we all know, are often negative and disapproving – we may call to mind the racist stereotype of the 'wild Irish'; the 'roarin' boy', the fighting Paddy, the figure of comedic ridicule with his 'bulls' and absurdities. We hope to demonstrate in this book that the 'wild' Celtic Spirit is as complex as it is sophisticated and is there for all to enjoy, learn from and contribute to.

There is an aspect of human nature – represented in the culture and colourful traditions of the ancient Celtic world – which yearns for freedom. It provokes a deep appreciation of the complexities of self and other, an imaginative, creative response to life and a deep connectedness with the earth itself, with the local place, with otherworlds. Despite dispiriting evidence to the contrary, this facet of our being is fundamental to our meaning as individuals and societies. That 'wildness', that joy in our immense capacity to care, to see sacredness, to understand ourselves as part of a much greater physical and even metaphysical universe, is not simply a Celtic 'preserve'. This perspective has deep resonances with many of the world's 'indigenous' spiritualities in the sense of simple, sustainable and interconnected ways of living on the earth and a respectful approach to the sacredness of the rest of nature and to understanding that he or she who is other is also part of the self.

From a Hindu perspective, it is the understanding that all of life is part of the Brahman, the 'Great Life', and within that 'Family of Being' we celebrate our place on the earth. So Celtic spirituality brings to life a way of living that is deeply connected to the natural rhythms of the earth and practices such as praying at holy wells and mountain pilgrimages recall the animistic perspectives of ancient indigenous cultures. Ultimately, the Celtic Spirit – as expressed within Celtic spirituality – is an experience of 'sacred presence' at the heart of life.

So, for example, Noel Dermot O'Donohue, in his book *The Mountain Behind the Mountain: Aspects of the Celtic Tradition*, speaks of this awareness of 'Presence' – not as some holy ideal, but rather as a celebration of the miracle in the ordinary:

It is a very ordinary, very physical, very material mountain, a place of sheep and kine, of peat and of streams that one might fish in or bathe in on a summer's day. It is an elemental mountain of water and fire, of sun and moon and wind and rain. What makes it special … is that it is a place of Presence and a place of presences. Only those who can perceive this in its ordinariness can encounter the mountain behind the mountain (O'Donohue, 1993, p. 30).

Over the centuries, the Celtic Spirit recycled itself, not in a narrow and prescribed fashion, but, as it began, open to the influence of the other; the early Celts wrought their motifs recalling patterns or contemporaneously open to civilisations thousands of miles away. Celtic Christianity was distinctive in its 'wild' allegiance to pagan classical frames of reference, when such allusions were not considered acceptable by Continental Christianity which had become increasingly rigorously theological and wary of anything that might seem even slightly heretical. After the Reformation, Church of Ireland clerics, members of the Anglo-Irish Establishment, found inspiration in the Celtic Spirit, making a journey, an immram, that was, also, a little wild – though for some not wild enough. What did 'other' mean? What did 'self' mean for these voyagers to the heart of darkness and lightness? As we enter the Celtic Twilight or Renaissance, there are, as we will see, even in a time of florescence for the Celtic Spirit, many differing, even contending definitions of what it was. The journey to the past, the journey between cultures was as hazardous as it was inspiring. After Partition we see yet more versions of the Celtic Spirit – some of them consciously mimicking older 'colonial' envisioning, others, mocking and ironic. But as we cross the threshold of the millennium, we find that somehow the Celtic Spirit is still recycling to meet the many questions of our own time. Key aspects of this ancient Celtic Spirit speak powerfully to the questions of our days. Can we reconnect with nature, never mind supernature and the spiritual? Is there such a thing as spirit in our world? How do we define self and other; how do we open our hearts to difference, to otherworlds that often seem invasive, foreign? What are the thresholds we need to cross?

This book links the Celtic Spirit and literature. So what of this Celtic Spirit as it manifests itself in literature? Whatever else may divide writers from this island, in many we find that a conception of the importance of some version of the Celtic Spirit informs not just their thought, but their imaginations. There is that love of place – in the past, a rural space and in more modern urban writers, an affection for the streets or districts of 'home' – and, of course, following on from the ancient Celtic *dinnseanchas*, a sense of the temporal associations of particular places. As time goes on, the palimpsest of what happened in local places becomes increasingly complex, even contentious; places are fought over, won, lost, sometimes imaginatively reclaimed in dynamic and surprising ways. And there is, in relation to place, also, a not infrequent tendency towards transcendence – a sensitivity, a tuning in to the metaphysical, to that otherworld just beyond the threshold of the real, the material – though always counterbalanced with a carefully observed, precise, verisimilitude. Patrick Kavanagh's epic kingdom is ironically and reverently named as the townland of Shancoduff, transfigured and not. Van Morrison's blues don't just roll down any city street, but down Royal Avenue – with all the historical resonances and claims that street name evokes. Counterpointing the love of place is the impetus for journeying out – whether it be the spiritual voyage of Brendan, the 'silence, exile and cunning' of young Stephen Dedalus or the imaginative explorations of 'otherworlds' in Colum McCann. The journey out, given our history, has remained a major motif. But what bendings and curvings and spirallings does that journey infer? Stephen Dedalus in James Joyce's *A Portrait of the Artist as a Young Man* understandably wishes to fly the nets of the nightmare of history. The nightmare is, of course, endless and fruitless repetition. But, as Joyce knew, when he got to *Ulysses*, repetition could have some creative possibilities.

If you stand half way up Croagh Patrick you can look down upon the sea and see, quite miraculously, that the sand forms itself in spirals. So natural and organic a pattern may have influenced the makers of early Celtic art. The natural spiral pattern of the sand produces its own drama. But, how can this elemental, organic shape relate to the nightmare of our history and how we might 'do' the present, never mind the future? Spirals betoken repetition as well as a curved rather than dialectic or oppositional view of life and of history. This provokes the suggestion that ideas can recycle in many forms, not excluding forms that are ironic or parodic.

Surely it is that it is only in the late twentieth century that an unbearable lightness of being has come to be – at least in certain parts of the island. Freed from the 'nightmare of history', the Celtic Spirit can dance and sing. There has been no scarcity of comic spirit, a legacy too of a long history of literary manifestations, prone, it must be said, to a 'wild' satiric turn, from Merriman to Swift to Sheridan to Wilde to Flann O'Brien and Samuel Beckett to Paul Muldoon. And, it must be said, there has been also a deal of dancing and singing; from *sean nós* to celtic rock and world music, from dream maidens to Riverdance and beyond. The remarkable thing is the tenacity of the Celtic Spirit. So, Seamus Heaney, in his last collection, *Human Chain*, reruns, recycles, enacts his own *recurscis* (Heaney, 2013) and Paul Muldoon sets his elegy to Heaney among the medieval monks of Northumbria (Muldoon, 2015).

But what does this unbearable lightness of being signify for the Celtic Spirit? As if, as always, with one foot in the local place and the contemporary, and the other deftly pointing into otherworlds, that spirit seems to hold fealty to a set of values that have their genesis in a conception of the function of the poet as apostolic, even sacral. By this we do not mean to imply that Irish writers are given to unquestioning allegiance to particular church institutions; indeed it might be fairly said that a number of them have been anti-clerical. Rather, there is we would argue a strong imperative among writers to celebrate or discover anew what seems in every era to be a hidden island. That may be Ireland; it may be some other island, England, France, Jamaica, America. And, of course, as time goes by, down through the long crescendo of the centuries, there is a sense of inevitable repetition, of an impulse to keep on *writing* the original island, and maybe also *righting* it. That the rebalancing, the righting, has had many contradictory and contesting agendas, we can hardly doubt.

So, we may say, that one aspect of the Celtic Spirit in literature is also about the drama of oppositions, contending playfully and fiercely with a drama of how, also, people contain these oppositions within *themselves*. As we will see, the Celtic Spirit speaks of the sort of hospitality which is about openness of heart, welcome and acceptance – not only to the other we encounter in the strangers we meet, but to the shadow-side of our own souls too. One of the great motifs in Celtic literature is the 'threshold', a powerful symbol of our potential for crossing over into new worlds of the imagination and of understanding how we ourselves may belong to one world and yet, also, to more than one cultural and political world. That 'threshold spirit' could shape a nuanced and imaginative attitude to ourselves, to others, to the earth, to what might be immanent, transfiguring, lit. That is a tough wildness.

CLONFERT CATHEDRAL DOOR

Thresholds: doors into the dark and into the light.

The Celtic Spirit embodies contention, as well as harmony; its arts recognise the repeating and cyclical patterns of history, wherein it appears that progress, enlightenment and justice are always subject to the tight vice of selfishness and cruelty. But these arts are our Resistance, because they are the resilience of the 'wild'; the enactment of imaginative freedom when freedom is constrained, as it always is. This book tells its own tale of how the Celtic Spirit has survived. In the finish up, it is only our local take on what we know to be a universal kind of spirit. But every universal spirit has, too, 'a local habitation and a name' to borrow from Shakespeare's *A Midsummer Night's Dream*.

So, in the twenty-first century we have the treasure of an ancient wisdom to guide us, expressed through writers and poets, artists and musicians, storytellers and teachers of spiritual wisdom down through the centuries. And we have too, the many interpretations of the Celtic Spirit – confirming and also challenging ancient wisdom, but reaffirming it for each time.

The book is divided into two broad sections. The first seven chapters set the context, offering a perspective on a range of facets of the Celtic Spirit. The next five chapters focus on the representation of the Celtic Spirit through the literature produced over many hundreds of years, right up to the present day.

Part One
In Chapter One: The Celtic Quest, we begin with a quest – a quest for identity – through history, language and archaeology. Who were/are the Celts? What is the Celtic Spirit? Where did this Celtic Spirit come from? Is there really such a phenomenon as 'The Celtic Spirit' – or is it a romantic vision invented in the nineteenth century in a 'Celtic Renaissance'? It is true to say

that much of our contemporary perspectives on what 'Celtic' means remain the subject of scholarly controversy in terms of an agreed historical Celtic identity. Traditionally, evidence for all things 'Celtic' is offered by ancient classical authors, linguistic scholarship and archaeology – yet the very fact that there are so many and such diverse fields of study involved makes the quest more complex. Keeping this reservation in mind, Chapter One will attempt a very brief overview of some of the contemporary scholarship about Celtic identity, past and present. We will trace the development of the Celtic Spirit through the many turmoils of history, the upheavals of invasion, rebellion and plantation, examining how the Celtic Spirit redefined itself across the eras.

In Chapter Two: The Celtic Spirit and Nature, we will focus on the importance of nature for the Celtic psyche, showing how, for the Celts, nature was sacral, the source of energy. Plants, animals, the seasons are all lovingly observed and appreciated for their own sake in an ecological outlook which does not take man to be the most important force. And nature, in the Celtic world, often has an extra dimension; the Celtic belief in an immanent nature, infused with the sometimes beneficent and sometimes hostile influence of the gods offers a richly metaphysical connectivity. This transcendent dimension enabled the Celts to conceive of an otherworld beyond their own, not always remotely distant, but on the threshold of the natural world. With the coming of Christianity, this sense of an immanent nature, blessed with the presence of God, was to be preserved. The similarity between the Celtic concept of nature and that of other ancient cultures will also be discussed. And we will ask what can the rich and dynamic Celtic attitude to nature teach us in the modern day?

Chapter Three: Hospitality and Heroes concentrates on the centrality of hospitality for the Celtic Spirit, especially in terms of its specific significance within a heroic warrior culture. But, as will suggest, hospitality and openness to others can still be a vital aspect of our way of being. And we will look at how, in later times, the concept of the heroic journey evolved, and how we too can enter upon our own voyage of self-discovery.

Chapter Four: Art and Creative Living offers a discussion of Celtic art and how it related to the sacral, and how, in our time, we may gain inspiration from the Celts for a way of living that is creative, in tune with nature and respectful of it. Many wonderful books have already been produced on the subject of Celtic art (Déchelette, 1913; Jacobsthal, 1944; Megaw and Megaw, 2001); what we would like to do is concentrate on how Celtic art and the manner of living of the Celts were connected. The chapter will explore the relationships between Celtic art, the Celtic calendar and Celtic festivals before going on to talk about specific examples of Celtic art. It will then move on to a discussion about how, in our time, we can espouse the principles and practices of creative living.

All great cultures encompass stories about journeys, sometimes physical, embodying the importance to the human spirit of discovering new worlds, of not limiting our horizons; and often, also, metaphorical journeys of the spirit, of the soul. So, in Chapter Five: The Celtic Spirit and Journey, we will follow the Celts in their various kinds of journey, and how difficult it was for a people with such a strong attachment to kin and to local place to leave it for the unknown world beyond. And we will reflect on what journey might mean for us in our time.

In Chapter Six: The Celtic Spirit and the Otherworld, we will explore how the Celts regarded the threshold between this life and the next and how, before and after Christianity, death was not regarded as an annihilation, but rather a natural passage, indeed, a homecoming.

Part Two

In Chapter Seven: Early Literature: Epic Imaginings, we will look more closely at the literary representation of the Celtic heroic culture, gaining an insight into the epic sensibility of the Celts, commencing with a closer look at the foundational creation myth poem, 'The Song of Amergin' (Amorgen). We will then move on to consider the impact of the coming of Christianity, specifically in terms of how this affected the kind of literature that was possible. And we will look at the early jewels of this new hybrid literature: early Irish poetry.

In Chapter Eight: Tales of this World and the Otherworld, we will look at how prose developed, concentrating especially on the compilation of tales into what are now known as cycles. In this chapter we will take a look also at voyage literature, echoing the earlier themes of the journey and the otherworld.

This book assays a broad historical perspective in arguing that the Celtic Spirit has survived a great many changes in the political and social nexus. In Chapter Nine: After the Normans: The Great Change, we will chart the impact of what was known as the 'Great Change' – the profound shift from the old Gaelic order to a new English order. We will look at how different poets from the old order responded to the change in language, in culture, in social and economic position. We will also look at the emergence of writing in English by the so-called Anglo-Irish writers like Swift and Oliver Goldsmith.

In Chapter Ten: The Celtic Spirit: New Forms, we will explore how the Celtic Spirit found new forms in the nineteenth century, through the 'invention' of new genres like the Big House novel and through the scholarly work of the Antiquarians who 'rediscovered' manuscripts and songs from the older Gaelic world. The Antiquarians created a new interest, a new fashion even, for the Celtic, which chimed with a European preoccupation with the 'primitive' and the 'exotic'. Nationalism was also on the rise across Europe and we will look at how some writers channelled their version of the Celtic Spirit into a more overtly political campaign. We will conclude by discussing the florescence of new configurations of the Celtic in the work of a range of writers from the so-called Celtic Revival, and how their work both related to and disconnected from the politics of the time.

CELTIC SPIRITUALITY LOGO
The enduring Celtic Spirit:
Logo for the Centre for Celtic Spirituality, Navan Centre, Armagh.

In the twentieth century one might have expected to bid adieu to the Celtic Spirit. But, in literature it has survived in all sorts of interesting and surprising ways. So, in Chapter Eleven: Celtic Spirit in the Twentieth Century, we will look at the work of writers like Joyce, Beckett and O'Brien and see how they critique the Celtic Spirit at times, presenting it through a comic and ironic lens. And we will discuss other writers like Kavanagh, who somehow managed to preserve the mystical aspects of the Celtic Spirit, that immanence of nature we spoke of earlier. We will conclude the chapter with reference to some contemporary writers like Heaney and Muldoon who have, in our day, found new inspiration through a return, a *recrusis*, to the subjects and figures of the Celtic past, and, in certain respects, to some of its literary forms.

In the twentieth century the Celtic Spirit lives on through a range of voices; sometimes contradictory, sometimes contentious, sometimes ironic, sometimes critical and sometimes shaped by returns and rewritings, both tender and inspiring. In a book of this size, we cannot possibly hope to offer an exhaustive survey of the literature from this island over hundreds of years; all we promise is that the reader will forgive our many omissions and will share our joy and appreciation of the sheer richness and complexity of the myriad-minded, multi-voiced Celtic Spirit.

PART ONE

CHAPTER ONE

The Celtic Quest
Grace Clunie

They also invited strangers to their banquets,
And only after the meal do they ask
Who they are
And of what they stand in need.
(Diodorus Siculus, quoted in Ó Duinn, 2000, p. 30)

We begin with a quest – a quest for identity – through history, language and archaeology. Who were/are the Celts? What is the Celtic Spirit? Where did this Celtic Spirit come from? Traditionally, evidence for all things 'Celtic' is offered by ancient classical authors, linguistic scholarship and archaeology – yet the very fact that there are so many and such diverse fields of study involved makes the quest more complex. Keeping this reservation in mind, this chapter will attempt a very brief overview of some of the contemporary scholarship about Celtic identity, past and present.

We begin with the classical sources (Greek and Latin) from the Pre-Roman and Roman era. Six names were used to define the 'Celts', three in Greek (Keltoi, Keltai, Galatai) and three in Latin (Celti, Celtae, Galli). The earliest written references were made by the Greek writers Hecataeus and Herodotus during the sixth and fifth centuries BCE. The writings of Hecataeus of Miletus, the well-travelled geographer, are lost, but others have quoted him. From them we discover that Narbon (Narbonne in southern France) was a Celtic city and trading centre. He also mentions Massalia (Marseilles) and a third city, Nyrax, as a Celtic city, though its location is uncertain. Herodotus mentions a people he calls 'Keltoi' who lived in Iberia and around the source of the Ister (Danube). In addition, Herodotus states that the Danube rose in the land of the Celts, near the city of Pyrene. Cunliffe comments:

> If Pyrene refers to the Pyrenees, then he is probably scrambling together different pieces of information he has learned of the Celts, that the Danube rose in Celtic lands and that the Celts lived near the Pyrenees ... It is not much to go on. At best it suggests that the early Greek geographers had only a vague idea of European geography and were content to lump together most of the Barbarians of Europe, from the Middle Danube to the Atlantic as Celts, while recognising that there were others within this region who were not Celts (Cunliffe, 2003, p. 9).

It is also worth noting that, although the Greeks called them 'Keltoi', Herodotus doesn't say what they called themselves. Originally encountered as trading neighbours with the Greeks and Etruscans, the Celts were a non-literate people, so that they left no written accounts of themselves. Nevertheless, their societies were both sophisticated and skilled in terms of art, religion, warfare, language and social customs.

The Romans also referred to them as 'Gauls' in describing fierce barbarian invaders who, around 390 BCE, sacked Rome, but were driven back to the Po Valley. They were called 'Gallia Cisalpina' ('Gaul this side of the Alps'). Another term is 'Galations', given to Celtic groups who invaded the Balkans and in 279 BCE attacked Delphi, at that time the Greeks' most sacred shrine. The records attest that they were beaten back into the region we now call Turkey, and were the Galations of the New Testament Epistle. It is clear from Livy and others that the Celts were regarded by the Romans as a terrifying and aggressive foes. For example, Livy, Polybius and Pausanias describe the Celts as huge in size (including the women!), strong, violent, fearless, hostile and susceptible to drunkenness. They also write about their strange, inadequate swords and shields, and the raucous din they made when going into battle – reminiscent of Cúchulainn's 'war-warp' in the Ulster Cycle of mythological tales. In addition, we read that they had red or blonde hair, that the men wore gold neck and arm rings, that they were skilled horsemen and that they frequently decapitated their enemies. They used war-chariots and trumpets, loved banqueting, seemed to have no prohibition on forming homosexual attachments and showed unquestioning hospitality to strangers (see the quote from Diodorus Siculus at the beginning of this chapter).

So, from Greek and Latin writers such as Herodotus, Strabo, Plato, Aristotle, Posidonius, Diodorus Siculus and Julius Caesar, it would seem that we ought to know a lot about the identity of the 'Celts' in antiquity. But for several reasons this is not the full picture. For example, although these writers attributed a common identity to these 'Celtic' peoples, we don't know whether they themselves perceived this or not. There is no preserved source that records the criteria by which these peoples were designated 'Celts'/'Galli'. Yet these ancient writers did perceive a difference between themselves and this cultural group they called 'Celt'. So, irrespective of whether they called themselves Celts, it seems they had, broadly speaking, a common identity in culture and language. In addition, the chiefdoms and societies of the pre-Christian world were organised much more loosely than the global conglomerates of the modern world and within them a range of related Celtic languages and dialects were spoken. Therefore, these classical sources offer evidence for Celtic peoples in ancient Europe, though probably in a much looser sense than the ways in which we would speak of ethnic identity today.

The second source of evidence is linguistic – the approach which seeks to classify as 'Celtic' those who speak an identifiably Celtic language. Modern Celtic language studies began with George Buchanan in the sixteenth century, but only really developed with Paul-Yves Pezron and Edward Lhuyd in the early eighteenth century. Edward Lhuyd's *Archaeologica Britannica* of 1707 noted similarities between Welsh, Cornish and Breton – but also stated that they differed from Irish (Lhuyd, 1707). In the nineteenth century, Sir John Rhys built on Lhuyd's work, identifying two families of Celtic languages: Q-Celtic or Goidelic (Irish, Scots Gaelic and Manx) and P-Celtic or Brythonic (Welsh, Breton and Cornish). This distinction is made on the basis of how the QU sound is pronounced or spelled. In Q-Celtic it remains as the hard 'Q' – or later 'K' sound – and in P-Celtic it softens to the 'P' sound, e.g. *Cethir* (Irish for four) and *Pedwar* (Welsh for four). So Irish, Manx and Scots Gaelic are Q-Celtic languages, whereas Breton, Welsh and Cornish are P-Celtic – though contemporary scholars now say that this is only one of various differences. Rhys, following on Lhuyd's work, perceived each language family as representing a wave of Celtic migrations from Central Europe into Britain and Ireland, though, as we shall see, more recent scholars have challenged this 'invasionist theory'.

After Lhuyd, not much further progress was made until the early nineteenth century when James Cowles Prichard published *Eastern Origins of the Celtic Nations* (Prichard, 1831). The title reflects European interest in 'the Orient', an understandable theme in an era of empire building, and approaches the matter from an angle of fascination for the indigenous cultures within the European empires. Then, in 1853, Johann Kaspar Zeuss published his *Grammatica Celtica* (Zeuss, 1853). This was a pioneering work on Old Irish, mostly using the glosses left by Irish *peregrini* on Latin manuscripts, and it created a new wave of interest in Celtic Studies in Germany, especially by Sanskrit scholars.

More contemporary linguistic scholars have identified an Indo-European language family, from which 'Proto-Celtic' or 'Common Celtic' has descended as one branch. Proto-Celtic is then subdivided into various branches: Lepontic, Celtiberian,

Gaulish (for example, Galation and Noric), Brittonic (Breton, Cornish and Welsh), and Goidelic (Irish, Manx and Scots Gaelic). Like other Indo-European languages, Proto-Celtic is described by a bundle of *isoglosses* (i.e. the geographic boundary of a certain linguistic feature such as the pronunciation of a vowel) which show innovations in Proto-Indo-European and so distinguish it from the other members of the Indo-European family. For example, the oldest diagnostic feature which reveals a language to be Celtic is the loss of the Indo-European 'P', as in Irish *athair* versus Latin *pater* and English *father*, or Irish *iasc* versus Latin *piscis* and English *fish*.

Some scholars distinguish between Continental and Insular Celtic, and indeed all surviving Celtic languages are from the Insular Celtic group, Brittonic and Goidelic. This highlights a problem for the study of the origins of Continental Celtic particularly because, originally an oral people, very little written Celtic from the pre-Roman era is available for scrutiny. Evidence is limited to a few sources such as place names, coins and inscriptions. However, scholarship has revealed that the Celtic languages were spoken over a vast geographical area. Previously it was assumed that this indicated large population movements and waves of invaders. However, the archaeological evidence is lacking for such a migratory movement during the Iron Age from the North Alpine area to places like the Iberian Peninsula and the British Isles. As Simon James says:

> We now also have a more sophisticated understanding of how such 'pre-modern' societies work, largely from anthropological research from living peoples which shows that they can and do change, often radically and quickly, for internal reasons as well as due to external contacts. We do not need to infer invasions to explain the appearance of similarities between the peoples of Ireland and Britain and the continental Celtic Gauls (James, 1999, p. 40).

So, linguistic scholarship reveals not one unified Celtic identity and language, but a variety of peoples over a large geographical area, sharing systems of values and beliefs and in contact with one another for various reasons, including agriculture and commerce, through networks of interaction such as the Atlantic seaways and rivers.

As Cunliffe says, this barbarian world was encountered by the Greeks

[and] what they saw was a kaleidoscope of different cultures sharing a broadly similar language and a set of values that conditioned their behaviour. It was not unreasonable, therefore, for the Mediterranean observers to regard them as one people and to give them a name – the Celts – the name by which one of the communities they came into contact with identified themselves ... so it was that the concept of Celts as the peripheral barbarians first passed into history (Cunliffe, 2003, p. 95).

The third source of evidence is archaeological, including 'Celtic' art, and traditionally archaeologists have identified several 'cultures' of the Neolithic, Bronze and Iron Ages. Bell-Beaker Culture is the term used for a defined culture of pre-historic western Europe from late Neolithic to early Bronze Age (2900 BCE–1800 BCE). Similar burial styles, housing, weaponry, ornamentation and coarse ceramic ware have been identified from this period. The Urnfield Culture (*c.* 1300–800 BCE) in the North Alpine zone is identified by a proliferation of hillforts where large numbers of urned cremations, including grave goods, were discovered. The Hallstatt C period was identified by a change in burial practice to inhumation with grave goods buried alongside. Both Urnfield and Hallstatt C indicate a hierarchical society, the elite being buried with four-wheeled wagons, sets of horse harnesses and long swords. By the sixth century BCE there were developing links with the

Mediterranean world and various trading posts, for example, at Marseilles. In this period, which the archaeologists call Hallstatt D, imported goods were more widely found.

KNOCKDRUM FORT

Mighty perspective: Knockdrum is a Bronze Age hilltop circular stone fort in west Cork and affords spectacular vistas over sea and land.

Following this period, Etruscan influence expanded into the Po Valley, allowing trade through the Alpine passes to the barbarian north. Again, elite graves have been uncovered containing large quantities of Etruscan bronze vessels, especially beaked flagons and stamnos-type storage jars (i.e. oval storage jar which tapers at the base and has two horizontal handles set on the shoulder). Speaking of these burials, archaeologists have used the term La Tène A or La Tène 1 period.

Arising out of the La Tène period is highly skilled artwork thought to have been created for the wealthy, which has become known as 'Early Celtic art'. Prior to La Tène, Hallstatt period art showed geometric ornament and patterns of straight lines and rectangles. By the La Tène period, the style is curvilinear and much more free-flowing, with vegetal and foliage motifs together with spirals, triskelles, s-scrolls, lyre and trumpet shapes and, on occasions, elusive face-like forms sometimes called the 'Cheshire-Cat' style. These decorative styles of the La Tène craftspeople spread rapidly across Europe, so that elements of the La Tène art style have been uncovered from Ireland to the Black Sea.

THE TANDRAGEE MAN

Palimpsests, Pagan and Celtic: 'The Tandragee Man',
St Patrick's Church of Ireland Cathedral, Armagh.

Art styles are deeply imbedded in society's beliefs and values. Art is a product of a place and time and of peoples who belong to particular self-identified social and cultural groups. Martyn Jope comments that

[their] artwork … is full of social implications … a means of communication between people … a means of displaying social rank … a potent factor in expressing cultural taste and human relations with the supernatural … [and] can sometimes also give clues to the lifestyle and living conditions of different social strata (Jope, 1995, p. 376).

More recently, there have been interesting new archaeological theories about the origins and identity of Celtic peoples, which moves the focus from Iron Age central Europe, Hallstatt and La Tène to the Atlantic Bronze Age. For example, John Koch tells us: 'For two of the three components of the Celts – namely, as people called 'Keltoi' and as speakers of ancient Celtic languages – there is earlier and better evidence in the Atlantic west than in the central European Watershed Zone' (Koch, 2008, p. 2). His in-depth studies of Tartessian inscriptions from south-west Iberia represent the earliest attested evidence of a Celtic language (*c.* eight–sixth century BCE) and so he suggests it ought to be added to the established list of ancient Celtic languages. Cunliffe supports this, using evidence for the development and expansion of the Atlantic zone of interaction and exchange. He suggests that contact from the Neolithic period onwards allowed Celtic trade languages to develop in the Atlantic zone and move eastward. This theory is also underpinned by genetic evidence which does not support the traditional view of Iron Age Celtic migration originating in central Europe.

Cunliffe intriguingly asks, 'Could it be that, far from being a language introduced by invaders or migrants moving in from central Europe, it was the language of the indigenous Atlantic communities, which had developed over the long periods of interaction beginning in the 5th millennium BCE?' (Cunliffe, 2003, p. 26). And as Koch says, 'West Britain, as well as remaining Celtic speaking longer, possibly became Celtic speaking earlier ... [and] the question "when did the Celts come to Britain" may have built into it an assumption that is no longer valid' (Koch, 2008, p. 2).

So the concept of 'the Celts' is both ancient and contemporary, forever evolving as new scholarship offers fresh insights into the ancient past and new controversies arise. Indeed, it may be that there are other dangers to be wary of in the search for ethnic certainties, such as the possibilities of racial and ethnic stereotyping when, in reality, we all belong to the one human family – for the evidence does not support the idea of a 'Pan-European Celtic society', but rather a mosaic of diverse societies across Europe.

Using this approach, which celebrates social diversity and a more loosely held notion of commonality, the classical, linguistic and archaeological sources offer evidence for Celtic peoples of ancient Europe. A people with a variety of common languages, common social, cultural and artistic expressions – and all perceived to represent a defined identity by the Greek and Roman writers of antiquity. Cunliffe comments:

> In the 4th millennium BCE the main centres of innovation were scattered along the Atlantic, in the Tagus region of Portugal, the Morbihan in southern Brittany, the Boyne Valley of Ireland and the Orkney Isles. Although each region had its own distinct characteristics, the degree by which they shared concepts of architecture, art, cosmology and belief is remarkable (Cunliffe, 2003, p. 21).

That this culture also produced 'literature' is undeniable. However, given that the nature of that literature was oral, it is not until the coming of Christianity that written versions of oral material became available. Christianity, crucially, brought 'writing' as the ancient stories were put down on manuscript by Christian clerics or scholars of the pre-existing Bardic order, or a combination of both. Regardless of their source, the preservation of that ancient culture was dependent upon its committal not just to a lineage of oral memory, but to a written form. As we will see in later chapters, the introduction of writing was no straightforward matter and had implications not just for content but for literary forms.

Celtic-speaking areas of continental Europe eventually came under the control of Roman civilisation, and because of the need to maintain peace and stability throughout so vast and varied an empire, the goal was to ensure as much homogeneity as possible – in customs, language and culture. Ultimately, this had a devastating impact on Celtic civilisation, both in terms of language and culture. One example was the Roman ban on Druidic practice. In AD 60–1, determined to break the power and influence of the Druids, the Romans attacked the British Druids on Anglesey (Ynys Môn), one of the Druids' last strongholds. Tacitus described how they eventually won the battle, subdued the Druids and cut down their groves of sacred oaks. In addition, as the Roman Empire gradually adopted Christianity after Constantine, the teachings of Christ ceased to be the practices of a persecuted minority on the edges of society and changed radically as it moved into the mainstream of popular culture and became the affluent religion of the nobility with all the trappings of power and hierarchy.

However, in the more remote regions of western Europe – Armorica (the part of Gaul that includes the Brittany peninsula), south-west Britain, Wales, Scotland and Ireland – indigenous Celtic-speaking populations remained intact. So it was that a distinct form of Christianity developed in early medieval Ireland, influenced by the poverty and simplicity of the Desert Fathers and Mothers, which initiated a golden age of learning and art, centred around the monastic settlements. Barry Cunliffe comments:

> The early Christian Celtic-speaking communities of the West were the direct successors of the pagan pre-historic Celtic speakers of the same region. In using phrases like 'Celtic-Christianity' or 'the Celtic West' archaeologists and historians are not being entirely outrageous (Cunliffe, 2003, p. 143).

The contrast between the manifestation of Christianity in these more rural and remote regions and the urban Continental Christianity was revealed in various ways. For example, in Ireland monasticism perfectly suited the small tribal units, or *tuathas*, of rural social organisation. This meant that Christian community living was focused more on the abbot in small communities, in contrast to the Continental emphasis on the more hierarchical and remote office of bishop. There was no war fought over the coming of Christianity to Ireland and indeed many of the old perspectives about the universe were retained. Perhaps there are indications of this in the earliest Irish mythologies, which often find a gentle coexistence – if not harmony – between the old religion and the new. One example is the story of *The Children Of Lir* – a story of pre-Christian shamanistic shape-shifting, which yet has the children being cared for, and baptised, by a Christian hermit monk. Only much later, in retrospective stories of Irish Christianity – such as that written by Muirchú in the late seventh century AD – *Vita Sancti Patricii* – do we find more controversy being introduced by the writer between Christianity and paganism. Of course Christianity brought positive and humanitarian changes to an ancient warrior culture, yet alongside this – as we shall see in the coming chapters – many customs and practices of pre-Christian Ireland survived.

ST BRIGID

The changing Celtic Spirit: pagan goddess, Christian saint.

A further example is in the person of St Brigid – both a pre-Christian Goddess (Brigantia) and a Christian saint. So that 1 February, the beginning of the old Celtic season of Imbolc/ Springtide, became St Brigid's Day. As we will discover later in this book, other overlaps between the Christian and the pre-Christian are evident in the early medieval voyage literature, the respect for wells, mountains and trees as places of prayer and a spirituality that celebrated the immanence of God in the

47

natural world and the ordinary. Celtic Christianity is so called because in distinctive ways it respected, embodied and absorbed the shape of the indigenous Insular Celtic culture in which it was nurtured.

From the fifth century AD, Ireland experienced a golden age of learning and art, prayer and pilgrimage, focused around a monastic expression of Christianity. Examples of this flowering are to be found in nature-focused poetry and inspirational prayers such as 'The Cry of the Deer' or 'St Patrick's Breastplate', as well as artistic masterpieces such as the illuminated manuscripts from monastic communities, the *Book of Kells* and the *Book of Armagh*. The chapters to come will explore more fully this golden age of Celtic Christianity, its roots in pre-Christian perspectives and influences from desert monasticism – and its inspirations for us today.

By the Synod of Whitby in AD 664, which aimed to bring the Church in these islands into line with the Continental Church in matters such as the dating of Easter, monastic tonsure, penitential practices and various other aspects, change was on the way – though very gradually.

Irish monasticism influenced Scotland (e.g. Iona) and Northern England (e.g. Lindisfarne) and also had a profound influence on the Continent – for example, Bobbio Abbey in Italy was one of Columbanus' institutions. However, because of close ties between ruling families and monasteries, reflecting the tribal nature of Ireland, the monastic system became increasingly secularised. In the later medieval period in Ireland Viking invasions had a devastating effect on the monastic settlements.

Yet, even in these times, there were interesting developments such as the reforming influence of the Céilí Dé (friends or servants of God), and the production of great manuscripts such as the *Book of the Dun Cow* and the *Book of Leinster*. From these we have the earliest written accounts of ancient oral stories, including the *Táin Bó Cúailnge*. There were also bardic schools of poetry mentioned as early as 1041, which seemed to have worked alongside the monasteries, perhaps with some crossover of personnel. Thus, although Church reform was gradually reflecting the Continental style, within its ways of being – its monastic organisation and ways of living, both communally and with simplicity, the practice of hospitality and respect for art and music – the Celtic Spirit was very much alive.

ROCK OF CASHEL

Doors into a Continental Christianity: The Rock of Cashel was the seat of the kings of Munster until 1101, when the site was presented to the Church. Among the venerable buildings on the site is Cormac's Chapel, Ireland's most remarkable Romanesque church. Cormac MacCarthaigh was King of Munster and built the chapel between 1127 and 1134. Also here is St Patrick's Cathedral, erected in the thirteenth century.

49

With the Protestant Reformation, new divisions arose in an Ireland which had already experienced the Norman invasion and an increasing polarity between the English colonists and the Irish. Allegiances were often very complicated with the Old English who, in some cases, derived their lineage back to the Normans and upheld Catholicism; thus, at least in terms of religion, they were on the side of the Gaelic chieftains – while perhaps not fully identifying with them in terms of political ideals!

At a profound level, the Reformation was to have its effect on the very essence of what Celtic writing was about and from which it derived both its authority and its particular world view. For example, Anthony Duncan, an English canon of Scottish descent, comments on the effect of the Reformation on the creative imagination:

> The focus of religion was effectively shifted from the heart to the head ... not only was the intellectual climate essentially non-mystical, it speedily became positively anti-mystical. The intuition was suspect – it became regarded as the realm of the devil and his angels. In Scotland alone, over the course of two and a half centuries, between four and five thousand people were to be burned alive for a 'witchcraft' which was often as not little more than the possession and use of higher than usual degree of intuitive perception (Duncan, 1992, p. 81).

In 1606 (a year before the Flight of the Earls) the old Brehon Laws, which had grown out of an ancient oral society and Celtic social organisation, were abolished. This was but a symbol of the widespread changes that were to occur for the Gaelic order in terms of land 'ownership', economic position and culture; yet for the advocates of the new Plantation order, the bringing to Ireland of English law, language, religion and customs was seen as a needful reform. Some made their own accommodation with the new order and prospered after a fashion. New plantations in the eighteenth century brought many new settlers from England and Scotland, bringing their own traditions.

Then in the nineteenth century came a revival of the Celtic Spirit, perhaps beginning in the least likely place: among the Anglo-Irish Protestants. We will explore this in more depth later in the book, along with the story of how the Celtic Spirit manifested itself in literature after the Plantation and Reformation.

Certainly in the late nineteenth century there was a rich, if romantic, flowering of some form of the Celtic Spirit, especially in music, language and literary culture. Celtic myths and legends were edited and published, traditional Irish music was revived, attempts were made to resurrect the Irish language and the Gaelic Society was founded in 1893. Writers such as AE/George Russell, W. B. Yeats, Lady Gregory and J. M. Synge, brought the Celtic Spirit to life – along with an explosion of creativity in the world of fine art. Lorna Reynolds comments on the impact:

> This is what Yeats himself was attempting, what he wanted to encourage in others: the expression of that ancient idealism; the rediscovery of a mythology that by marrying the race to rock and hill would give it unity; the recovery also of the sense prevalent in ancient Ireland of the sacredness of the land, of every spring and stream, mountain and tree, of the indivisibility of all life, past and present, dead and living (Reynolds, 1981, pp. 393 & 395).

In terms of a renaissance of Celtic spirituality, the publication of *Carmina Gadelica* was of enormous significance. In the late nineteenth century, Alexander Carmichael, an islander himself from the Isle of Lismore in Argyll, travelled all over the Scottish Highlands and the Hebrides collecting prayers, hymns, incantations, work-songs, charms and cures of the

Gaelic people. An oral tradition captured on the page, *Carmina Gadelica* contains a strange and powerful blend of the pagan and the Christian, preserving an ancient culture and ways of living for future generations.

During the twentieth and twenty-first centuries, this heritage of Celtic literature and spirituality has continued to flourish, develop and inspire. Continuity is especially strong in areas which still speak a Celtic language. For example, the connections between Scotland and Ireland were so continuous and unbroken that we can talk of a Gaelic language continuum that lasted until the beginning of the present century. In the 1870s, Irish speakers from County Antrim attending the fairs on the Isle of Arran in Scotland were able to converse quite easily with the local Gaels.

In terms of Celtic spirituality, the resurrection of intentional community on Iona, with its Wild Goose liturgical publishing wing, has been very influential, and thousands – of all faiths and none – make pilgrimages to Iona annually. Many of the old pilgrim paths, once traversed by Irish *peregrini*, have been reopened in Europe, and pilgrimage as a practice is becoming re-evaluated as an approach to spiritual journey. Other examples of the flourishing of Celtic spirituality in our time are the Community of Aidan and Hilda based on Holy Island, Lindisfarne, the Northumbrian Community and the thousands who pilgrimage to Ireland each year in search of the Celtic Spirit. There is also a proliferation of writers on Celtic spirituality such as David Adam (1989), Noel Dermot O'Donoghue, Ian Bradley (2003), John O'Donoghue (2007), J. Philip Newell (2008), Ray Simpson (2014), to name but a few. There are also Celtic Studies departments in many universities and recently 'The Classics of Western Spirituality' series published *Celtic Spirituality* (Davies and O'Loughlin, 1999). In fact, there is a virtual explosion of interest in the relevance of many aspects of Celtic spirituality for the twenty-first century search for inspiration and meaning.

CHAPTER TWO

The Celtic Spirit and Nature
Grace Clunie

We have looked at an overview of aspects of ancient Celtic civilisation – the classical sources, language, geography, archaeology and some characteristics of Celtic identity.

In this chapter we will have a closer look at the Celtic Spirit and nature, focusing on what we can decipher about the ancients' understanding of their relationship with nature and its power over their daily existence.

Celtic civilisation – at least in the Insular Celtic world – was lived close to the land and intimately shared with animals and birds. Their very existence depended on the world of nature: being able to grow and harvest food for living, nurturing animals for milk, wool and food and knowing which plants would bring healing for various ailments in times of sickness.

They were deeply connected with the cycle of the seasons because they had to be. Their life depended on it. This is not the romantic pastoral scenes of the nineteenth-century poets, for whom nature was a source of beauty and delight. This was a practical relationship for daily existence and an approach to the powers of nature that bordered on awe. And what they observed was the waxing and the waning of everything: the tides that came in and went out – full tide, ebb tide; the moon, that went from being a small sliver in the night sky to a full moon; the cycle of life and death; the rising of the sun in the morning to its full height at midday and its setting in the evening, plunging the world into darkness. Where the sun came up was east, where it set was west and they learned to tell the directions from the place of the sun in the sky, and at night from the place of the stars and the constellations. And so, they read the signs of creation, and behind it all they encountered a powerful and creative energy, which was represented in many forms.

For example, Lugh, the God of Light, is one of the major Celtic deities. There are many stories about Lugh in the old Irish mythologies, not least that he fathered Cúchulainn, the great warrior of Ulster. He is considered a sun god because his name derives from the Proto-Indo-European root, *Leuk*, 'flashing light', and he has given his name to many places, for example Lyon in France was originally *Lugdunom*, meaning 'stronghold of light'. One of the four major festivals of the Celtic year was named after Lugh – Lughnasa on 1 August.

The point is that the Celtic peoples revered the power of the sun because they knew how dependent their lives were on its light and heat. This reverence for the power of nature is evident in some of the most ancient of the Irish mythologies, originally part of the oral culture before being written down many centuries later (and most likely changed forever in the process). An example is *The Second Battle of Maigh Tuireadh* from the Mythological Cycle of Irish myths and legends. In summary, Lugh, on the side of the Tuatha Dé Danann, defeats Balor, the one-eyed champion of the Fomorians, whose king, Bres, pleads for mercy. Quoting from Lady Gregory's translation King Bres says: 'If you spare me, the men of Ireland will reap a harvest of corn every quarter.' But Maeltine for the Tuatha Dé Danann, respecting the natural rhythms of the earth, replies: 'The spring is for ploughing and sowing, and the beginning of the summer for the strength of the corn, and the beginning of autumn of its ripeness, and the winter for using it.' So Lugh then asks Bres, 'tell us what is the best way for the men of Ireland to plough and to sow and to reap' (Gregory, 1902, p. 52). And after this he lets Bres go free.

As John Moriarty (1999, p. 43) has said, this was a battle 'between a people intent on shaping nature to suit them and a people who, surrendering to it, would let nature shape them to suit it'. So the Celtic peoples had a deep reverence, even awe, of the power of nature.

For them, the natural world was full of what we would call 'sacred power'. This, for them, was represented in the attribution of deities to the rivers, the streams, the lakes, the springs, the mountains, the trees, and all of nature.

Another of the ancient mythologies of Ireland captures this concept beautifully – *The Coming of the Gael*. The story tells of a people called 'The Gael', or 'The Sons of Miled', who came from 'the South' to invade Ireland. When they landed they were met by the Tuatha Dé Danann, who, for the ancients, were a semi-divine people. In summary, because of a slight of honour a battle ensued and ultimately the Tuatha Dé Danann were defeated – but this is what the old writings say:

> As for the Tuatha Dé Danaan, though they had been defeated by the Milesians … they did not leave Ireland. They went underground to inhabit the mounds and earthworks known as Sidhes that are scattered all over the country. Above them, in the upper kingdom, the human inhabitants of Ireland … lived and died, helped, and sometimes hindered, by the people of the Sidhe. From time to time, down through the ages, these mysterious, imperishable people entered the world of mortals. Sometimes they fell in love with human beings and at other times they held humans enthralled with their beauty and their haunting music. But their kingdom was that Happy Otherworld under the earth and they always went back there to the Land of the Ever Young (Heaney, 1994, p. 55).

So the Celts believed that the Tuatha Dé Danann – the people of the Goddess Danu – inhabited the underground world of the Sidhe and the very earth itself. To this day, there's still a folk memory of that – in a sense, they still reside in the earth and they still hold power. For example, many farmers would still hesitate before attempting to cut down special trees – even if they're awkwardly placed in the middle of a field that needs to be sowed and harvested – if that tree is locally known as 'a fairy tree'. This could be regarded as just a superstition; however, underneath resides an age-old respect for the power of nature herself and a desire to work in harmony with that power.

Indeed, this could be why so many of the ancient sacred sites in Ireland have never been eroded or destroyed, for example, Newgrange, Tara (though under threat of motorway in recent years), Emain Macha (though under threat of quarrying in the 1980s) and the old dolmens, which still exist in their hundreds in the landscape of Ireland. Today this is a gift for Irish tourism, because people travel to Ireland from all parts of the world to visit these places and ancient sites and to experience them at first hand. But they are also an indicator that the earth and the land remain centrally important in the psyche of the Irish people.

Perhaps it could be compared to the respect for the sacredness of the earth felt by many indigenous people throughout the world. For example, this chant comes from the Native American peoples – the Omaha:

Remember, remember the sacredness of things,
Running streams and dwellings,
The young within the nest,
A hearth for sacred fire,
The holy flame (Exley, 1997, p. 12).

In his book *Where Three Streams Meet*, Seán Ó Duinn speaks about this awe of nature which the ancient Celts had in terms of the concept of *neart* (Irish for 'strength' or 'power'). He says:

Behind this extraordinary cycle of decay and growth, the cyclical movement in nature, the death of one form and the birth of another, the Celts must have seen a strange energy … filling everything, invigorating everything … creative energy or neart (Ó Duinn, 2000, p. 78).

And so this *neart* was the living energy at the heart of everything, including human beings. Another example is a poem written by Dylan Thomas, the Welsh poet:

The force that through the green fuse drives the flower
Drives my green age ... (Thomas, 2000, p. 13).

The 'force' – as Thomas calls it – or the *neart* – was in the flower as well as the human being.

For the Celtic peoples the world was charged with this power and the *neart* presence was everywhere. The mountains and rivers weren't just called after gods and goddesses – they were actual manifestations of the sacred.

This sense of sacred power in everything – even the rocks and stones – is what is called an animistic perception of life, and this understanding of existence is shared by other indigenous peoples throughout the world – for example, the Native Americans for whom all species of the earth were their relatives, their family, their kin. From Black Elk of the Sioux:

Hear me, four quarters of the world – a relative I am!
Give me the strength to walk the soft earth,
In beauty may I walk,
A relative to all that is!
Give me the eyes to see and the strength to understand
That I may be like you.
With your power only can I face the winds (Exley, 1997, p. 7).

Looking at this ancient perception of life from a modern scientific world view, there are interesting insights to consider. For example, scientists have discovered that human beings share DNA with all living organisms and that the three letter words of the genetic code are the same in every creature. All life is one! We are literally 'kin' to all that is. As well as that, the physicists tell us that at the subatomic level the classical distinction between matter and energy disappears. All matter is energy (*neart*?), moving in defined patterns of relationality.

At this level everything is a web of relationships in which the whole universe is interconnected and in which the observer also stands as part of the process. We cannot observe anything objectively, for the very act of observation affects what we observe. Therefore, all so-called solid objects at this micro level are a matrix of dancing energy. Even our own bodies, despite the appearance of continuity over time, are continually dying and being reborn in every second. In fact, according to the work of Swedish molecular biologist Dr Jonas Frisén on carbon-14 and body tissue renewal, over a period of seven years every molecule of your body is replaced (Frisén et al, 2005).

So this interconnection with the rest of the universe and this dancing energy at the heart of life may be linked to what the Celts experienced and expressed in poetry and story, and what we are rediscovering in scientific language. Sadly, though, in our daily living, we've forgotten our complete connection with everything else and we see ourselves as somehow separate from the rest of nature.

In contrast, the beautiful, ancient poem of Amergin, often called Ireland's oldest poet, brings to us a gift of connectedness in powerful images of nature. The poem will be discussed more fully in Chapter Seven. We may note here that the poet isn't singing *about* nature, in an objective way, he is totally identified *with* nature. There is no distance. He doesn't say, 'I am *like* the wind on the sea', or 'I am *like* the wave on the ocean.' He says, 'I *am* the wind on the sea; I *am* the wave on the ocean.' This is reminiscent of a reference in the Book of Exodus in the Bible when Moses asks God what is His Name – and God replies 'I Am' – 'Tell them "I Am" has sent you' (Exodus 3:13–14). It is a name that signifies *Being*; and Being in the present tense. So it is with Amergin in this poem of nature. There is no objective distance between himself and the rest of nature.

SHAMAN FIGURE WITH ANTLERS

Singing forth Ireland: Amergin celebrates his new land.

Thom Hartmann, in a fascinating book called *The Last Hours of Ancient Sunlight*, speaks of meeting an aboriginal elder who had this same ancient, non-dualistic perception of existence. The following comes from a discussion lecture about Hartmann's book:

I remember the first time I met somebody who lives inside the older culture story, instead of the one our society believes. I was sitting in a dry riverbed, talking

59

through a translator with Tommy George, a 90-year old Aboriginal king. I was asking about 'spirit' and 'sacred places,' which led to a lengthy exchange between Tommy George and the translator, back and forth and back and forth. Finally I asked, 'what's going on?' and the translator replied, 'I had to explain your concept. They don't have a word for sacred.' 'Why?' I asked. 'Because there is nothing that isn't sacred', was the reply. 'They don't make the distinction' (Hartmann, 2007, unpaged).

He also discovered, in his conversation with Tommy George, that they didn't have a word for 'nature'. Why? 'Because there isn't any "not nature". Everything is, so there is no need for the word. Humans, animals, plants, soil, the sky – it's all one thing.' In this way aboriginal or indigenous cultures – of which Celtic culture is one – experience the rest of creation as kin. Another example from the Native American peoples:

Hills are always more beautiful than stone buildings, you know.
Living in a city is an artificial existence.
Lots of people hardly ever feel real soil under their feet, see plants grow, except in flower pots, or get far enough beyond the street light to catch the enchantment of a night sky studded with stars. When people live far from scenes of the Great Spirit's making, it's easy for them to forget His laws (Exley, 1997, p. 32).

So these 'Laws' mentioned here were also very much part of the Celtic way of living.

They believed there was a natural cycle to the year and a way of living in tune with nature that had to be respected; a pattern of right relationship at the heart of life.

One could argue that this speaks to the very heart of today's ecological crisis. We have lost a balanced and a right relationship with the rest of the earth. Our greed pushes us to exploit nature for all we can get – just as Bres suggested getting milk and crops at every season of the year in the old mythology of *The Second Battle of Maigh Tuireadh*. Yet as Ecclesiastes in the Old Testament says, 'for everything there is a time and a season' (Ecclesiastes 3:1). And indeed the Old Testament sets up rest for humans, the land and the animals – the seven-day cycle (Sabbath), the seven-year cycle, and the seven-year-times-seven-year cycle or jubilee – of which Jesus speaks in his teachings (Luke 4:18–19). The message is clear – we need to work *with* nature and not in opposition.

This view of existence, then, was not only animistic but also panentheistic, meaning that, although the gods and goddesses were *in* the rivers and the wells and the mountains, they were also beyond and greater than any one thing. So the Celts had a respect for the sacredness of the earth and a deep understanding of the cycles of nature.

Let's consider now some of the influences of this ancient perspective on the first manifestation of Christianity in Ireland. It needs to be remembered that the first Irish Christians were people who were coming from the perspective of the animistic and panentheistic view of existence and, although attempting to understand the new faith and its teachings, they would surely have also been deeply respectful of their ancestral heritage. This seems clear when the phenomenon of early Christianity in Ireland is examined, because it seems to contain much of the indigenous or ancestral perspective. For example, in writing down the old myths and legends, passed down the centuries through an oral tradition, the Christian monks were clearly fascinated and impassioned by their colour and power. True, they introduced Christian elements into the old stories, yet the old myths and legends retain their vibrancy and speak clearly of an ancient way of being and thinking. An example is the stories of the Fianna, where the hero Oisín meets 'St Patrick of the bells' and two worlds of thought come together with mutual respect – though in the end Oisín's beautiful lament is for the end of the old ways of the Fianna:

There is no one at all in the world the way I am;

It is a pity the way I am;

An old man dragging stones;

It is long the clouds are over me tonight!

I am the last of the Fianna, great Oisin, son of Finn,

Listening to the voice of bells;

It is long the clouds are over me tonight (Trans. Gregory, 1904, p. 308).

We have noted that the Celts practised a great reverence and awe for the natural world. This was an aspect which was also clearly evident in early Christianity in Ireland. In Celtic Christianity, we find an approach to nature that is inclusive and non-dualistic. An example is this ancient poem-prayer, 'The Little Gray Crow':

The Little gray Crow with a bald head,

And the Lark whose bed is in the sky,

Must go where the fame of men must go,

And where men themselves must go.

All who have come, have gone,

All who now come, must go,

All who will come, shall go

To where the grace of God flows forever (Van de Weyer, 1997, p. 33).

Here is, simply captured, an approach to nature that is all-inclusive in the salvation spectrum. Nothing is outside of God's grace, everything has the potential to be full of the sacred, and salvation isn't just about human beings. The poem encapsulates a universal theology of grace and healing represented in the Bible itself. For example, in Paul's letter to the Romans we read that 'the whole creation ... will obtain the freedom of the glory of the children of God' (Romans 8:21).

And the Psalms speak of the creation 'telling the glory of God' (Psalm 19:1).

As an ancient saying traditionally attributed to St Columbanus expresses it: 'If you want to know The Creator, first get to know His creation.' The opening pages of the Bible present a picture of all that exists, coming from the same divine source, and the phrase 'it is good' is repeated six times! This picture is of an original goodness at the heart of everything – all emerges from the same sacred source.

This perspective on nature is echoed in the theology of John Scotus Eriugena, an early medieval Irish theologian (*c.* 815–77). In his great ninth-century work, *Periphyseon*, republished by

ARDBOE MONASTERY CHURCH

Thresholds: Nature returns to clothe the ruined church arch. The monastery church at Ardboe, Co. Tyrone. The church dates back to the seventeenth century and was founded in 590 by St Colman Muchaidhe.

Thomas Gale in 1681 under the title *De Divisione Naturae,* Eriugena says that the created universe is the manifestation of God, a God in process. He says that the creation of the world is in reality a *theophania* or 'showing forth' of the essence of God in the things created and ultimately all things will return to God. His view is panentheistic as it holds that all is *in* God, not that all *is* God. He says: 'Creation is God's emanation from Himself and return toward Himself. Thus going forth into all things in order He makes all things and is made in all things, and returns to Himself, and while He is made in all things He does not cease to be above all things' (Eriugena, *c.* 862–867, 683b).

So God is in all things, yet also above all things, and all things are sacred. Christ's coming is about reconnecting us and the whole of creation with our essential sacred nature, our original goodness. In this sense Christ is the cosmological saviour and not just human-centred. One of the fullest expressions of this cosmological Christology is found in Colossians 1:15–20:

> He is the image of the invisible God, the firstborn of all creation; for in him all things in heaven and on earth were created ... all things have been created through him and for him. He himself is before all things and in him all things hold together ... for in him all the fullness of God was pleased to dwell and through him God was pleased to reconcile to Himself all things (Colossians 1:15–20).

This hymn of Christ and creation brings together the two dramas of nature/creation and redemption in the figure of the cosmological Christ. This understanding that redemption was for all of nature and of respect for the sacred earth was strong in the prayers and practice of Celtic Christianity – in its prayer life and artwork. Another example is the beautiful prayer-poem 'The Tree of Life', which sees Eden in the earth and all of nature.

O, King of the Tree of Life,
The blossoms on the branches are your people,
The singing birds are your angels,
The whispering breeze is your Spirit.

O, King of the Tree of Life,
May the blossoms bring forth the sweetest fruit,
May the birds sing out the highest praise,
May your Spirit cover all with his gentle breath (Van de
Weyer, 1997).

Another more contemporary source of Celtic Christianity
is *Carmina Gadelica*, a collection of ancient prayers, hymns and
incantations gathered from the Highlands and islands of
Scotland by Alexander Carmichael in the nineteenth century.
They are wonderfully full of awareness of sacred presence/
neart in the whole of creation, not just human beings, and they
also contain an immanent view of the sacred, or as we might
say, God in the ordinary. Not a faraway, transcendent God, but
an Emmanuel/God with us.

This example of 'common prayer' – 'Driving the Cows' –
values the sacred in the simplicity of the humble cow. Notice
that the saints and angels are invoked for their protection and
that among the saints is 'Maol Dúinne' – hero of the longest of
the Irish immram tales (see Chapter Five) and St Brendan the
Voyager.

Closed to you be every pit,
Smooth to you be every hill,
Snug to you be every bare spot,
Beside the cold mountains …

The fellowship of Mary Mother be yours,
The fellowship of Brigit of kine be yours,
The fellowship of Michael victorious be yours,
In nibbling, in chewing, in munching (Trans. Moore,
1992, p. 337).

In this approach to nature, all is sacred. Creation is sacrament – all that we see is a visible reminder of an invisible grace. So, how can we sum up what the Celtic Spirit has to say to us in our twenty-first-century lifestyles?

Firstly, that there is this intimate relationship (kin) between all the species of nature – all life is one. All things have come from the same sacred source, therefore all things are sacred. We're living in an age and at a time when we have lost our connection with the rest of nature. Our lives are cut off from the natural cycles of the earth. More worrying for the future, we're living at a time of environmental change and major extinction of species, and the loss of even one species impacts upon us all. The Celtic Spirit reminds us of our relationship with the sacred earth and our need to find a new reciprocal relationship with nature. We can't just keep on taking. We need to give back. In this sense Celtic spirituality is a call *to right relationship*, not just with our human neighbours, but with the whole of creation.

Secondly, the Celtic Spirit reminds us of the power at the heart of all life. Everything is imbued with the living *neart* – or as Christians might say, 'in *Him* we live and move and have our being' (Acts 17:28). In Celtic spirituality this is not just about human beings – the whole earth is alive with the sacred presence; to quote from Gerard Manly Hopkins: 'The world is charged with the Grandeur of God' (Hopkins, 1918; rpt 1995, p. 101).

So Celtic spirituality reveals clearly that life on the earth is not just about human beings; in fact in terms of evolution we are newcomers to the earth compared to some of the most ancient species. This leads us to ask searching questions about the ethics of our relationships with other species, to value and respect the earth and to recognise that a healthy environment also has implications for human health and well-being. The point is that modern science has revealed something that the ancient indigenous people and the Celts already knew instinctively through experience; namely, that we are all part of the one interconnected ecosystem and when one life form dies and becomes extinct, it has a profound effect upon us all. It is a challenge to practise, as far as we possibly can, right relationship with all of creation and a simpler approach to daily living.

Thirdly, the Celtic Spirit recalls us to the experience of the sacred in every moment of life. Non-dualism is an approach to living that recognises the continual potential for the sacred. Life isn't divided up into sacred/profane, holy/unholy, ordinary/miraculous. Rather, everything has potential for the sacred – as King Tommy George illustrated in his conversation with Thom Hartmann. This ethos of seeing the sacred in the 'ordinary' is also in other ancient spiritual approaches to existence, such as Buddhism, which speaks of the beauty inherent in fully living the present moment with the conscious gratitude of an open heart.

This deep awareness of sacred presence and power is at the heart of the well-known 'St Patrick's Breastplate' in which the invocation of the Christ is nine-fold.

Christ be with me, Christ within me,
Christ behind me, Christ before me,
Christ beside me, Christ to win me,
Christ to comfort and restore me,
Christ beneath me, Christ above me,
Christ in quiet, Christ in danger,
Christ in hearts of all that love me,
Christ in mouth of friend or stranger (Oxford University Press, 2000, p. 597).

Finally, a personal story. A few years ago I went to Donegal to stay with a wonderful lady who is a herbalist, writer and ecologist. I wanted to learn from her wisdom, along with others who were also staying with her to learn about the healing earth. She lives very simply – using rainwater, a windmill and a solar panel. There is nothing she does not know about the healing energies – the living *neart* – of the earth. I mention this because for me she exemplifies the Celtic Spirit. Not that she has studied Celtic spirituality – she doesn't have to because she just lives it. She told us that the earth provides for our healing if we have eyes to see it. On the first morning of our time with her, she began with these words: 'I'm in love with the earth.'

There is deep healing in the earth – for those who spend time in nature and who experience that deep connection with sacred presence. Indeed in a sense the earth is our 'wider body', the outer world which nurtures our existence: Mother Earth. And in terms of a new and more positive relationship with the earth, the real way forward is for all of us to experience the healing power of nature for ourselves, and to 'fall in love' with the earth. Because when you are in love, you do not deliberately hurt the one you love. You naturally do the right thing. The Celtic Spirit opens our eyes to the joy of a much wider belonging within the huge and gloriously diverse family of nature. We are never alone in this world. Every day is filled with sacred presence if we have eyes to see it; as David Adam's poem 'I Have Seen the Lord' reminds us:

Where the mist rises from the sea,
Where the waves creep upon the shore,
Where the wrack lifts upon the strand,
I have seen the Lord (Adam, 1989, p. 28).

CHAPTER THREE

The Celtic Spirit: Hospitality and Heroes
Grace Clunie

God bless the poor,
God bless the sick,
God bless our human race.

God bless our food,
God bless our drink,
All homes, O God, embrace (Van De Weyer, 1997, p.
53).

The offering and receiving of hospitality was one of the
centrally important aspects of Celtic community – and indeed
of many indigenous tribal peoples to this day. Feasting and
hospitality marked many aspects of daily life – for example,
welcoming visitors, honouring heroes and celebrating festivals.
In the Ulster Cycle of mythologies, the High King, Conor Mac
Nessa, who established the Red Branch warriors at Emain
Macha, is said to divide his day into three parts, as follows:

> He would spend a third of his day watching them
> training at arms and playing hurley on the green at
> Emain Macha. Another third of the day the king would
> spend playing chess. The last third in feasting and
> entertainment (Heaney, 1994, p. 73).

What a life! Yet to refuse hospitality was not only insulting
to the host, but almost a taboo. An example is the story of
Bricriu's Feast, again, one of the stories from the Ulster Cycle of
mythologies. The story begins:

> Bricriu 'poison-tongue' spent a whole year preparing a
> great feast for Connor Mac Nessa and his followers ...
> Bricriu was notorious for causing strife among the

69

guests at any feast he attended … the rest of the Ulster chiefs did not want to go to Bricriu's house because they mistrusted him and his mischievous tricks (Heaney, 1994, pp. 147–8).

EMAIN MACHA

A place of heroes, hospitality, an apple and a Barbary ape: Emain Macha (Navan Fort) is one of the great legendary sites of Celtic mythology. Associated with the Red Branch Knights and the Ulster Cycle of tales, the site dates back to 95 BC. Among the archaeological findings was the remains of a Barbary ape, suggesting very early international commerce, and an apple. To this day, Armagh is known as the orchard county.

However, Bricriu threatens his invited guests with a *geis* or curse and so they decided to accept his invitation. The Ulster chiefs knew that by refusing Bricriu's hospitality and breaking the taboo, they left themselves vulnerable to the curses of Bricriu. And so begins a very lively tale.

Repeatedly, in the old mythologies, when hospitality is not respected, bad things happen.

For example, even when Cúchulainn, with his loyal friend Laeg, was on his journey to what turned out to be his death, he still couldn't refuse hospitality:

> On their way south they came upon three wrinkled hags, blind in their left eyes, bending over a fire. They were cooking an animal on a spit made of a Rowan branch and as Cúchulainn came up to them he saw that the animal was a hound (Cúchulainn is named after the hound). He made to pass them for he knew they were not there for any good and moreover there was a 'Geis' on him forbidding him to eat the meat of a hound, since it was his namesake. But one of the crones called out to him, 'Come here to us, Cúchulainn, and do not pass us. Stop and eat with us!'
>
> 'I won't stop with you!' Cúchulainn cried.
>
> 'You won't eat with us because the food we're cooking is only a hound and this is a poor cooking hearth. If it belonged to an important man you would stop! Shame on you for shunning the poor!' Cúchulainn was stung by these words, so he ordered Laeg to pull up the horses (Heaney, 1994, pp. 99–100).

To refuse hospitality, in whatever circumstances, was worse by far than the strongest *geis*. Cúchulainn was *compelled* to accept their hospitality.

Underlying all of this was a mindset of welcome and genuine hospitality as a mark of respect for a person. It was a way of honouring a person and it has remained part of the identity and psyche of the Irish until this day. Ancient classical sources, describing the Celtic and Gaulish peoples, also make much of this aspect – the hospitality of the Celtic Spirit and their love of feasting. For example, Strabo (*c.* 64 BC–AD 21) wrote of the Celtic peoples:

> Their houses are large and circular, built of planks and wickerwork, the roof being a dome of heavy thatch.

71

They have such enormous flocks of sheep and herds of swine that they afford a plenteous supply of Sagi and of salt meat, not only to Rome but to most parts of Italy (Ó Duinn, 2000, p. 28).

Diodorus Siculus comments:

They also invite strangers to their banquets, and only *after* the meal do they ask who they are and of what they stand in need (Ó Duinn, 2000, p. 30).

This is interesting because it was common practice to consider foreigners without a local host to be lacking legal protection and therefore 'fair game'. But there is evidence that under the Brehon Laws, hospitality was customarily granted to foreigners. Examples of this ethos of Celtic hospitality are the Spanish Celtiberian inscriptions on *Tesserae Hospitales* (Hospitality Tablets) which indicate a practice of granting hospitality to foreigners.

The practice of hospitality was also an integral part of Celtic Christianity. It was rooted in a scripture from the Letter to the Hebrews:

Do not neglect to show hospitality to strangers, for by so doing some have entertained angels unawares (Hebrews: 13:1).

This was a reference to the Old Testament story of Abraham and Sarah's encounter with three angels, to whom they extended the usual gracious hospitality for strangers, and then later discovered that they were Messengers of God (Genesis 18:1–15).

Hospitality was also a centrally important part of the ministry of Jesus himself. The Scribes and Pharisees found fault with Jesus because 'he came eating and drinking, a glutton and a drunkard' (Luke 7:34). However, much of his ministry and parable stories centred on hospitality as a symbol of the love and acceptance of God. For example, in the story of the rich man and Lazarus, the rich man's sin is his failure to acknow-ledge and offer hospitality to the one who sat at his gate in terrible need. After death Lazarus is welcomed into the heavenly realm but the rich man is turned away (Luke 16:19–31). Another example is the meeting between Jesus and the despised tax collector, Zacchaeus. Being small of stature, Zacchaeus hides in the branches of a sycamore tree to get a glimpse of Jesus as he passes by in the crowd below. But Jesus stops right under the tree, gazes directly into the eyes of Zacchaeus and says: 'Zacchaeus, hurry and come down; for I must stay at your house today' (Luke 19:5). It is a miracle of hospitality.

Another beautiful example is the visit of Jesus to the home of Simon the Pharisee. Jesus notes that Simon fails to offer the usual marks of hospitality such as the kiss of greeting and the water to wash dusty feet. However, he says nothing of this until a woman enters the house, uninvited, with a perfumed jar of ointment. As she weeps, she proceeds to wash the feet of Jesus with her tears, dry them with her hair and then anoint them with the ointment. Simon, outraged, protests at Jesus allowing such a sinful woman to even touch him. Jesus responds by comparing her true hospitality of heart with Simon's judgmental attitude and lack of love for, he says, 'Her sins which were many are forgiven, for she loved much' (Luke 7:47). She is the one Jesus values though she is not respected by society. Authentic hospitality is all about the motives of the heart and not about outward show, and in the Christian tradition it is particularly blessed when directed to the weak, the vulnerable and the powerless in society.

Indeed, at the heart of Christian devotion is the Eucharist or Holy Communion or Mass. This is God's invitation of hospitality to remember the Christ within – the Christ who is *in* the host and *is* the host. The Book of Revelation to John portrays heaven and the afterlife as 'the marriage supper of the Lamb' (Revelation 19:9) – another scene of Divine hospitality.

So, in this great tradition – both of hospitality at the heart of Celtic society and at the heart of Christian devotion – the Celtic monastic settlements were places of refuge and hospitality for the poor and the needy. They had an open door to welcome strangers. They fed the poor – it is said that St Columba's monastery in Derry fed up to a thousand people every day. They offered refuge to fugitives from justice, giving them some months of respite to prepare their case against their accuser. This also allowed a 'cooling period', hopefully enabling a more measured and just outcome. They also offered medical help to the ill – for in those ancient times finding help in times of sickness and pain was not as easy. To this day at Glendalough, in the mountains of County Wicklow, visitors can still see the ruins of this Celtic monastic way of living and the old infirmaries where the sick were treated. It was their way of identifying with the words of Christ: 'Whatever you do, to the least of these your brothers and sisters, you do to me'(Matthew 25:40). In other words, hospitality is about recognising the sacredness in the other – no matter how humble they may be – because in Christ's perspective, the more humble the person, the more they need welcome and kindness.

There's a wonderful ancient poem called 'St Brigid's Feast', which, above all, identifies the Christian heaven as a place of hospitality:

I should like a great lake of finest ale for the King of kings.
I should like a table of choicest food for the family of heaven.
Let the ale be made from the fruits of faith,
And the food be forgiving love.
I should welcome the poor to my feast, for they are God's children.

I should welcome the sick to my feast, for they are
God's joy.
Let the poor sit with Jesus at the highest place,
And the sick dance with the angels (Van De Weyer, 1997,
p. 53).

A lovely ancient Celtic Rune of Hospitality, used by the Iona
Community says:

I saw a stranger yestereen.
I put food in the eating place,
Drink in the drinking place,
Music in the listening place,
And in the Sacred Name of the Triune,
He blessed myself, and my house,
My cattle and my dear ones.
And the lark said in her song,
Often, often, often goes the Christ in the stranger's guise
(Ferguson, 1998, p. 25).

At the heart of this practice of hospitality within Celtic
Christianity was an understanding that within each person
resides the sacred soul. Rooted in the opening chapter of
Genesis where God says, 'Let us make humankind in our
image' (Genesis 1:26), both male and female are made in the
Divine image and to offer hospitality is to recognise the
sacredness of another.

A contemporary writer in the Celtic tradition, John Philip
Newell, puts it like this:

At the beginning of the Hebrew scriptures, the book of
Genesis describes humanity as made in the 'image' and
'likeness' of God (Genesis 1:26) ... Everything else that
is said about us in the scriptures needs to be read in the
light of this starting point. The image of God is at the
core of our being (Newell, 2008, p. 3).

He goes on to tell a story:

> A nineteenth century teacher in the Celtic world, Alexander Scott, used the analogy of royal garments. Apparently in his day, royal garments were woven through with a costly thread, a thread of gold. And if somehow the golden thread were taken out of the garment, the whole garment would unravel. So it is, he said, with the image of God woven into the fabric of our being. If it were taken out of us we would unravel. We would cease to be. So the image of God is not simply a characteristic of who we are, which may or may not be there, depending on whether or not we have been baptized. The image of God is the essence of our being. It is the core of the human soul. We are sacred, not because we have been baptized or because we belong to one faith tradition over another. We are sacred because we have been born (Newell, 2008, pp. 3–4).

In the history of the world there have been many occasions when attempts have been made to 'remove the golden thread' – from an individual or from a race of people. For example, the treatment by the Nazi regime of the Jewish people, gypsy people and those of a homosexual orientation in the years of the Second World War in Europe. By reducing these peoples to 'inhuman' status they gave themselves carte blanche to do whatever they liked to them. In our day it continues in holocausts and injustices – especially to those vulnerable peoples who have no voice of influence and are therefore silenced and exploited.

In contrast, this practice of hospitality, a treasure of sacred wisdom from ancient Celtic peoples and from the life of Jesus and the practices of Celtic monasticism, speaks of a different way that seeks the sacred – the golden thread – in the other.

In a world that is increasingly multicultural in its identity, hospitality speaks to us of the welcome and the open heart. An acceptance of others for who they are, rather than prejudging people based on labels of gender, race, religion, sexual orientation and all the other labels we attach to people nowadays. Hospitality is a way of living and relating to others which understands that beneath all the labels is the common humanity that we all share – the sacred soul.

There's an old story from the early Christian tradition in Europe about St Martin of Tours, a well-known personality in the early Church (indeed, part of the *Book of Armagh* is devoted to him). The story goes that he was out on his horse one day when he encountered a naked beggar by the roadside. Overcome with compassion for the man, he took off the cloak he was wearing and gave it to the naked beggar. That night he had a dream in which Christ appeared to him, wearing the very cloak he had placed around the shoulders of the beggar. And the words of Christ to him in the dream were: 'Whatever you do, to the least of these your brothers and sisters, you do to me' (Matthew 25:40).

Hospitality as a way of living is beautifully represented by Mother Theresa of Calcutta who, when asked how she sustained her compassion for her work among the poor of Calcutta, is quoted as saying: 'I see Jesus in every person. I say: This is sick Jesus I must feed him. This is poor Jesus, I must help him' (Ortberg, 2012, p. 27). In the same way, hospitality, in the Celtic Spirit, is the practice of an open and non-judgmental heart in our encounters with others. It is about treating others as if they were Christ himself.

Nevertheless, it must also be said that it takes courage to have an open heart. Because, no doubt, sooner or later someone will abuse your hospitality and when that happens it takes courage not to shut down your open heart. Indeed hospitality is also a journey of risk and courage that requires a foundation of compassion and wisdom; and this is a further step in exploring the concept of hospitality within the ethos of the Celtic Spirit: hospitality as a courageous journey.

We have noted that the practice of hospitality is about respecting the sacredness of the other, yet such a practice originates in something even deeper, which is all about respecting the self or self-respect. There's an old saying 'charity begins at home', and if we are unable to have self-love and self-respect, it's difficult to offer it to others. For without that foundation of self-respect, our relationships with others will always be needy – seeking the fulfilment of something we feel is somehow missing within our own souls, through relationships with others, and therefore having expectations of the other that may not be possible for that person to fulfil.

There is a lovely expression of hospitality to the self in Celtic spirituality that speaks of coming home to the hearth of your own soul. To be rooted in this deep homecoming of self-acceptance, love and embrace, is the ultimate homecoming.

For many people, though, this journey of hospitality to the self takes a lifetime for all sorts of reasons. Sometimes there can be many obstacles which stand in the way of that ultimate homecoming of personal love and self-acceptance. Such obstacles may be connected with childhood years, the family, schools, churches or other social institutions; influences and experiences that may have instilled self-dissatisfaction, even self-repulsion.

The journey to the homecoming of personal hospitality may also be inhibited by adolescent experiences or career choices made and lives lived to please others instead of following the call of our own gifts and talents. So for most of us, to come home to the hearth of our own souls requires a lifetime's journey of self-discovery, eventually leading to self-acceptance and self-embrace – coming home to the hearth of your own soul. This is a journey that often requires great courage because it may require letting go of ideas, people or experiences that no longer serve us in any positive and health-giving way.

This is the essence of the heroic journey, first written about by the American psychologist and mythologist Joseph Campbell, who examined many of the indigenous mythologies of the ancient world, including the Celtic myths and legends. There he discovered a common theme running through all of these ancient stories, including the Hebrew stories of the Old Testament. It is the story of a journey which transforms the traveller forever – a heroic journey. This same story outline – though with variable details – has been repeated again and again in all the old myths and legends of the world's ancient cultures. That is why one of Campbell's books about the heroic journey is called *The Hero with a Thousand Faces* (Campbell, 1949; rpt 2008).

It could be said that the word 'hero' may seem a bit remote to many people. Like the word 'saint', it's hard to see ourselves as either a saint or a hero. Yet in the way of Celtic storytelling, each person is the hero or heroine of their own life story.

The basic outline of the heroic journey (Vogler, 1985, p. 49) is as follows:

Figure 3.1: Heroic Journey (Vogler, 1985, p. 49)

The hero is presented with a challenge or adventure and hears the call to the quest (1), but is reluctant at first to heed the call (2). However, eventually with the encouragement of another, the hero leaves the familiar place and is now committed to the journey (2) and (3). He/she goes through a time of testing (4) and reaches the heart of the matter (the innermost cave where the treasure lies) in enduring a supreme ordeal (5). Through this suffering the treasure is achieved (6) and the hero returns to the familiar place (7) – but returns as a transformed person, with a new perspective and a healing treasure to share (8).

An example of such a story from the Celtic Mythologies is *The Voyage of Bran*. The story begins with Bran at home, in the familiar place. But Bran has an urge 'to get away from the noise' – and sometimes, in order to hear the voice of our hearts, we need to 'get away from the noise' in our lives, whatever that may be. For Bran, this choice changes his life. In this quiet place he hears the ancient music:

> [G]lad of the silence and glad to be alone. Suddenly at his back he heard music. Not the sound of the harps he had just left, but a music stranger and sweeter than anything he had ever heard ... the music from the Happy Otherworld (Heaney, 1994, p. 56).

He hears the ancient music calling him out on a journey to a different way of being. So the story continues and Bran is called by a new music – the music of the silver branch from the world of the Tuatha Dé Danann – to enter a new experience of life and set out on the voyage that would change him forever. The stories and legends of Celtic Ireland are full of such heroic journeys, in which the hero is tested to the ultimate and, through the suffering, is transformed forever.

The Bible is also full of such heroic journeys. Abraham and Sarah, who 'went out not knowing where they were going' (Hebrews 11:8); Jonah, who tried to ignore the Call – and ended up in a perilous place; Mary, mother of Jesus, who heard the call and accepted it in humility, though not knowing where it would lead. It is this 'unknown' aspect of the heroic journey that requires courage to take the first step out of the familiar place. The heroic journey is about having the courage to listen to your heart and to follow its call, as Joseph Campbell said:

If you can see your path laid out in front of you step by step, you know it's not your path. Your own path you make with every step you take. That's why it's your path (Campbell, 2011, p. 22).

To the Celtic Christians, Christ was the ultimate hero, the one who left God's realm to follow the sacred call. With his disciples, he went through a time of testing in his confrontation with the religious authorities of his day. He suffered alone the supreme ordeal – crucifixion – and achieved the treasure – returning from the dead. Through this heroic journey Christ achieved the treasure of salvation for the whole earth.

In terms of the Celtic Spirit, the heroic journey speaks to us more personally and profoundly of the ultimate journey to find our own particular destiny and to come home to ourselves. In this sense the heroic cycle has the potential to be a source of inspiration and insight for all of us because it's at the heart of everyone's life. All of us encounter challenges, difficulties and times of trouble as we go through life. Our supreme ordeal may be physical or mental illness, divorce, bereavement, rejection, abuse or a multitude of other difficult life experiences. Yet these suffering experiences are the dark caves that offer us real treasure – the treasure of compassion, wisdom and understanding. As Henri Nouwen states, true healers are wounded healers – and the hero of the heroic journey carries his wounds (Nouwen, 1994).

A personal story, which I tell often and which I found profoundly life-transforming, is to do with a dream I had many years ago. Dreams are often gateways into the truth of the soul, and certainly this dream held deep wisdom for me. In the dream I was walking down wide stone steps, leading into a huge pyramid structure. At the bottom of the steps, dust and sand covered the floor and I took up a broom and began to sweep. As I swept away the layers of sand and dust, gradually and to my complete joy a beautiful colourful, mosaic-tiled floor began to be uncovered. Its symmetry and glorious colour were breathtaking. The experience of the dream was one of sheer joy, healing and bliss. I awoke with all of the joy and peace still within me, and remained still for a long time, absorbed in the beauty of the dream and wondering about its meaning.

As I reflected on the dream in the days afterwards, it seemed clear to me that the mosaic floor represented the beauty of the authentic soul. Through life's experiences our soul-beauty may get covered over with the dust and the dirt of living. Yet the beauty of the soul – our sacred authentic self – remains intact, no matter what life throws at us, to be uncovered and revealed as we realise our own sacredness and learn to value and love ourselves. This dream revealed to me – as does the vibrancy of the Celtic Spirit – that ultimately our potential for healing in this life is *within* our own souls. True hospitality begins with listening to one's own soul and embracing its giftedness and beauty.

A year or so later, I was attending a conference at which the guest speaker was a psychologist and writer from County Cork. I had the opportunity to tell him about my dream and his response was even more enlightening. Firstly, he agreed with my interpretation and marvelled about what a wonderful, insightful dream it was. However, he also said that I was lucky that in this dream all I had to do was to sweep away some dust and dirt – and there, uncovered, was my authentic soul! He said that for many people, some of whom he had worked with in therapy, their authentic soul is, as it were, encased in concrete because of the experiences of horror and abuse they have gone through in their lives. Just to survive they have had to hide who they truly are. For such people, to let down their defences – even enough to begin to hear the voice of their own soul – is a terrifying journey. It is the hero's story of facing the dragon! Though, as Joseph Campbell said of the lessons of the hero's journey: 'It's inevitably the cave you fear to enter which holds the treasure you seek' (Campbell, 1991, p. 8). The psychologist also said that the important thing to remember is that no one can ever deface or destroy your sacred soul. Your authentic self and voice is always there, intact, no matter what experiences you have been through, to be revealed and celebrated in all its glory. And from the perspective of the heroic journey we are never victims – no matter what has happened to us – but heroes of our own heroic life journeys. Indeed it is the suffering experiences of life, and the things about our life that make us vulnerable, which have the potential to become the pathways to the greatest healing treasures, reconnecting us with the soul. The heroic journey is about coming home to the fire of your soul. As Joseph Campbell said:

> People say that what we're all seeking is a meaning for life. I don't think that's what we're really seeking. I think that what we're seeking is an experience of being alive, so that our life experiences on the purely physical plane will have resonances with our own innermost being and reality, so that we actually feel the rapture of being alive (Campbell, 2011, p. 43).

The fire of the soul and the rapture of being alive is the music of the Celtic Spirit – the music that calls to us from the otherworld of our authentic souls:

Years later, when Oisin was an old, old man,
And when all the other Fianna were dead,
He was asked by St Patrick

What was the music that Finn and the Fianna loved best to
hear.
Remembering those days
And the sunburnt companions who were long gone,
He told the holy man
That the best music was
The music of what happened (Heaney, 1994, p. 170).

CHAPTER FOUR

The Celtic Spirit: Art and Creative Living
Grace Clunie

'In the beginning,
God created …' (Genesis 1:1)

As we have already discovered, the ancient Celts lived close to the rhythms and patterns of the natural world and from this intimacy with nature, based on both reverence and survival, came a cyclical perception of time. This is illustrated in artwork and by the Celtic calendar and in Celtic Christianity by the creativity of illuminated manuscripts, metalwork and sculpture. In this chapter we explore the phenomenon of Celtic art, its relationship to the Celtic calendar, the Celtic festivals, and the call to creativity.

Figure 4.1: The Celtic Calendar (Ó Duinn, 2000, pp. 222–326)

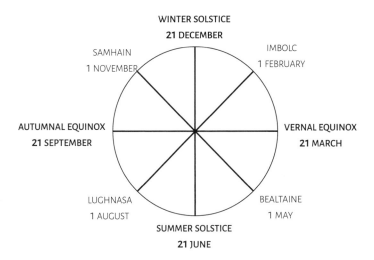

The year was divided up according to the seasons and the festivals that marked them, and in this way the Celtic peoples celebrated the sacredness of time. In addition, this cyclical concept, also prevalent in the very shapes of nature herself, was an integral part of Celtic artwork. Life was full of sacred meaning and the rituals that gave shape to the year also produced the distinguishing features of Celtic art – knotwork, spirals, curving lines and intricately balanced, ornamental patterns. Diagrammatically, the Celtic calendar (Ó Duinn, 2000, pp. 222–326) is as displayed on page 81.

The basic four quarters of the year follow the progress of the sun from the darkest and shortest day of the year on 21 December, when the sun is almost absent from the earth, through the spring equinox, to the summer solstice, the longest day, on 21 June, when the sun appears to be at the height of its powers, onwards to the autumn equinox when, once again, the sun is in decline and the days grow shorter. The vital import-ance of the sun to the life of the earth was understood by the Megalithic and Neolithic peoples. So much so, that much of their art and ritual was connected with the path of the sun.

One of the prime examples is the ancient site of Newgrange in County Meath, which is dated to around 3,200 BC, making it older than the pyramids of Egypt. The large circular mound with interior chambers is accessed by a narrow passageway. It was built to align with the rising sun and on the winter solstice, at the time when the sun reaches its zenith, light floods the inner chamber. For many this is an indicator that these ancestors had a deep knowledge of astronomy and the position of the sun, moon, stars and planets in relation to the earth. Exteriorly, the site is circled by standing stones, which archaeologists say date to a later period. Upon these standing stones are carved various circular motifs familiar to Celtic art, and, which some say, indicating the cyclical year and the cycles of life and death. The stones display a range of carved art including circles, spirals, arcs, chevrons, radials and parallel lines. Among the most amazing are the circular *triskele* carvings on the huge stone at the entrance to the passage way that leads to the inner chamber. And for contemporary artists in the Celtic style, this ancient design has become an icon of inspiration. The point is that Newgrange, a ritual ancestral site, is a symbol of the connection for the ancient peoples between sacred time and sacred art.

The Celtic peoples added four more festivals to the year, Samhain, Imbolc, Bealtaine and Lughnasa, each of which marks the subtle changes of the Irish seasons.

In many of the ancient mythologies, events of particular significance happened at the beginning of these sacred times. For example, *The Voyage of Bran* from the Mythological Cycle begins with a gathering of chiefs who had assembled 'to celebrate the great feast of Bealtaine, which falls on the first of May' (Heaney, 1994, p. 56). And in the Fenian Cycle when Finn joins the Fianna, the events begin on the night before 'the solemn day of Samhain' (Heaney, 1994, p. 164).

The year begins with Samhain on the first of November, which is the winter quarter when the Insular Celtic world goes into hibernation. It's a time for rest, for remembrance of the ancestors and equated with old age. The year moves through the winter solstice and on to Imbolc, celebrated on the first of February, which is a time of new beginnings and equated with childhood. Time moves on through the spring equinox to Bealtaine on the first of May and is a time of vitality associated with the vigour of young adulthood. Finally comes Lughnasa on the first of August – the time for harvesting which is equated with mature adulthood in the human life cycle.

Caitlin Matthews, to whom I am indebted for this information about the Celtic year, in her beautiful *Celtic Devotional*, says:

> The Celtic year may be likened to the life-progress of the soul itself: it starts at the time of cold and darkness and

proceeds through the many seasons of life until it reaches fruitful maturity ... Each season provides us with many doorways of opportunity for fresh spiritual revelation and personal response (Matthews, 1996, pp. 9–10).

It may also be of interest to know that an actual surviving Celtic calendar was uncovered in 1897 in woods near Bourg in the Ain region of France. 'The Coligny Tablet', as it is now called, has revealed to scholars important information about the ways in which the Celtic peoples observed the annual seasons. For example, the Tablet confirms that the Celtic year began in October/November with Samonios, during which Samhain was celebrated. Each day was measured from sunset to sunset – not midnight to midnight, as in the modern Roman calendar – and each month started at the full moon. The names for the months revealed details of the lives of the Celtic peoples; for example, November/December was 'The Darkest Depths', January/February was 'Stay-Home-Time' and June/July was 'Horse-time' (Matthews, 1994, pp. 91–3).

The essence of this approach to living, marking the seasons with festivals and rituals, is an acknowledgement of the sacredness of time. So early Christianity in Ireland continued this pattern and approach to living through the daily round of monastic prayer and the annual Christian festivals. The main manifestation of early Christian organisation in Ireland was monasticism, and the practice of daily prayer was based upon the 'Liturgy of the Hours' or the 'Divine Office'. Originally this grew from the Jewish practice of reciting particular prayers at set times of the day. Based upon Psalm 119:164 – 'Seven times a day I praise you for your righteous laws' – seven 'Offices' developed – Lauds, Prime, Terce, Sext, None, Vespers and Compline – with a night office sometimes called Vigils. However, it also seems possible that the pre-Christian approach to marking the sacredness of the seasons would have supported the Christian monastic practice of 'sacred living'. Indeed, many of the Christian festivals have residues of those more ancient festivals and are even celebrated around the same times.

An interesting example is the festival of Samhain. In pre-Christian times this was regarded as a 'thin-time' of the year. This referred to the perception that the otherworld was an invisible yet parallel world of the gods and the ancestors, which sometimes burst into human experience at particular significant times. Indeed at times such as Samhain it seemed that there was only a thin veil between this world and the otherworld. For example, in the Fenian Cycle of Irish mythologies, Finn says: 'Men of Ireland, tomorrow is the solemn day of Samhain when the doors of the Otherworld stand open and the Tuatha Dé Danann come out and mix with mortals' (Heaney, 1994, p. 164).

Samhain was a time for remembrance of all who had gone on to the otherworld and who might possibly return at this marginal time of the year. In the Christian Church at this season 'All Saints' and 'All Souls' are celebrated. Many traditions also have 'Remembrance Sunday', with special prayer services to remember those who have died during the year, and 'Graveyard Sunday', to visit and pray at the family graves. In the secular world there is the celebration of Hallowe'en (All Hallows Eve) during which people dress up as mythical figures – ghosts, witches, phantoms and fairies – all representing well-known otherworld figures. In addition, around the time when pre-Christian practice marked the darkest day of the year at the winter solstice and the rebirth of the sun at the year's turning, Christians mark the birth of Christ, the Light of the World.

Again, around the time of the spring equinox, between Imbolc and Bealtaine, which both emphasised the fertility of the earth and celebrated the increasing power of the sun,

Christians celebrate Easter, the rising of the Son from the dead. Indeed, when I was a child we had some practices at Eastertide that were certainly of pre-Christian origin. For example, we boiled eggs in the yellow whin (gorse) flowers and, when they were hard-boiled and their shells yellow, we painted faces on them, then took them to the highest hill around and competed to see who could throw their eggs the furthest. Then, gathering up the broken eggs, we would shell them and eat them! I have often wondered if this was a remnant of some ancient fertility rite.

At Christmas time most of us bring a tree into our homes and, according to many sources, this originates in a pre-Christian practice. Ancient peoples brought evergreen trees into their dwellings during the winter solstice, when the land was in the icy grip of winter, so that the inhabitants would receive protection and blessing from the spirit of the evergreen tree.

The point is that all of these ancient rituals and festivals underline an approach to living which is connected to the earth. This remind us that we are all part of the bigger picture of the earth family and acknowledges the sacredness of time – that each moment, day and season brings its challenges and blessings. It is this approach to existence that underlined the artwork of the Celtic peoples. Art was not just for decorative purposes, but also represented deeper symbolic significances. For example, at Newgrange archaeologists have uncovered intricate artwork on some of the standing stones which they say was hidden under the earth and would not have been visible. Therefore, its purpose was not solely decorative as it was not ever visible above the ground to the human eye.

The Irish-American artist and researcher Martin Brennan, who studied the artwork in the Loughcrew passage tombs in County Meath, discovered that the beams of the rising sun at the spring and autumn equinoxes illuminate the artwork on the backstone, which, he says, holds astronomical significance.

His research identified a clear and distinct link between megalithic art and the astronomical events that animate megalithic structures, giving them meaning and function (Brennan, 1983).

The symbolic nature of Celtic art is underlined by Barry Cunliffe, Professor of European Archaeology at the University of Oxford. He says:

Celtic Art was far more than purely decorative art-for-art's sake. The choice of motifs and their arrangement will have held meaning for those who could interpret them. It is highly probable that they communicated identity and status as well as endowing the owner with a degree of Divine protection (Cunliffe, 2003, p. 67).

Modern archaeology has been able to use remaining artefacts as one way of tracing the identity of a people called Celts, before any written records. Although Celtic art had a variety of styles of centuries there are some familiar commonalities. For example, Celtic art avoided straight lines and used knotwork, spirals, weaving patterns, representations of animals, such as the Boar and patterns visible in the natural world, such as circles on the bark of ancient trees, ripples on a pool of water. They also frequently represented the human head.

Their artwork was in metal, wood, leather and stone. These were used to make, for example, fine jewellery, the torc for the neck, weapons, utensils for daily use, decorated harnesses for horses, glass, enamelling – and also sacred items such as the standing stones around ritual mounds like Newgrange. The Celts were very skilled artists and craftsworkers.

In his book, *The Celts*, Peter Beresford Ellis comments on Celtic coinage:

One of the richest expressions of Celtic Art is to be found in the production of Celtic coinage … To put the Celtic development of Celtic coinage into context, the Celts were minting their own coins some 50 years before Rome started to do so (Beresford Ellis, 1998, p. 139).

In ancient Celtic society artists, craftsmen and poets had a very high standing. Indeed, along with Druids and bards and those skilled at healing, the craftsworkers were included in the ruling class.

In the ancient myths and legends, the Celtic God of the Blacksmiths, Goibhniu, reveals interesting aspects of the status of the smith, who had high status because they were perceived to possess some otherworld knowledge, alchemy: by fire, water and their art they forged strong metal. So in Ireland the smith appears as a triune god – Goibhniu, Luchta and Credhne – perhaps this meant that the Christian concept of a triune god was already familiar to the Celts? Lugh (God of Light) in Celtic mythology is blessed with all the skills of a craftsman.

In the story of Lugh coming to Tara – part of the Mythological Cycle – King Nuada has managed to regain the kingship from Bres, the unjust Fomorian king, and Lugh comes to Tara, seat of the High King, to be on the side of the Tuatha Dé Danann. It transpires that Lugh possesses the gift of all the arts and so they call him *Samildanach*, meaning a master of all the arts.

This practice of creative arts and skills, so valued in Irish society, was also an integral aspect of Celtic Christianity, and we are very fortunate in our time to still have so much of this inspirational artwork with us. For example, in many Irish villages elaborately carved stone high crosses still stand. A lovely example is in the village of Donaghmore, County Tyrone, which has a beautiful high cross displaying the life of Christ, from his birth to his ascension into heaven. At one time the people would have gathered around these crosses to hear the gospel stories. In an age when people did not read or write they were a great visual aid.

DONAGHMORE CROSS

Still stand: The High Cross at Donaghmore, Co. Tyrone.
A monastery is reputed to have been founded here in the sixth century by
St Patrick, for St Columba.

From the monasteries of early Christian Ireland came iconic
and inspirational artworks in the form of illuminated manuscripts. In *The Celtic Way* Ian Bradley says:

The Celtic monasteries were not just religious institutions in the narrow sense. They opened their doors to
seekers and scholars of all kinds and became important
centres of learning and culture. In this respect they took
over the role which had been fulfilled by communities

of bards and filid in pre-Christian times … If the monks had a scriptural inspiration for their work, it was surely Paul's injunction to the Philippians to hold unto whatsoever things are pure and lovely and good. This meant keeping alive native traditions of poetry and folksong as well as copying the Scriptures, practicing the art of manuscript illumination, studying classical authors, both for their philosophy and their theology and fashioning exquisite brooches and rings (Bradley, 1993; rpt 2003, pp. 73–4).

CELTIC SPIRAL CERAMIC

A pattern of spirals: One of the most characteristic motifs in Celtic design is the spiral.

Monks carefully copied the gospels, embellishing them with fantastic ornamentation – spiral markings, knots, animal and human heads, plants and birds, all drawn in vivid colours. Today, in our time, thousands travel from all over the world each year to see the *Book of Kells* in Trinity College Dublin. It is well over a thousand years old – dated to the ninth century – and is an exceptional example of the illuminated manuscripts produced by many of the Celtic Christian monastic settlements. It is a richly illustrated Latin manuscript version of the four gospels and, according to legend, Columba was its creator on Iona.

This insular style of Celtic art, as it is called, evolved and flourished in Northern Britain and Ireland. Another wonderful example is *The Lindisfarne Gospels*. The artwork was created using a variety of colours – red, yellow, green, blue, pink, purple, white, black and brown – from a variety of natural sources. For example, red from red lead; yellow from egg yoke; green from copper; purple from a Mediterranean plant; blue from a precious stone called lapis lazuli.

The *Book of Kells* also contains beautiful calligraphic art and is decorated with all sorts of interlocking spirals and weaving designs, along with representations of birds and animals, insects, fish and mythical creatures. These iconic gospel books were lovingly and painstakingly created by various artists and craftsmen over many years. They used vellum or calf skin as 'paper' and it is said that it took the skin of one hundred calves to make the *Book of Armagh*. They worked with poor light so it was most likely younger monks with good vision who worked on these intricate creations under the tutorage of an older monk. Sometimes there are comments in the margins, some humorous, which give insight into the daily lives of the monks in these places. In Armagh the scribe is said to have been Ferdomnach, who took over the work from Patrick's heir, Torbach, and their likenesses have been represented in two beautiful stained-glass windows on the north side of the main

BOOK OF KELLS, BLESSED VIRGIN AND CHILD

Supreme artistry: detail from the *Book of Kells*, Trinity College Dublin.

sanctuary of the old cathedral. Of course there was a status attached to owning such illuminated manuscripts, and monastic communities which housed such great works, therefore, had higher status.

The *Book of Armagh*, also known as the *Canon of Patrick*, is a collation of several books – some of which are a life of St Martin of Tours and the earliest copy of the gospels in Irish, a life of St Patrick and also the *Book of Angel* (*Liber Angeli*). Through the *Book of Armagh*, the Christian monastic community in that place made retrospective connections with both St Martin of Tours and, of course, St Patrick. This was often done to establish the status and authenticity of a monastic community, so the tradition is recorded in the *Book of Angel* that Patrick had decreed that Armagh be the centre of the Christian Church in Ireland. It was certainly a great centre in Patrick's time, based around the reputation of Emain Macha, seat of the King of Ulster. To this day it remains the 'ecclesiastical capital of Ireland' and both the Roman Catholic and Anglican Archbishops reside there.

In terms of understanding the place of the artist and craftsperson in Celtic Christian society, there is a lovely example of a small Celtic monastic community called Nendrum near Comber in County Down, which, in ancient times would have been on an island but now is accessible by car via a road bridge linking the island to the mainland. It is interesting because of the circular way in which it is organised and laid out. In the centre circle is the church, the tower, the sundial and the graves of the monks who were always buried where they had lived and worked. In the next circle were the craftsmen and the artisans who practised their artistic skills and in the third circle out crops were grown and animals grazed. It was a very sustainable community of simple living, and more recently remnants of the world's oldest tide-mill have been discovered there – using the ebb and the flow of the tides they powered a mill that would have ground flour for bread. So, Nendrum also illustrates the place of artisans and creative people within the life of the Celtic monastic community.

Having noted the central importance of art and creativity to the Celtic Spirit and to Celtic Christianity, what inspirations are there in all of this for us today? Celtic art is a vital and important part of Irish heritage, but it also may have other gems to offer to us in the light of modern psychology. For example, modern psychology, in particular since Carl Jung, has revealed that the human psyche has a left-brain and a right-brain way of being and encountering experience. This is now a familiar concept to most of us – and indeed the following will oversimplify something that is actually quite complex. Nevertheless, briefly, and from the perspective of a non-specialist, it appears that the right brain processes the artistic, intuitive, sensual and emotional side of human experience whereas the left brain processes the analytical, scientific, logical and mathematical side of human experience. Clearly, both are important to the totality of our life experience. However, it has to be said that the contemporary emphasis in western society is predominantly on left-brain approachs based upon the scientific world view and empiricism. For universities and colleges, funding is often much more widely available for scientific subjects than for the world of the arts, and indeed the creative wisdom of spiritual, artistic and poetic insight and experience has sometimes been pushed to the margins. The fact that the poet, the storyteller and the Druid were highly valued by their society gives us an insight into the perspectives of the Celtic Spirit and explains why in the earliest manifestations of Christianity creativity flourished.

There is a particular prayer-poem called 'The Hermit and the Blackbird' from the Celtic Christian hermit tradition that expresses beautifully the contrast between these two ways of being. On the one hand, the mathematical approach to prayer that is bound to counting the Liturgy of the Hours – represented by the hermit – and on the other hand, the sort of prayer which wells up out of the very nature of creative being – represented by the Blackbird:

> I need to watch the sun, to calculate the hours that I should pray to God.
> But the Blackbird who nests in the roof of my hut makes no such calculations:
> She sings God's praises all day long.
>
> I need books to read, to learn the hidden truths of God.
> But the Blackbird who shares my simple meals needs no written texts:
> She can read the love of God in every leaf and flower (Van de Weyer, 1997, p. 31).

The Celtic Spirit, with its emphasis on art and creativity, speaks to us of a balance between left and right brain. However, in our modern educational systems the experience of knowledge is about analytical, academic ways of learning and so, for artists and creative people, this has often meant being compelled, to some extent, to fit in by suppression or compromise. In addition, there is also the idea of the expert in the world today, which often inhibits people from practising their arts and skills because they view themselves as unworthy amateurs, only the expert can authoritatively comment on what 'good' art is. Sometimes, in today's very materialistic culture, art has become more of a commodity for sale and investment, rather than being valued as an expression of the soul of a person or a society. But the Celtic Spirit and Celtic art seem to speak with a different voice about art, which is an expression or *embodiment* of gift and skill, an integral part of identity and being. In this sense, creativity and art are spiritual paths for the unfolding of the gifted self – and all are gifted.

In her wonderful book *The Artist's Way*, Julia Cameron says that creativity is the essential nature of God. Think, for example, of the opening words of the Bible: 'In the beginning God created ...' So we begin with a picture of God as creator/artist. Julia Cameron says that in expressing our creativity as human beings we are aligning ourselves with the creative power of the universe. This creative power is also the *neart*, referred to earlier, of the pre-Christian world. She says:

> For most of us the idea that the Creator *encourages* creativity is a radical thought. We tend to think, or at least fear, that creative dreams are egotistical, something that God wouldn't approve of ... This thinking must be undone. For creativity is *spiritual experience*. It is 'spiritual *chiropractic*.' We undertake certain spiritual exercises to achieve alignment with the creative energy of the universe (Cameron, 1995, p. 1).

In this sense creativity is a pathway to connection with the Divine as Cameron says:

> Creativity is the natural order of life. Life is energy, pure creative energy. Creativity is God's gift to us. Using our creativity is our gift back to God. Our creative dreams and yearnings come from a Divine source. As we move toward our dreams, we move toward our Divinity (Cameron, 1995, p. 3).

Other ancient religions also recognise the spiritual value of the creative arts. Personally, I love the symmetry and colour of Islamic art and also the music and Mandala artwork of Tibetan Buddhism. So this creativity, so important for Celtic spirituality, and for many spiritual paths, is inspirational for us today because all of us have this creative aspect of our humanity. To uncover our creativity is to follow in the footsteps of the Celtic Spirit and to find the voice of our own authentic selves. This is not about academic study or objective learning.

Rather, it is about the creative art of living – *being yourself*. For me it is summed up by an old word in the Irish – *dán* – which means both your poetry and your destiny. That word expresses a deep wisdom that one's destiny is somehow bound up with the practice of one's poetry, and that life is about the joy of *embodying* our gift or skill – not just working for money or killing time.

The Celtic Spirit gives us the example of Lugh, who, in the Mythological Cycle is presented as someone whose many gifts were integrated into his very way of being. This beautiful description of Lugh, perceived by King Nuada as being alive with light, is part of the story *Lugh Comes to Tara*:

> One day ... Nuada was looking out across the ramparts of his fort when he saw a troop of warriors coming towards him. His eyes were dazzled by a bright light as if he had looked full into the sun, but then he saw that the brilliant rays shone from the face of the leader of the troop and from his long golden hair. Darts of light came off the young man's armour and off his weapons and the gold-embossed harness of his horse. A great jewel blazed from the front of the golden helmet he wore on his shining hair, and Nuada knew that Lugh had come back to Tara (Heaney, 1994, p. 15).

This image of Lugh, shining with light, is reminiscent of the story of the Transfiguration of Christ in the gospels. As the mythologist Joseph Campbell has said: 'We save the world by being alive ourselves' (Campbell, 1988, p. 120).

This idea of the giftedness of the self is also located in the Christian tradition in 1 Corinthians 12 which talks about varieties of gifts and varieties of service. So all of us are gifted in different ways, and to be alive is to hear and follow the voice of your own unique inner creativity and to live out of that power or – in the words of the Celtic Spirit – to live your *dán*.

Ancient words from Psalm 139 express it like this:

> You knit me together in my mother's womb … My frame was not hidden from you, when I was being made in secret, intricately woven in the depths of the earth. Your eyes beheld my unformed substance. In your book were written all the days that were formed for me when none of them as yet existed (Psalm 139:13–16).

All of us are unique individuals – biologically and in every way – and no one else can be us. Only we can offer our particular gift to the world in our particular way. So the best thing anyone can do in this life, for ourselves and for others, is to *be yourself*. Julia Cameron says: 'No matter what your age or your life path … it is not too late or too egotistical or too selfish or too silly to work on your creativity' (Cameron, 1995, p. xii).

In whatever way your creativity expresses itself, it is the path to your authentic self and to being alive. This is one of the great wisdom insights of the Celtic Spirit – to be truly alive, discover, celebrate and practice your *dán*!

CHAPTER FIVE

The Celtic Spirit and Journey
Grace Clunie

Here is the 'Prayer of a Breton Fisherman':
Lord, the sea is so wide
And my boat is so small.
Be with me (Hutchinson, 2000, p. 3).

In Chapter One of this book we explored the ways in which the evolving civilisations of the Celtic peoples were associated with wide areas of Europe over many centuries. Indeed, it seems that Celtic civilisation, in all its variety, at particular times, represented peoples on the move. One example is that documented by Greek and Roman historians concerning the movement of Celts from north of the Alps into the Mediterranean lands in the period from about 400 BCE. Perhaps it was this feature within the history and experience of Celtic peoples that resulted in the urge to journey, represented in the echtrae and immram journey stories of the Insular Celts. Yet, at the same time, the Insular Celtic peoples were very rooted in place, with regard to kin and identity.

In this sense it could be said that they held together two important aspects of their way of living: firstly, a deep sense of rootedness and place in terms of kin and tribal identity; and secondly, a nomadic yearning which led to the undertaking of long journeys and the valuing of epic stories about voyages to unfamiliar places. This chapter will explore some examples of echtrae and immram and the manifestation of *peregrinatio* in Celtic Christianity, as well as considering some aspects of the nomadic way of being for our inspiration today.

One of the best known of the old mythological journey stories is *The Voyage of Bran*. The story is a fascinating one. It

begins at the great feast of Bealtaine, the first of May, a propit-
ious time:

> As his guests listened to the musicians and poets, and
> cheered on the champions ... Bran left the gathering to
> get away from the noise ... he stood looking across the
> plain, glad of the silence and glad to be alone. Suddenly
> at his back he heard music ... a music stranger and
> sweeter than anything he had ever heard ... he realized
> he was listening to the music of the Sidhe and became
> afraid (Heaney, 1994, p. 56).

So here we have the beginning of a great journey. Bran is
the one who is brave enough to leave the usual and familiar
occupations of the tribe, and step out on his own, and in the
silence and the moments of aloneness he encounters a doorway
into a new world. The journey always begins with the leaving
of the familiar and the longing for something other than the
familiar. Bran is called by the song of the people of the Sidhe,
the otherworld. He falls asleep – for the call often comes in
dreams, the deepest place of the unconscious – and when he
awakes, the story continues:

> As he looked around the familiar place, something
> gleamed in the grass beside him – it was the branch of
> an apple tree, made of silver, that shone with a frosty
> brightness (Heaney, 1994, p. 57).

The familiar place has changed and when he enters the
great hall carrying the silver branch a silence falls on the
gathering. Then a woman of the Sidhe appears – 'one of those
ageless ones who lives under the great mounds and under the
waters of rivers and lakes' (Heaney, 1994, p. 57). She begins to
sing and her song ends with these words:

> Though all can hear me, Bran, my song is for you,
> Don't let tiredness delay you,
> Don't wait to drink wine,

Begin the voyage across the clear sea
To the beautiful land I have promised (Heaney, 1994, p. 58).

So Bran gathers thirty sailors and they row off across the ocean to seek the fair land. During their voyage they meet the God of the sea, Manannán Mac Lir (after whom the Isle of Man is named) and, among many adventures, they discover the island of joy and the island of women. There they have great contentment for a year until one of their number, Nechtan, begins to feel homesick and they eventually decide to bring him home. Then the story ends with a strange twist of fate. When they reach the shores of Ireland the people call to them from the shore, asking their identity and Bran responds with his name and kin-name. But the people respond:

We have heard of Bran, son of Febal ... He set out hundreds of years ago in a curragh to seek a magic land ... He has not been heard of since, but The Voyage of Bran is a story known to us all. It is one of our oldest tales (Heaney, 1994, p. 62).

Then Nechtan leaps out of the boat and wades to the shore, but:

As soon as his foot touched the earth he turned into a handful of dust the same as if he'd been buried there for centuries (Heaney, 1994, p. 62).

So there is a sense in this wonderful story that when someone goes out on a journey they enter a different time frame and they become different people from those who remain in the tribe and the familiar. Not only do they feel restless in the old home place, but actually they no longer belong there and they can never truly go back – for everything has changed and the familiar place knows them no more. Perhaps it was a bit like this for those who left home to go to America during the great famine in the nineteenth century, so that this sense of the nomadic and of the mystery of journey is part of both ancient Celtic identity and more contemporary Irish experience.

In ancient times the world was a strange, dark and dangerous place, largely unmapped territory. To the Celtic mind – an insular island people – around any corner could possibly come an encounter with the otherworld, the people of the Sidhe, who inhabited the mysterious and secret parts of the earth and the ocean. In this sense, journeys in the old mythologies were always adventurous, dangerous, heroic and life changing and they represented much more than just a physical journey. They were also about the spiritual journey, the search for the authentic path or voice, the inner quest for spiritual rebirth, and journey as a pathway to the sacred source of the soul.

FIGURE OF TINY MAN AMONG THE WAVES

Casting upon the waters: The immram was often a journey of the spirit.

According to the scholars, there are two different types or genres of journey story. The first is echtrae (meaning 'adventure'), and is about a hero's adventure in the otherworld – but usually an otherworld that is not particularly Christian in its presentation. Indeed, although *The Voyage of Bran* is known as *Immram Brain*, it is more accurately an echtrae because the otherworld of the hero is pre-Christian, with the gods and goddesses of the Sidhe calling the hero on his journey. Secondly, there are early Irish journey stories known as immrama (from *immram*, literally 'rowing about'). These are tales of sea voyages arising from a period when Irish Christian monks practised exile, both as a form of subjection to what they perceived to be the will of God and to spread the gospel of Jesus Christ.

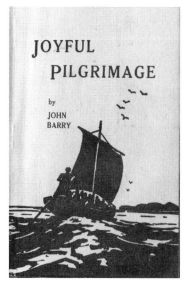

COLUMBA VOYAGE TO IONA

A joyful pilgrimage: In 1963 the Church of Ireland organised a commemorative voyage to honour the journey of Saint Columba, undertaken fourteen hundred years before. Volunteers came from all over Ireland to build a curragh and sail it to Iona.

107

One example of the immram genre is *Navigatio Sancti Brendani* (*The Voyage of St Brendan*), c. AD 900. St Brendan's journey is undertaken not so much as a heroic adventure, but to seek for 'the Promised Land of the Saints' (O'Meara, 1976, p. 4). The promised land is described as a place already 'not far away' and fasting for forty days is part of the preparation for the journey, which is blessed by the holy St Enda. As they take leave, the name of the Trinity is invoked and the voyage seems surrounded by a sacred light. As St Brendan and his brethren journey on the ocean to many islands, they are clearly guided by God, and Brendan himself is portrayed as a serene, saintly figure, similar to the calm of Christ in the boat on the Lake of Galilee recorded in the gospels. It is a world located in the liturgy and daily prayer of monasticism and the Bible.

Another interesting example is *Immram Curaig Máele Dúin*, written in Old Irish around the end of the first millennium, which is viewed by some scholars to be a secular imitation of *The Voyage of St Brendan*. These two immrama have much in common in terms of the content and layout of their stories but are also markedly different in ethos. Ultimately, both tales espouse the Christian message of love and peace in subjection to the will of God. However, whereas *The Voyage of St Brendan* is located in the world of Christian monasticism from beginning to end, and the journey is about seeking for an otherworld similar to the biblical promised land, *Immram Curaig Máele Dúin* contains a different ethos.

Máele Dúin is a truly human being who remains truly human and his journey is about reconnecting with his true self by God's grace – his own community – rather than the longing for an 'otherworld' or promised land somewhere else. And whereas St Brendan is presented as a saintly figure, it has to be said that Máele Dúin takes his humanity along with him. So in this sense *Immram Curaig Máele Dúin* merges the secular and the sacred and elevates the material world to a place of wonder and divinity. Indeed there are undertones of Erigena in the sense that humanity and the earth are not ultimately evil and sinful, but rooted in goodness and potential for the Divine. In addition, Máele Dúin harbours a yearning for the ancient ways and the Celtic Spirit. *The Voyage of Muldoon* is recycled satirically in Flann O'Brien's *An Béal Bocht* (*The Poor Mouth*). We will be discussing that extraordinary book in Chapter Eleven.

The yearning for the adventures of voyage and journey is represented in early Irish Christianity by the *peregrinatio*. Early Irish Christians practised a form of self-sacrifice to the will of God by willingly leaving home and kin and going into exile for the gospel of Christ. This self-imposed exile was particularly difficult because values of kinship and tribal allegiance were central to the identity and status of a person. To abandon homeland, tribe and family for the sake of Christ was a huge sacrifice and even regarded as a type of martyrdom.

In her book *A World Made Whole* Esther De Waal outlines three types of Celtic martyrdom:

- ♭ Red Martyrdom: separation from the soul at death (martyrdom by sword or fire was very rare in the Celtic churches).

- ♭ Green Martyrdom: separation from one's desires (penance as a spiritual exercise was widely practised).

- ♭ White Martyrdom: separation from one's beloved homeland (self-imposed exile was common and very painful for these home lovers) (De Waal, 1991, p. 44).

Thomas Owen Clancy comments:

One of the most important aspects of early Irish society was Kinship … To go outside this structure was dangerous. To leave one's homeland involved not only travel in the wilderness, the dwelling place of beasts and brigands, but travel into another territory. To settle there

meant loss of status, protection and loss of basic rights
... This displacement from the kin group into the
unknown was openly courted, indeed seen as a type of
martyrdom by early Irish monastics (Clancy, 2000, pp.
194–226).

There were rules of kinship and belonging that had to be
respected, especially by anyone planning to leave the tribe.
Leave-taking had to be done ritually and properly. Phyllida
Anam-Aire from County Donegal has written about these old
traditions, emphasising what a massive decision it was to leave
the tribe. She says:

Before leaving the tribe in Celtic times, permission had
to be granted by the grandfather. The elders listened
carefully without judgment, and usually the young
person was able to leave with a blessing, but not before
they were initiated into a ritual of leaving the father's
house. Six tasks were necessary. They had to:
State why they wanted to leave.
Ask forgiveness from the ancestors.
Ask for their father's blessing.
Thank their mother for giving them life.
Ask for the goodwill of their siblings.
Tell the community (Anam-Áire, 2007, p. 131).

This deep sense of tribal identity and belonging which can
be found in many of the Celtic mythologies – and indeed
exemplified by the genealogies within the literature – can still
be experienced in Ireland to this day. We have a rich, cultural
heritage and it lives in our bones, so that still, wherever you
go in Ireland you will always be asked: 'What's your name,
and where do you come from?' This is all about placing the
stranger in the context of tribal identity and kinship – the place
of belonging. This deep sense of rootedness is captured in the
poetry of Patrick Kavanagh, who is quoted as saying:

To know fully even one field or one land is a lifetime's experience. In the world of poetic experience it is depth that counts, not width (Kavanagh, 1977, p. 8).

That sort of *knowing* is about depth of understanding and feel of place. It is the opposite of the person who says: 'I saw the whole world in a month!' They may have travelled great distances in miles, but very little in depths of understanding. So, this deep rootedness of place is tied up with identity and belonging and yet, parallel to this, there's also the phenomenon of *peregrinatio* – an example of the nomadic aspect of the Celtic Spirit. Indeed, to this day Irish people have journeyed all over the world, so that there is hardly a city anywhere in the world without an Irish pub!

There is a sense in which that word 'be-longing' seems to sum it up: the restlessness of *longing* that leads the soul out on a journey, like Bran or Brendan or Máele Dúin, coupled with *be*, just being in one place. Longing and belonging – two aspects of the same Celtic Spirit. In terms of Celtic Christianity, it may be that early Irish Christians perceived some aspects of this nomadic spirit within the Bible itself. The ancient Hebrew people were, like Abraham and Sarah, nomadic peoples – 'A wandering Aramean was my father' (Deuteronomy 26:5). They journeyed through the desert regions, like the Bedouins of the Sahara desert, pitching their tents as they went – but always with the hope of a promised land of belonging up ahead. Yahweh, their portable God, travelled with them in the Ark of the Covenant, in the cloud by day and the pillar of fire by night. They had to trust in God for the journey. And then later, when the people were more settled in the land and they wanted to appoint a king, God was not very pleased about it. 1 Samuel 8 records how the elders of Israel said: 'Appoint for us a King to govern us, like other nations' (v. 5). And when Samuel the prophet asked God about it, God replied, 'Let them have what they want for they have not rejected you, they have rejected *me* from being King over them'(v. 7). So that was the first step towards a more institutionalised way of being.

Then came the kings – first of all Saul, then David, then Solomon – and it was they who decided to build a temple for God. King David wanted to build the temple – but God said no. Then came his son Solomon and he was chosen as the temple builder, so Yahweh ceased altogether to be the nomadic, portable God of the Ark of the Covenant and became this 'God in a House' – still seen our churches and buildings today. It is as if the more settled the Israelites became, the more secure they felt.

In the gospels of the New Testament there are also aspects of this nomadic spirit of journey. Christ himself was a wanderer from place to place who said at one point in his ministry: 'Foxes have holes, and birds of the air have nests; but the Son of Man has nowhere to lay his head' (Luke 9:58). In addition, the first Christians were actually called 'People of the Way' (Acts 9:2), suggesting that their spiritual path was inspired by the ethos of journey.

When you are travelling there are all sorts of uncertainties and insecurities. You don't know where you'll end up at the close of a day. But when you are settled, life becomes more predictable and you start to gather 'stuff' around you. And so your God becomes settled too and starts to gather stuff too – all the trappings of buildings and churches and what we call organised religion.

In contrast, the *peregrinatio* of Celtic Christianity were inspired by the nomadic spirit, evident in the early part of the Old Testament and in the ministry of Jesus, and left all that was familiar to follow Christ into the unknown. In this way Christianity spread and monasteries were established in Great Britain and continental Europe. In Ireland, the period known as the Dark Ages was actually a time of light and learning that profoundly influenced the whole of Europe.

One early example is Columba of Iona. Columba or Colum Cille was born around 521. Our knowledge of him derives largely from the *Life of Colum Cille*, written by Adamnán about one hundred years after his death. He was linked with the powerful Uí Néill tribe of Northern Ireland and with the royal dynasty of Leinster. He founded monasteries in Derry and Durrow and, in 563, left Ireland to found a community off the Scottish coast at Iona. The story goes that Columba had broken rules of copyright, which led to a battle in which many were killed; this resulted in him being banished from the shores of Ireland. His journey led him to a tiny, obscure island off the west coast of Scotland, now called Iona. It is hard to imagine what it must have been like for Columba to leave his kin and country – or for all those who set out as wandering ascetics for the sake of Christ. At that time, Iona was still in the sphere of influence of the Picts, but in the course of time Gaelic language and culture dominated the whole of the western part of Scotland. Iona itself became a very influential centre of Irish Christianity from where the Celtic influence passed to Northumbria and took root at Lindisfarne and elsewhere and even extended down into parts of East Anglia.

Another major *peregrinatio* figure was Columbanus (543–615), who was born in Leinster, trained in Bangor, County Down, and left Ireland in 587 for Gaul. In contrast to Colum Cille, we have a number of works written by Columbanus that give us a picture of an able and strong Christian leader. Columbanus brought Celtic Christianity to the Continent, and was the founder of monasteries such as Luxeuil in south-east France and Bobbio in Northern Italy. During the seventh century, those who came after Columbanus founded several monasteries in the regions that we now call France, Germany, Belgium and Switzerland. One of the best known is St Gall in Switzerland and Mont-St Michel in France. The lifelong and voluntary commitment of Columbanus to exile from his homeland is an outstanding example of *peregrinatio pro Christo,* or wandering for Christ, but his sacrifice brought a great harvest in terms of the spread of monastic Christianity in Europe.

For Celtic Christians who left behind their kin and country to set out, for the sake of the gospel, as wandering ascetics into a largely unmapped, unknown world holding all sorts of dangers around every corner, this was a truly heroic journey. The pilgrim of today has the comfort of the travel itinerary, the knowledge of places to stay – booked well ahead – and a mobile phone to keep in touch. There were no such luxuries for the Celtic pilgrim, and yet *peregrinatio* is one of the most important features of Celtic Christianity. For a people who had a very strong sense of place and kinship connection, this exile for Christ was a very costly form of discipleship – almost a mini-death. It's clear, though, from Celtic monastic writings that this exile was far more than just a physical journey, hard though that was. It was, most importantly, an inner journey, leaving behind all that was familiar, including one's kinship identity – literally becoming a 'nobody' for the sake of the gospel. It has echoes of Philippians 2 where it says that Christ 'emptied himself, taking the form of a servant' (v. 7). It is with this same attitude of kenosis that the Celtic pilgrim set out, trusting in God alone. In a sense it was a sacramental journey – an outward and visible sign of an inward and spiritual grace.

This is part of an ancient prayer attributed to St Brendan the Navigator, as he prepared to leave his home and set sail:

Shall I abandon, O King of mysteries, the soft comforts of home?
Shall I turn my back on my native land, and my face toward the sea?
Shall I put myself wholly at the mercy of God,
Without silver, without a horse, without fame and honour?
Shall I throw myself wholly on the King of Kings,

Without sword and shield, without food and drink,
without a bed to lie on?
Shall I take my tiny coracle across the wide, sparkling
ocean?
O King of the glorious Heaven, shall I go of my own
choice upon the sea?
O Christ, will you help me on the wild waves? (Van De
Weyer, 1997, p. 20).

There's a sense of being so small, even a bit lost on the huge
sea of life. Like a prayer attributed to the Breton fishermen:
Lord, the sea is so wide
And my boat is so small.
Be with me (Hutchinson, 2000, p. 3).

So what does this nomadic aspect of the Celtic Spirit have
to teach us today – with our maps and our mobile phones and
our holidays with their carefully planned itineraries? Can we
gain any inspiration from the nomadic ways of the Celtic Spirit
for contemporary living?

Speaking personally, in my work with people coming to
Ireland on Celtic pilgrimage – mostly from North America and
Canada – I can see that having the courage to go out on a
journey, to leave the familiar place and routine and to step
outside your door into a strange world, is good for the soul. It
gives space and time for a slight readjustment in the safe and
predictable routines of life in order to experience being a
stranger in a strange place – and all the uncertainty that goes
along with that. And just that experience of strangeness and
uncertainty can radically alter the inner perspective of a
person. During the journey we're called to trust that our steps
will be led by the ever-unfolding presence of guidance in our
lives – that which brings us hope, healing and transformation.
Like the hero on the heroic journey, you will not return to your
place as the same person, but you *will* return with treasure to
share. I remember travelling in Zimbabwe in the 1990s, being

shocked by my first experience of being the only white person on a street in Harare. When I returned home I looked with new eyes of understanding and compassion at the only black person walking down a street in Belfast!

In our day, sacred journey and pilgrimage is finding new expressions. For example, the Santiago de Compostela pilgrimage route through the Pyrenees to Spain has been written about by people as diverse as the Brazillian writer Paulo Coelho (Coelho, 2005) and the actress Shirley Maclaine (Maclaine, 2001). Many people today – of all faiths and none – are visiting these ancient sacred places because they predate all our religious labels and are filled with sacred presence.

The Celts talked about 'thin places'; by this they meant particular places or experiences that were full of sacred presence or power, where it feels as if there is only a thin veil between this world and the next. The old Celtic saying is: 'Let your feet follow your heart until you find your place of resurrection' (Simpson, 2014, p. 75). Celtic monks sought their places of resurrection in this world by journeying to find the place where they could best fulfill their mission.

There's a story about St Jarlath who was told by St Brendan that he should drive his chariot until the wheel broke. Wherever it broke, there he should build his monastery. Jarlath's chariot wheel broke at Tuam and so he built his monastery there. It's now the seat of the Diocese of Tuam and the episcopal ring bears an engraving of the broken wheel. I like the idea that it is when things *break down* that you are closest to your place of resurrection – not when things are perfect! It echoes the cycle of the heroic journey and the supreme ordeal that many go through in their life experience, which transforms them forever.

So these early monks of the Irish Church wandered the earth, both in Ireland and across Europe, looking for their place of resurrection. They believed they would be shown by God where they were to settle and this would be their place of resurrection. In the same way, all of us can find the place in this life where we can best share our gifts if we listen to our heart and if we follow its call. It's your heart that reveals your passion. So let your feet follow your heart.

But whether you go out on a physical journey of pilgrimage or not, this nomadic spirit that's part of the Celtic way of being holds something inspirational for us all because, ultimately, the nomadic spirit is a path of the soul. It is a way of being that is about being flexible and not stuck in a rut; about being open to new vision, new ideas and new perspectives. When we get too stuck in a rut we lose our flexibility. Physically that leads to arthritis; mentally it leads to intransigence.

There's an old Chinese proverb that says, 'The reed that will not bend will break.' The equivalent for me is revealed by the wonderfully artistic, stone-built walls in the Mourne mountains in County Down. They are not solid walls but are deliberately built with holes between the stones because of the high winds in the mountains. If the walls were solid they'd fall over, but the holes allow the wind to pass through – and so they stand for hundreds of years. The walls are a lesson about the benefits of not being too solid and inflexible in our approach to life. In the same way, nomadic spirituality is about flexibility. It's also about learning to trust that all shall be well and that our steps through the journey of this life are sacred and guided.

A lovely part of *The Voyage of St Brendan* is about the monks rowing hard against the wind out on their Curragh on the wide ocean. Then St Brendan says:

Don't row so hard or you will exhaust yourselves. Is Almighty God not the helmsman and captain of our ship? Do not strain yourselves, since he guides us where He will' (O'Meara, 1991, p. 10).

And when they ceased rowing the wind died down and they were brought to the shore they were seeking. So this is the true nomadic spirit – especially if there's some area in your life where it feels like hard work and you're not achieving much. The lesson is to stop rowing, to let go, and go with the sacred flow. As the Beatles song says, 'Let it be, let it be'; words of course that originally belong to that wise woman, Mary the mother of Jesus.

In his beautiful blessing 'For the Traveller' John O'Donohue says:

A journey can become a sacred thing.
When you travel,
A new silence
Goes with you,
And if you listen,
You will hear
What your heart
Would love to say (O'Donohue, 2007, p. 70).

This is the essence of the nomadic spirit for our age, which is so full of noise and often meaningless activity. To find the 'thin place' where there is opportunity to be still and listen to the voice of your own heart. The Celtic Spirit, combining both the nomadic and the rooted identity, calls us outwards on a journey to come home to the hearth of our own authentic soul. This is an excerpt from an immram chant composed by Caitlin Matthews, an inspirational writer on Celtic spirituality which draws together beautifully the power of the old mythologies and the ocean journeys of the early Irish Christians:

I do not know where I am bound,
I journey far across the foam.
I seek my soul, where is it found?
I watch the star to guide me home.

A branch of silver in my hand
With crystal bloom and golden fruit,
The mother tree grows on the strand,
It's there that I shall find my root (Matthews, 1999, p. 120).

CHAPTER SIX

The Celtic Spirit and the Otherworld
Grace Clunie

May your soul smile
In the embrace
Of your Anamcara (O'Donohue, 1997, p. 261).

One of the profound and often bitter realisations about life, for every individual and every culture in every age, is that one day, not too far away, our life will cease to be – at least in this form. The Celtic peoples were well aware of death in the midst of life; in those times, life was hard and subject to disease, accident and warfare and generally people did not live as long. Yet the Greeks and Romans observed of the Celts that they seemed not to be afraid of death. Diodorus Siculus comments:

> For their journeys and in battle they use two-horse chariots, the chariot carrying both charioteer and chieftain. When they meet with cavalry in the battle they cast their javelins at the enemy and then, descending from the chariot, join battle with their swords. Some of them *so far despise death* that they descend to do battle, unclothed except for a girdle (Cunliffe, 2010, p. 57).

For the Celtic peoples, death did not mean annihilation, because the soul did not perish but passed from one body to another. So death was an evitable part of life and not to be feared because it was, in essence, a rite of passage to the otherworld, the blessed realm of the gods and ancestors and the eternal home of the soul.

DROMBEG STONE CIRCLE

Monument to an afterlife: Stone circles were ritual sites, often associated with human burial. It is thought that the remains of a youth were interred here. The site dates back to *c.* 1100–800 BC, later Bronze Age.

We have seen in a previous chapter how the otherworld, in pre-Christian Ireland, was intimately connected to the earth – a parallel world, invisible, but part of this world – not the more transcendent and remote heaven of Christianity. In the mythology of the Tuatha Dé Danann, the semi-divine inhabitants of Ireland, they reside in the otherworld of the Sidhe within the earth itself.

> But as to the Tuatha Dé Danaan after they were beaten, they would not go under the sway of the sons of Miled, but they went away by themselves. And Manannan ... chose out the most beautiful of the hills and valleys of Ireland for them to settle in; and he put hidden walls about them, so that no man could see through, but they themselves could see through them and pass through

them. And he made the Feast of the Age for them, and what they drank as it was the ale of Goibniu the Smith, that kept whoever tasted it from age and from sickness and from death (Gregory, 1904, reprint 1994, p. 61).

So the Celtic otherworld is an invisible realm within this visible realm of the material world. Only a thin veil inhibits us from seeing it, except for those who have the second sight and for those times and places which are called thin times and thin places – when a glimpse of the otherworld is possible.

The Celtic otherworld was also the place of poetry and music – the special artistic gifts of the most skilled. It was the haunting music of the otherworld that called out to Bran and changed the course of his life forever. Bran listens to the song of the woman from the otherworld describe its beauty:

From one ancient tree, a chorus of birds sing out the hours.
All is harmony and peace in this fertile, well-tilled land.
Music sweetens the ear and colour delights the eye.
Brightness falls from the air and the sea washes against the cliffs
Like a crystal veil.
In this fair island there is nothing rough or harsh.
No weeping or sobbing is heard there and treachery is unknown.
There are no cries of lamentation or grief, no weakness or illness.
No death (Heaney, 1994, pp. 57–8).

So the otherworld is a place of beauty, peace, harmony and eternal life. It is also a place integrated with the earth itself – a place where everything is possible.

This reverence for the earth as the place where the Divine reside, coupled with a belief in the afterlife of the otherworld is evidenced in the Celtic rituals for the dead. Archaeologists are aware of the practice of carefully interring bodies from the

Paleolithic period and Mesolithic period, the individuals often buried with grave goods, such as red deer antler, shell beads and red ochre.

Barry Cunliffe comments about extended rites of passage for death and burial exemplified by the megalithic chambered tombs. He uses the example of the West Kennet Long Barrow:

Here it seems that the body of the newly deceased was placed in the main passage until such time as another person died, when the remains of the earlier body were cleared away into side chambers to make space for the new arrival. This went on for some time until the moment of closure, which here involved the placing of a massive stone slab across the entrance (Cunliffe, 2010, p. 20).

Cunliffe also notes that, as well as inhumation, Celtic burial practices would have involved excarnation:

that is, the exposure of the body to the elements and to predatory birds ... the implications are interesting. One sector of the populations was consigned to the earth – to the chthonic deities – the other to the sky (Cunliffe, 2010, p. 21).

He also says:

[A] simple underlying pattern can be discerned which may be characterized as the balance of opposites bet-ween the earth and the sky – the fertile earth providing the sustenance essential for the community's well-being; the ever consistent sky offering the signs that chart the passage of time (Cunliffe, 2010, p. 18–19).

This respect for the earth and the sky is also part of the ritual of cremation for the Celtic peoples, which was more common from the middle of the second millennium BCE:

On the funeral pyre, the spirit of the departed is released into the sky while the physical remains, the ashes, are placed in ceramic containers and buried in the ground (Cunliffe, 2010, p. 21).

All of this archaeological evidence underlines what the ancient mythologies tell us of the reverence of the Celtic peoples for the natural world and also of their belief in an afterlife.

In our time the scientists have revealed the essence of the material in the atom. Atoms are the building blocks of all matter including our human bodies, so that, after death, when our bodies are returned to the earth or cremated, and the ashes scattered or buried, we are literally reunited with the earth from the perspective of the atomic material. It could be said that this knowledge was intuitively understood and represented by the ancient ritual practices of Celtic peoples at death.

Many people today also believe in the eternal life of the spirit or the soul of a person. For the ancient Celtic peoples this spirit was the energy or the *neart* at the heart of all life, which came ultimately from the origin of all life and at death would return to that source. Ecclesiastes in the Bible describes death as the parting of soul and body and puts it beautifully like this:

When the silver cord is snapped, and the golden bowl is broken, and the pitcher is broken at the fountain, and the wheel broken at the cistern, and the dust returns to the earth as it was, and the breath returns to God who gave it (Ecclesiastes 12:6 & 7).

Celtic Christianity, drawing on the teachings of scripture, also believed in the continuation of the soul in life after death. The understanding of the next life was based upon the descriptions of heaven in the Bible. For example, the reference that Jesus made to the afterlife in John's Gospel, when he speaks of heaven as 'My Father's house'. He says, 'In my Father's house there are many dwelling-places' (John 14:2).

Or the descriptions of heaven from the Book of Revelation to John the Divine:

> Then I saw a new heaven and a new earth; for the first heaven and the first earth had passed away, and the sea was no more. And I saw the holy city, the new Jerusalem, coming down out of heaven from God, prepared as a bride adorned for her husband. And I heard a loud voice from the throne saying, 'See the home of God is among mortals. He will dwell with them: they will be His peoples, and God Himself will be with them. He will wipe every tear from their eyes. Death will be no more; mourning, crying and pain will be no more; for the first things have passed away' (Revelation 21:1–4).

Celtic Christians understood the afterlife to be, most importantly, the place where the soul returned *home* to God. In their liturgies and practices surrounding death and dying there are references to the final journey of the soul and the importance of allowing the soul to depart in peace, and for the living to let go of the loved one, so that the soul can be guided by the angels into the fullness of the Divine presence.

Death in the Celtic tradition was not a journey to be feared, but a transition to the place of eternal rest of the soul. This excerpt from a prayer within the collection of *Carmina Gadelica* sees death as going home – the final homecoming of the soul – and immersed in the natural rhythms of the earth.

> I am going home with thee
> To thy home! to thy home!
> I am going home with thee
> To thy home of winter …

> I am going home with thee,
> Thou child of my love,
> To the dear Son of blessings,
> To the Father of grace (Moore, 1992, p. 311).

It was also important to prepare for your death by living a good life, remembering, even at the most healthy moments of life, that your time for death would also come. As this excerpt from an ancient prayer-poem reminds us:

Remember, O friend, your end.

Remember you are made of clay,
And to clay you will return.

Remember your life is the breath of God,
Which at death will depart.

Now your life on earth is solid and stable;
But soon it will dissolve,
Your body crumbling to dust.

Remember, O friend, your end (Van de Weyer, 1997, p. 61).

It was also important to prepare for a good death by prayer and penitence:

Death with unction and with penitence,
Death with joy and with forgiveness,
Death without horror or repulsion,
Death without fear or shrinking …

The seven angels of the Holy Spirit
And two attendant angels
Be shielding me, and be this night the night
Till brightness and summer-tide shall come! (Moore, 1992, p. 311)

The process of dying itself was seen as part of the journey of life, and along the path of that journey the Christian is supported by the presence of the saints and the angels, who surround the living as a source of help and encouragement. An individual was never an isolated soul. Rather, they were a part of a huge family – the family of the communion of saints which the 'Letter to the Hebrews' in the New Testament speaks of as 'the great cloud of witnesses' (Hebrews 12:1):

When your eyes are closing and your mouth opening,
May God bring you comfort on that day.

When your senses are fading and your limbs growing cold,
May God save your soul on that day ...

Pray that the virgin will reach out and embrace you,
That Michael will reach down and lift you up,
On the day of your death (Van de Weyer, 1997, p. 61).

In his wonderful book *Anam Cara: Spiritual Wisdom from the Celtic World,* John O'Donohue says:

There is a presence who walks the road of life with you. This presence accompanies your every moment. It shadows your every thought and feeling. On your own, or with others, it is always there with you. When you were born it came out of the womb with you; with the excitement at your arrival nobody noticed it. Though this presence surrounds you, you may still be blind to its companionship. The name of this presence is death (O'Donohue, 1997, p. 243).

He goes on to speak of the fear of death in modern western culture – a fear which leads people to deny death, to deny the ageing process and indeed to disparage the gifts of old age:

Though death is the most powerful and ultimate experience in one's life, our culture goes to great pains to deny its presence. In a certain sense, the whole world of media, image and advertising are trying to cultivate a cult of immortality; consequently, the rhythm of death in life is rarely acknowledged (O'Donohue, 1997, pp. 249–50).

Speaking personally, I remember recently feeling moved by a poem by W. S. Merwin called 'For the Anniversary of my Death', which speaks of a deathday as well as a birthday and begins:

Every year without knowing it I have passed the day
When the last fires will wave to me
And the silence will set out
Tireless traveler
Like the beam of a lightless star (Merwin, 2003, p. 85).

The Celtic Spirit speaks of the remembrance of your death as well as your birth.

Another gift of the Celtic Spirit is the wonderful insight that, truly, the dead are not too far away. For the ancient Celts, the otherworld was really a familiar part – if an invisible part – of this world. So that death wasn't a leaving for a strange place far away, but instead, like the story of the prodigal son, it was a homecoming of reconciliation and joy. In this sense, the past – and all that is yet to be – is part of the present moment. O'Donohue comments:

In the Celtic tradition there is a great sense that the dead do not live far away. In Ireland there are always places, fields and old ruins where the ghosts of people were seen. That kind of folk memory recognizes that people who have lived in a place, even when they move to invisible form, somehow still remain attached to that place (O'Donohue, 1997, p. 255).

Other gifts of the Celtic Spirit are the gentle rituals around the journey towards death and dying. In Ireland we still have the tradition of the wake, practised in different ways by different traditions. When a loved one dies, although the undertakers need to do their job, the 'sacred shell', the body of the deceased is brought back home – sometimes even laid on their own bed. So the dead person is accompanied on their journey towards death by their family and friends and by being in the familiar place. Connected with this is an ancient understanding of the process of soul departing from body taking a period of time. As the Bible speaks of Jesus being three days in the tomb before his resurrection, so people often chose that period of three days to allow the soul and the body time for leave-taking. Again, O'Donohue comments:

> The soul does not leave the body abruptly; this is a slow leave-taking. You will notice how the body changes in its first stages of death. The person does not really leave life for a while. It is very important not to leave the dead person on his own. Funeral homes are cold, clinical places. If at all possible, when the person dies, they should be left in their familiar surroundings, so that they can make this deeper transition in a comfortable, easy and secure way. The person who has entered the voyage of death needs more in-depth care (O'Donohue, 1997, p. 260).

This approach also gives the family and loved ones the space and opportunity to take their farewell and to allow the soul to depart in peace.

The ultimate gift of the Celtic Spirit in terms of death and dying is to recognise death not as an enemy, but as a friend of the soul, facilitating the onward journey of the soul to its ultimate healing. In his book *Before We Say Goodbye: Preparing for a Good Death*, Ray Simpson advises: 'Make death your Anam Cara. ... Friendship with our death would enable us to celebrate the eternity of the soul which death cannot touch ... ' (Simpson, 2001, p. 8).

The practices of Celtic Christianity encourage us to reflect on death and dying and the otherworld with an approach that is healing and helpful for the twenty-first century and to look differently at the meaning of death, for ourselves and for our loved ones – for the experience of death inevitably comes to us all. All of these ancient traditions speak to us of deeper wisdom, help and inspiration along the journey from life to death. The heroes and the heroines of the ancient stories had the courage to follow the call of the heart to search and find the treasure that is the authentic soul. The first Christians followed the call of Christ to journey out into an unmapped world. Through all of this, the Celtic Spirit speaks to us profoundly about the adventure of living as well as about the journey home, through death and dying.

John O'Donohue, who had many wise insights about the path towards death and beyond (and he himself died suddenly and at a relatively young age) puts it very beautifully:

> If you are striving to be equal to your destiny and worthy of the possibilities that sleep in the clay of your heart, then you should be regularly reaching new horizons. Against this perspective, death can be understood as the final horizon. Beyond there, the deepest well of your identity awaits you. In that well, you will behold the beauty and light of your eternal face (O'Donohue, 1997, p. 261).

So the Celtic Spirit is both ancient and contemporary and carries the wisdom of the ancestors for modern generations. So far we have explored the relationship with nature, the open heart of hospitality, the sacred cycle of the year, the power of creativity, the call to journey and the perspective of death as our ultimate Anam Cara.

From this understanding of the wisdom of the Celtic Spirit, we continue on this soul-journey, seeking to unveil more of the Celtic Spirit within the literature of the centuries in Ireland.

PART TWO

CHAPTER SEVEN
Early Literature: Epic Imaginings
Tess Maginess

'The Song of Amorgen'

There is an epic folk metal band based in Holland called Amorgen. There is also an early Celtic poem called 'The Song of Amorgen' (or Amergin). Evidence, if any were needed, of the tenacity and variety of the Celtic Spirit. It might be an idea to begin a consideration of the Celtic Spirit in early Irish literature with an example of it, for that may help us to lose our bearings as quickly as possible and thus allow us to enter, imaginatively, a world very different from our own. But, we might well discover, paradoxically, a few home truths, for we will recognise features of this world that are still profoundly familiar.

Amorgen's claims are hardly modest. A modern poet announcing himself in such terms would likely be run out of town. But, of course, this is not a modern poem. Indeed, it is perhaps one of the earliest lyrics that have come down to us. As for Amorgen himself, did he exist or is he a pretty invention of Celtic scholars determined to escape the ineffability of their subject matter by having to assign, once again, under the category of author that baffling, defeating and recursive word, 'anonymous'? For whatever else may be made up, the plain truth is that an awful lot of early Celtic literature is anonymous. And we will go into the reasons for that a bit later. But what of this Amorgen or Amergin? He was a mythological character who appears in one of the cycles of tales we will be discussing in a later chapter. Amorgen/Amergin Gluingel (white knees)/Glunmar (big knee) was a Druid, bard and judge for the Milesians. Professor Robert Welch informs us that 'Amergin' is the name given to several legendary poets in medieval

Irish literature, that is, at a time when a great deal of oral poetry was transcribed and, arguably, rewritten (Welch, 1996, p. 12). The name signifies 'wonderful birth'. One poet of this name was *ollam* (*ollamh*) to King Conchobor of Ulster. An *ollam* represented the highest rank of poets or *fili*. Amergin is included in the pseudo-historical accounts of the settlement of the Gaels in Ireland, as found in the *Lebor Gabála* (*Book of Invasions*). This compendium, sometimes also known as *Lebor Gabála Érenn* (*Book of the Taking of Ireland*), appears in its earliest form in the *Book of Leinster*, compiled around AD 1150 and constituting the first 'chronicle' of Irish history (Macalister, 1938–1956). This Amorgen was, evidently, amongst the sons of Mil who landed in the south-west of Ireland at Bealtaine (springtime). Coming ashore, he sings a cosmic hymn, in which he identifies himself with the whole of nature. Indeed, the song sings Ireland into being and, as such, can be identified as a creation myth. When the sons of Mil defeat the Tuatha Dé Danann, Amergin negotiates the transfer of sovereignty with Éiru (an ancient name for Ireland) and his chanted invocation to the land of Ireland calms the wind raised by the Druids to prevent a further landing. It is hard to miss the mix of myth and realpolitik conferred by or upon this Amorgen in the *Book of Invasions*, but like so many other figures in Celtic literature, Amorgen was subsequently 'translated', in more senses than one, in different political and historical contexts. Just take a look at the many versions on the Internet. Indeed, quite beyond literature, the Irish rock band, Horslips, named their sixth album *The Book of Invasions* (1976). Perhaps this makes our first point again about the tenacity and myriad forms of Celtic figures, and we may add, by way of prolepsis, that the recycling is not infrequently ironic. That, we may hazard, is one of the legacies of a colonial history. And we will explore that cultural phenomenon in a later chapter.

But let us return to, as it were, the literary genesis. There may have been others, but they are lost to us now. The fact that the poem titles itself as a song begins to allow us to understand the context. For this would have been an oral poem, recited or sung, perhaps at some ancient court. And the singer is, as he says himself, a god and, amounting it would seem to near enough the same thing, a Druid. And, as such, he is simply voicing, quite literally, the sacral shape and function of poetry in his time. But we need to understand this, perhaps, not through an exclusively modern lens where the poet, in our time, could not or would not lay any claims to the vatic and godlike status. Amorgen is not an ironic Joycean God, hovering over his handiwork. Here in this poem, in its time, there is no ironic distance between nature and God as there is for Joyce's Stephen Dedalus. Nor is Amorgen a Romantic like Shelley, proclaiming the revolution from an upstairs window in Dublin's Sackville Street in the early 1800s. The Romantic poets were, of course, looking back at the ancient Greek and Celtic poets and attempting to reassert the vatic function, and contingently, the political influence of shaman, seer and Druid. That this valiant appeal for the restoration of the crucial importance of the poet and behind that, the imagination itself, did not result in a glorious revolution has as much to do with the entire world view of that time as with the particular and disastrous 'causes' Shelley and Byron espoused.

Amorgen begins with nature:
I am a wind in the sea (for depth) ...
I am a stag of seven combats (for strength)
I am a hawk upon a cliff (for agility)
I am a tear-drop of the sun (for purity) ...
I am a salmon in a pool (for swiftness) ...
I am the excellence of arts (for beauty) ...
Who explains the stones of the mountains?
Who invokes the ages of the moon? ...
I invoked a satirist ...
A satirist of wind (Trans. Carey, 2003).

And we may say that unlike Joyce and unlike the Romantics, there was nothing else for him to begin with, since he is composing at a time before there were cities in Ireland, or for that matter, concepts such as nationality. However, that would be a mite ungracious and, in any case, would also fail to appreciate what this poet gives us that has now, largely, been lost.

Amorgen can proclaim himself a wind, a wave, a stag, a salmon, a lake because, as we have seen in Chapter Two, of his complete identification with the natural world. Poet and nature interpenetrate each other to a degree we find, nowadays, very difficult to comprehend. And this, we will see, is a foundational feature of early Celtic literature. Not surprisingly, the Romantic poets wrote a great deal also about nature, but their distance from it requires a supernal imaginative leap that Amorgen does not have to make, because he is already *in* and *of* nature. So, his words are not boisterous boasts of mastery, but simply the expression of a state of being in which the natural and the human are much less separated than they are in our world. To underscore the point, let us remind ourselves of those lines from Wordsworth's famous sonnet:

The world is too much with us late and soon
Getting and spending we lay waste our powers,
Little we see in nature that is ours ... (Wordsworth, 1807; rpt 1994, p. 307).

Or, closer to home, Yeats:

I will arise and go now, and go to Innisfree,
And a small cabin build there of clay and wattles made ... (Yeats, 1892; rpt 1994, p. 31).

And what kind of nature is it that Amorgen both articulates and embodies? The note is profoundly celebratory. More specifically, Amorgen concentrates on those aspects of nature that are the grandest, noblest and most terrifying. And it is the sublimity of nature which, so many centuries afterwards, another man from this island, Edmund Burke, so praised. Burke's encomium, partly based on French inspiration, was, of course, the seminal philosophical bible for the Romantics. Could Shelley's 'Ode to the West Wind' with its dynamic whirl and power and majesty have been written without Burke's *On the Sublime* (1757; rpt 1968), or, perhaps without Amorgen's song? For poetic winds do not come from thin air, but rather from a rich, if not always acknowledged, tradition.

There is something else about Amorgen's registration of nature that is remarkable, and that is his particularity. There is not one whiff of vapidity in it. Amorgen's nature is most particular, not some generalised invocation of a sublime nature. And the very individuation is what makes his incremental catalogue so compelling.

It may be argued that most of the items in Amorgen's list are all rather, well, clichéd. We would say two things about that. One is that winds and hawks and stags were likely a great deal less jaded in Amorgen's own time. The subsequent poetic circus might merit a desertion of them, but who are we to argue with the Elizabethan poets, whose fair parade of just such favourites drew no disdain? There is, maybe, another point. The animals and birds and fish which inhabit the poem are not chosen for their originality; quite the reverse. These are creatures that Amorgen's audience would see frequently around them. The Druidic-god poet is not trying to be precious, to go for the rare collector's item. We will return to rare collectors in a later chapter, when we discuss the Antiquarians. Amorgen knows that when it comes to nature, there is no point being obscure; plenty of room for that in the more vatic parts of his job. He needs to connect directly and simply with his audience, hence the choice of common species.

And, of course, we must also bear in mind, as the allusion to the salmon implies, that nature's creatures often also have a symbolic or metaphorical significance. Here we begin to glimpse another aspect of this Celtic world, which will be discussed in greater detail later. And that is the contiguity if we may so call it, of the symbolic and the natural. To put this another way, the symbolic or spiritual dimension is not, as it is mostly nowadays, at a vast remove from the natural and human world, but an organic extension of it. The natural and the supernatural are not two different worlds in this Celtic way of being, but intimately connected. The natural and the super-natural are, as it were, two levels within the same order.

That sounds very abstract. Let us try and come at what we are trying to say in another way. The story of the Salmon of Knowledge is very well known in Ireland. It is told in the Fenian Cycle. The salmon is a magical fish which the poet, Finn Eces, mistakenly tastes as he is cooking it. As a result, he is given all the knowledge of the world. The story is similar to that told about the Welsh poet Taliesin, whose poems appear to date back to the sixth century. Magic, the supernatural, emanates from the natural, the domestic even. The otherworld is not sealed off, but a logical extension of the natural world.

When the more explicitly supernatural aspects of Amorgen's ministry are then invoked we can see that there is a free foot and a foot planted firmly upon the earth. Late in the poem we have: 'I am the excellence of arts (for beauty).' Amorgen claims to be the essence of poetry and the arts. And the sharp edge is there, too, in his function as poet: 'I invoked a satirist ... A satirist of wind.' But the poet is also a prophet, a fore-teller, vatic: 'Who invokes the ages of the moon? Where lies the setting of the sun?'

The natural and supernatural are melded and mingled; there is no sense of two distinct worlds as there are these days. This world is next door to the otherworld. The portal or threshold is crossed by a magic that uses nature and language itself for its alchemy. So language, words, are part of this immanence too.

Limitations of space forbid a more detailed analysis, but let us summarise a few of the more salient aspects of the Celtic

Spirit as they are enunciated in this poem: the close relationship to nature; the particularity and sharpness of the imaging
of it; the fondness for catalogue, the proximal relationship
between this world and the otherworld; the position of the poet
as transcending, magic medium and the investiture of magic
and sacral power within language itself.

The Coming of the Writing Men

'The Song of Amorgen', we may speculate at least, was
originally a song, performed to a public court and only written
down much later. The crucial game changer here – and the one
which enables Celtic literature to survive a particularly
dramatic set of vicissitudes – is the writing down of it. And
what brought writing was Christianity. This, of course, did not
happen overnight, but the consequences were profound.
Before Christianity there existed a system of signs, known as
ogham. Ogham marks were often inscribed on wooden pillars
or standing stones (rather than paper) and, given the practical
limitations of such a canvas, we cannot be surprised that the
hieroglyphics were a shade terse. They may well have signified
a densely symbolically charged rune which connected at one
stroke the natural and the sacral. We do not know. What we
think we know is that poems and stories (sometimes in verse
form) were not written in or on stone.

And, as noted earlier, literature was not in any case viewed
by the early Gaels as something to be written down, for artful
as these poets were, and deeply schooled in their bardic forms
as they were, they surely would have devised a written form
if they thought it was needed. The poets were performers, who
recited or sang their words to a court. They were public, not
private figures, part of the ruling order and incredibly
influential in matters of governance. As Muireann Ní Bhrolcháin points out, this highly regarded order contained Druids

and jesters and female satirists (Ní Bhrolcháin, 2009, p. 10). The poets attached or withdrew their fealty in relation to a tribal king. And, as Mac Cana states, the clearest reflex for their literature was eulogy or satire (P. Mac Cana, 1991, p. 1). The eulogy drew on genealogy and much later a lot of this lore is gathered in what is called the *dinnseanchas*.

In a culture that is not literate, people have, arguably, a far greater capacity to memorise. Think of our grandparents or great-grandparents who often got very little schooling, but could recite fluently from the local paper to the Bible, from a story or a poem. So, this may well have meant that in early Ireland, literature was more widely disseminated than it is now. And, there are also the bardic schools, training up the *fili*, or bards or *ollamh* in the strict conventions and metrics of the various kinds of literature. It may have been, as David Greene, argues, that there were *fili* in the monasteries too (Greene, 1954, p. 25). This added, undoubtedly, to the conservatism of the oral forms, preserving them from one generation to the next.

Now what happens when in come the Christians? At the heart of Christianity from its earliest formation, is a very strong belief in the importance of writing. Think of all the Epistles. And, of course, that valorisation of the written word stretches away back into Judaic tradition (The Old Testament). The early Christians were on a mission from God (a bit like the Blues Brothers, but without the great 'gospel' tunes, if I may risk an irony). It was a very extensive mission and there were only a few apostles at the start, so writing epistles to far-flung congregations was a way, quite literally, of keeping the faith – on all sides. So, it is not so remarkable then that when Christianity arrived in Ireland, the importance of writing was already hardwired. And at this time there is an international community of Christians and they keep in touch by writing – in Latin.

Within Ireland itself, the monks evidently discovered that there was a very rich oral culture and a parallel community of scholars. Different commentators have different views about the relationship between the new and old orders. However, we can probably ditch the rather roseate Christian version of events in which the people of Ireland embraced the new religion – and more trickily – its ideology on such matters as kingship and governance, without so much as a 'who are you?' (Flower, 1947; rpt 1978, p. 4) Mac Cana ventures that there was probably increasing practical cooperation between the extant learned *fili* class and the Christian clerical writing men. But, he argues that the *fili* 'continued to assert their independence and the priority of their professional fraternity in matters of social and political concern' (Mac Cana, 1991, p. 1). It is always in some sense about power. And those who hold power do not easily surrender it. J. E. Caerwyn Williams opines that there may have been harmony between Christian and pagan, but also keen competition. He argues that this is what led to the success of Ireland in becoming the seat of Christian learning and the object of admiration for the rest of Europe between the sixth and ninth centuries AD (Mac Cana, 1991, p. 4).

Muireann Ní Bhrolcháin notes that the earliest poem in Old Irish, 'The Lament for Colm Cille', was composed by a bard, Eochad Dallan Forgaill and that Colm Cille led a movement at Druimm Ceit to defend the poets in danger of being expelled as too expensive (Ní Bhrolcháin, 2009, p. 13).

One of the finest commentators on Gaelic literature was Ulsterman Proinisas Mac Cana. Not only is Mac Cana scholarly, he writes with enormous grace and suppleness. Mac Cana tells us that between the sixth and twelfth century there was on this island a literature 'unparalleled in volume and variety in the rest of Western Europe' (Mac Cana, 1991, p. 1). Written literature can be traced back to the late sixth century. But, of course, behind this stretches a very long tradition of orally composed poems, many of them lost and many mere fragments of a larger enterprise. Mac Cana tells us that the monasteries became the cradle of the new written literature, but he enters this caveat:

> It is inconceivable that this literature could have flowered so rapidly and profusely had there not existed a manifold oral tradition and a professional learned class to care for it. Constantly the written text presupposes a living tradition that is both its source and its continuing referent; this enduring interaction of the oral and written is a crucial fact of Irish literary history. From the outset, the relationship was a complex one. When writing came, it brought not simply a new technique but also new values and to some extent a new concept of literary aesthetics ... and the task of creating a fruitful symbiosis of native and Christian culture fell to the scholars of the monasteries, some of whom, in the process, developed new perspectives on vernacular tradition (Mac Cana, 1991, pp. 1–2).

And, of course, we would know very, very little about that anterior oral tradition were it not for the Christian clerics who embraced the vernacular of their new mission country and who must have been prepared to listen again and again to the bardic poets reciting and then write this material down.

And, as Mac Cana and others like James Carney have noted, they did not write verbatim. Carney provocatively suggests that the clerical poems 'show every sign of being composed fictions which can have had no existence in Irish oral tradition (Carney, 1969, p. 7). Muireann Ní Bhrolcháin cites James Carney's comment that the coming into being of Irish vernacular literature, 'in the face of the dominant Latin culture, was something of a miracle; its continuation for nearly fourteen centuries no less so' (Ní Bhrolcháin, 2009, p. 5).

There was one thing the clerics changed radically, and that was verse metre. That might seem a small technical matter, but just think of the revolution in prosody in the twentieth century.

We have T. S. Eliot and Ezra Pound and ee cummings and all the other big beast Modernists rejecting rhyme and breaking up regular metres like iambic pentameter. However, many people even now do not regard anything that was not in regular rhyme and regular accentual rhythm as a poem at all, seeing no art in it. Poetry, for earlier generations was a thing meant to be easily understood and easily memorised, hence the rhyme and regular rhythm, a concept that stretches back in many respects to the view the bardic poets would have had of their art. And here we go again – that interconnectedness of the oral and the written.

But there is one small difference. Up until the seventh century Irish poetry was accentual; that is to say, like those poems favoured by older generations, where the rhythm is based on counting stresses. However, the lines were not end-rhymed. According to James Carney, the lines tended to be short and also incorporated heavy alliteration (which constitutes a sort of internal rhyme). But, under the influence of the clerics (schooled, of course in the metres of Latin hymns), that prosody was replaced with syllabic verse. This means that the accents are not counted, but rather the number of syllables in the line are, as in modern French poetry. According to James Carney, this syllabic verse, known as *dán dírech*, spread out from the monasteries and became the characteristic metre of the bardic schools right up until their break-up in the seventeenth century (Carney, 1969, p. 29). As accentual or stressed poetry is a natural metrics for a poetry that is sung or recited in public, so syllabic poetry is a natural metrics for poetry that is read off the manuscript (and later printed) page – and in private rather than in public. It is a much more interior sort of experience and consonant with a clerical culture which is not primarily (except in the sermon) orientated towards a public discourse and which does not see itself, at this stage in history, as occupying the centre ground of the tribal court.

Indeed, the organisation of the Irish Church in the sixth and seventh centuries was, according to P. L. Henry, either within smallish monastic settlements, or right out at the edge of the world in anchorite cells. The development of the 'disert' in close proximity to the monastic church, was part of a reform movement, influenced by Egyptian monasticism of the third and fourth centuries, with holy men literally living in the desert (Henry, 1966, p. 41). In the eighth century the Céile Dé was, Henry argues, a distinct institution of the reform movement (Henry, op. cit., p. 42). To this day we have in Armagh an area called Desart and a housing estate called Culdee Crescent.

So the consequence might naturally be that the clerics would write and transcribe the oral material that came before them. They did so through a habit of mind, a training in carefulness and cheerfulness learned from inter alia the tradition of epistle writing and a social positioning that if not enclaved, was not exactly at the heart of the courts. Thus, a contemplative, private sensibility would have been likely to develop in a markedly different way from the public, collective, ceremonial voice of the bardic poet. And was that, in turn, not likely to produce a poetry that was meant to be read rather than recited, thought upon rather than memorised?

So the public tone and the cosmic register of 'The Song of Amorgen' begins to be replaced by a more intimate, lyrical approach. Of course, paradoxically, we must concede that we only know this poem because it has a written form (indeed many written forms or versions).

And, we may note, the vast majority of the corpus, whether poetry or prose tales or a mix of both, was anonymous. That is perhaps the strangest concept of all to a modern sensibility, in which everything must be owned by the individual. Neither Celtic society nor the Christian clerics seem to have considered this to have a great deal of meaning.

To return to metrics, it was not until the *amhrán* or song metres became universal in the eighteenth century that natural stress accent became again dominant. And this we may add was, doubtless, influenced by English poetry, as English language and literature gained a purchase in Ireland. For all that the bardic schools represented a resistance to this new order, just as centuries before they had, they came under influences from outside.

By the eighth century Irish had emerged as a fully fledged literary language. And, Carney tells us, in the Romance-speaking areas of the Continent, the ordinary language was still a merely debased form of Latin and did not become a vehicle for literature until the twelfth and thirteenth centuries. Conversely, in Ireland, Latin was so completely a foreign language that it was learnt thoroughly without danger of contamination from the spoken dialect. This meant that the standard of Irish Latinity was higher (Carney, 1969, p. 34).

One interesting consequence was, according to Carney, that the Irish monastic clerics were able to accommodate hellenic and pagan mythology while the Western Church otherwise deprecated it (Carney, 1969, p. 34; Caerwyn Williams, 1958; rpt 1992, p. 3). What seems to have resulted, by Carney's analysis, was a poetry that both draws attention to its local habitation and name (all that was learned from the bards) and to its cosmopolitan influences.

So, what were the poems about? As Gerard Murphy tells us, while many were Christian in tone, the scope widened to encompass an old woman's sorrow recounting the loss of days gone by, to the blackbird's beauty, to a satire on a lady mourning the loss of her pet goose (Murphy, 1956; 1998, p. xv). Very often the poems were about nature. There is a huge body of lyrical verse focusing on this very subject. As Gerard Murphy argues, 'Irish lyric poetry is unique in the Middle Ages in its freshness of spirit and perfection of form' (Murphy, op.

cit., p. xiii). And when we think back to 'The Song of Amorgen', we can understand it as part of that tradition. Much of this poetry, however, was not transcribed or written down by traditional bards. If it was, they adopted the persona of the private, often hermetic monk, alone in his cell, writing or illustrating manuscripts. The poems are often set up as digressions, as it were, from the arduous business of copying and scribing. Here are a few little examples:

The Scribe out of Doors
A hedge of trees overlooks me,
A blackbird's lay sings to me;
Above my lined book
The birds chant their song to me.

The cuckoo sings to me lovely and clear
In a grey cloak from the ramparts of bushes.
Well indeed does the Lord look after me
As I write with care in the woodland shade (Trans. Mac Cana, 1991, p. 48).

May-time
Lovely season of May! Most noble then is the colour of trees; blackbirds sing a full lay, when the shaft of day is slender (Trans. Mac Cana, 1991, p. 34).

Winter
I have tidings for you: the stag bells,
Winter pours, summer has gone.

The wind is high and cold, the sun low;
Its course is short, the sea runs high.

The bracken has reddened, its shape hidden;
The wild goose has raised his familiar cry.

Cold has seized the wings of birds;
It is the season of ice – these are my tidings (Trans. Mac Cana, 1991, p. 36).

The Blackbird at Belfast Lough
The little bird which has whistled from the tip of his
bright yellow bill,
The blackbird from its branch heaped up with
yellow sends out its call over Belfast lough (Trans. Mac
Cana, 1991, p. 48).

As we saw in 'The Song of Amorgen', there is a close
identification of man with nature. And though the hermit is
not operating in the same incantatory register as Amorgen,
nonetheless, the aim is to make as fluid as possible the
boundaries between the human and the natural and the
supernatural. Though the hermit is enclosed in a cell, the focus
is not on the interior at all, but upon the natural world outside
and the supernatural world above. And there is that same
immanence, the infusion of nature with a sacral presence and,
correspondingly, the infusion of the sacral with the natural. The
hermit, far from being cut off in a Platonic cave, is part of
nature and supernature.

And, as in 'The Song of Amorgen', we have particularity.
Nature is individuated, seen up close, rather than from a
remote, pastoral and abstracting distance. As Mac Cana
observes, what we have here is an emotional response to
nature rather than the Naturalist's classification. As a result we
get, as he suggests, a succession of vivid images (Mac Cana,
1991, p. 3). Sometimes this lyric poetry has been described as
Impressionist; but the effect is not the blurry, light-drenched
atmosphere that the Impressionists give us, but rather
something much more crystalline and distinct. Perhaps Kuno
Meyer is closer to it when he ventures that 'like the Japanese,
the Celts were always quick to take an artistic hint; they avoid
the obvious and the commonplace' (Meyer, cited in Carney,
1969, p. 11).

Mac Cana, as always so graceful in his ability to glide
between the particular and the more general, observes that this

hermit poetry represents an idealisation of a retreat from society (Mac Cana, 1991, p. 3). And, there can be no doubt that the clerical monks, whether in a large scriptorium or a tiny cell, felt a need to articulate the joys of a life that must often have been rigidly disciplined, aesthetically demanding and lonesome. But they were, after all, appealing for converts, attempting to communicate the joys of the clerical life. And just maybe, for some of them, these little poems were sometimes hard enough wrought, however lightsome their tone and apparently simple their construction.

Perhaps one of the most mellifluous celebrations of nature is 'King and Hermit'. The poem is a colloquy between King Guaire and his brother, the hermit, Marbhan (Marban). Though beginning along the lines of a classical dialogue, the floor soon belongs entirely to Marbhan. And small blame to him, for this rhapsodic paean to the plenty of nature is propelled by an energy and amplitude of near visionary proportions, taking us back to the 'lift' of 'The Song of Amorgen'. Nature is depicted as an almost prelapsarian cornucopia. This device or trope is to appear not infrequently in Irish literature, sometimes, as with Brian Merriman and Flann O'Brien, for satiric purposes. There are obvious biblical undertones in the image of a wondrous land of plenty and the trope is also to be found in many American writers, for example Ernest Hemingway's *A Farewell to Arms*. We may note also in this poem the cataloguing technique we saw too in 'The Song of Amorgen', and this too is a device much favoured by Irish writers, whether in Irish or later in English. Think of the piling up of vivid particulars in Swift's *Gulliver's Travels*. There, obviously, the device is being used satirically. Unsurprisingly, Guaire is so beguiled by the paradisal plenum Marbhan conjures that the King forsakes his kingdom for Marbhan's luscious domain. The sheer sensuousness of the nature to be feasted upon within the hermetic life almost overtopples the Christian subtext with a playful irony – intentional or not.

The poem also embodies another theme that is at the heart of the Celtic Spirit, and that is hospitality. That theme is implicit in the poem about King Guaire and Marbhan, for the saint is inviting the king to share the plenty that nature provides. And this is rather a cheeky Christian touch, for the clerics had learned well and truly that a keystone of the Celtic concept of kingship was hospitality. The bards played it for all their worth, for they owed their power and prestige to the patronage of the tribal king. An interdependent relationship, existed then, in which the bard or *fili* inflated the virtues of the king with fantastic eulogies, emphasising his legitimacy by an astute reading of the genealogies. But if the king was parsimonious and failed to practice the *fili*'s invocation to ancient Celtic hospitality, the poet had vinegar as well as honey and could draw his satiric weaponry to ridicule his patron without remorse. In today's world that might not seem much worse than ending up as the butt in *The Thick of It* or *Spitting Images*. But we cannot underestimate the Druidic origin here and a bad rhyme could kill you. For these bards meant business. In a world where magic was as tenable as the power of the Internet today, the bards held enormous power.

And with the coming of Christianity, that shamanic power did not disappear. As David Greene points out, even after Christianity, as it were, assumes power over the otherworld, the *fili* still maintain considerable prestige. Greene notes that the bards can still damage physically, or even kill, by satire (Greene, 1963, p. 24; Bergin, 1970, p. 8).

The cleric may have tried to harness the power of the *fili* to their own version of the supernatural. Thus, for example, we have a pagan goddess reassigned as St Brigid. Her little miracle with the cloak is, in itself, a fantastic fusion of the two orders. It is a pretty tale, that does not cloak the political realities of that era. 'Give me', says the inexpressibly beautiful and wily Brigid, 'only enough land to build my church as would be the length of my cloak.' 'Fair enough,' says the native king, not wanting to be mean-spirited or inhospitable to a stranger. But the cloak miraculously extends until Brigid has in her train, a very substantial bit of native real estate.

In the ninth-century poem *Buile Suibhne* (*The Frenzy of Sweeney*), the Christians also win the day, or so it seems. The poem begins with an altercation between St Moling and Sweeney. Sweeney, rather truculent about all this new 'book' stuff, flings the saint's psalter into a river. The consequences for Sweeney are disastrous. The saint, apparently as able as any Druid to deploy a cast of words into a curse, condemns the recalcitrant to a life where he must, thereafter, be half man, half bird and, on the top of that, frenzied. But not for the first or last time in Celtic literature, the accursed, as Blake said of Milton's Satan, has the best lines. Sweeney's lament is one of the most trenchant and melodious in any language. Significantly, Sweeney's verse deploys the same immanent, fluid connection with nature and a focus on its vivid particularities. Hospitality – and the importance of it for the stranger, for the outcast – is another theme adumbrated in this poem. And Sweeney is, even in his exile, in his forced retreat from the social and political world, the compelling voice that somehow renders the actions of the saint a paler kind of mystery than the magic the bird-man invokes through language itself. Did the clerics who transcribed/composed this poem understand it as, in certain respects, ironic? And if so, what does that say about their own subversiveness – or am I misreading it? Is the poem a cautionary tale? If so, why is Sweeney presented as so sympathetic a figure?

SWEENEY

Clashing spirits: The Frenzy of Sweeney

We still have an awful lot to learn about the subtleties of that encounter between pagan and Christian Ireland, between the *fili* and the clerics. And there are perhaps lights here to a new understanding of the work of the Anglo-Irish Antiquarians, who might, in curious ways, bear some resemblance to those early Christian clerics, and indeed the *littérateurs* of the so-called Celtic Revival, or the Celtic Twilight. We will examine these questions in a later chapter.

Reiterating the point made about the tenacity and variety of the Celtic Spirit, and the tendency to recycle or 'resurrect' in renaissances ironic and otherwise, figures and tropes from early Celtic literature, it may be noted that Sweeney is destined for just such an investiture. Flann O'Brien (Brian O'Nolan) is to recycle his MA study of this fine poem in his comic novel *At Swim-Two-Birds* (1939). Seamus Heaney has also featured Sweeney in a number of poems. We will be able to have a closer look at these *ricorso* in a later chapter.

Perhaps part of the appeal of the figure of Sweeney is that his retreat from the world, unlike that of the anchorite, is not voluntary, but rather an imposed outcasting. For a variety of reasons which we will explore in later chapters, this theme of outcasting came to be imbued with a very special meaning for Irish writers. They saw in Sweeney a kind of artist analogue, banished for his independence and questioning of clerical and political authority.

It is, of course, Mac Cana, who draws attention to the theme of exile and retreat in this early Irish poetry. It is a theme echoed too in the prose tales, most notably *Deirdre and the Sons of Uisneach* but that is for another chapter. We have not space or time here to do anything but gesture towards the variations on this theme in the early literature, to say nothing of later writing in English, inspired, doubtless, by earlier literature.

The many poems ascribed to Colmcille (Columba) also inscribe this journey theme with the terse economy of the haiku. Though the poems of Colmcille offer us a glimpse of the extraordinary reach of the Irish clerics, bringing, as they did, not only Christianity but a rich literature to Britain and the Continent, here the predominant note is threnodic, a beautifully controlled, epigrammatic expression of the pain of loss – the loss of small places and of friends. Here is Kuno Meyer's translation:

> Great is the speed of my coracle,
> And its stern turned upon Derry:
> Grievous is my errand over the main,
> Travelling to Alba of the beetling brows ...
>
> There is a grey eye
> That will look back upon Ireland:
> It shall never see again
> The men of Ireland nor her women (Meyer, 1969, p. 17).

We will conclude this chapter with a poem that some of you might have encountered, or been subject to in some form at school. We say in some form because the other big point, maybe the biggest of all, about this literature is its fundamental instability. To put the matter another way, it has a capacity to reappear across the centuries in a very diverse, even contradictory, series of renderings and redactions. That might seem a curious thing to say after all the emphasis on preservation and conservatism. But we need to bear in mind that so much of what was written down, even from the earliest times, by those clerics or by bards who had learned to write Gaelic, was a not straightforward transcription. We have already drawn attention to what must have been a seismic shift in the matter of metre. And to the equally fundamental change from a poetry that is public to a poetry that is 'made' and read in private. We will talk more about words like 'redaction' later, because there is also the whole issue of how the oral material was handled by the literate clerics (and maybe bards) over the course of several centuries. There are huge questions here about how the oral literature was written down, how that complex material was organised and how it might have been changed and inflected. And that, in turn, will raise some further questions about authenticity and about identity.

The poem is called by many names, including 'The Cailleach Beare', 'The Old Woman of Beare' and 'The Hag of Beare'. Interestingly enough, the one constant is the place, the specific location. Not for the first time, we are forced to question, by modern-day standards, what exactly these monks were up to. For here is a poem which celebrates the sexual freedom of women with a frankness that *Fifty Shades of Grey* can only blush at. And here is a poem that confronts old age with a searing eye. Botox is not an option; quietism is not an option. But defeat is not an option either. It may be argued that it is a poem ahead of *our* time.

I am the Nun of Beara Baoi. I used to wear a shift that was always new. Today I have become so thin that I would not wear out even an old shift.

It is riches you love, not people; when we were alive, it was people we loved ...

I wasted my youth to begin with, and I am glad I decided it thus; even if I had not been venturesome, the cloak would be new no longer ...

Well might the son of Mary spend the night and be under the roof-tree of my pantry; though I am unable to offer any other hospitality, I have never said 'No' to anybody ...

Happy is the island of the great sea, for the flood comes to it after the ebb; as for me, I expect no flood after ebb to come to me (Trans. Mac Cana, 1991, p. 33–4).

In a later chapter we will discuss the so-called prose narratives, though some of them are peppered with poetry. And we will hear more about the three cycles, which is how later scholars subsequently grouped stories that had been earlier classified more by theme or what we would now call 'genre' (adventure, raiding, elopements). That classification was, of course itself the result of a medieval sensibility that favoured collection into manuscript books or compendia. Doubtless, as is the case today with oral storytellers, and with us all in our own 'networks', we tell and write stories that are both more local and, paradoxically, more protean. They evade, or are simply unaware of, the particular prevailing hegemony that would classify and register that which supports its own 'narrative'. And yet, of course, we cannot tell stories or write them without some seepage from that hegemony, without being, as it were, of our own time. Perhaps it was ever thus, but the great stories, the great literature is that which reflects both its own time and speaks forth vatically (like those bards) to the future, maybe ironically in an ironic time, maybe refreshingly, excitingly, in times of dynamic hope.

Whatever the issues that Christianity created, it cannot be denied that as a result of the coming of the writing men, we have an extraordinary corpus. These new Irish, in the form of the clerics, carried through Europe the magical and ferociously eloquent – albeit adopted and changed – burden of a Celtic civilisation far in advance of what was available on the Continent. This was not to be the last encounter between the Celtic Spirit and the otherworlds of newcomers. That encounter continues to this day. Amorgen's singing of the land he had come to – the poetic, mythical shaping of it in the form of they who come – continues, as does the mythical and expedient urge to repulse further landings. Was nothing there before Amorgen? That song is lost, inevitably, because somebody had to come, it seems, from somewhere else in the Celtic mythos and overwritten it. We did not, like the Aborigines, form ourselves out of the land, make song lines from a mythos of organic growth out of the land. Thus, for they who would declare themselves native, authentic, Celtics, they too were, to quote John Hewitt, 'once alien here' (Hewitt, 1991, p. 386).

CHAPTER EIGHT

Tales of this World and the Otherworld
Tess Maginess

Arts of the Storyteller: The Spoken Tale and the Written Tale
One of the things we explore in this chapter is how we tell
stories in these parts and, in the process of considering that
question, we look at what influence the Celtic Spirit –
hardwired or imbibed – has had on our love of narratives and
on our way of constructing and reconstructing or recycling old
narratives. Thomas Kilroy maintains that the chromosome of
story, the anecdote, is in the DNA of the Irish fictional tradition
from at least the end of the eighteenth century (cited by Brown,
2010, p. 104). Maria Edgeworth agrees about the central
importance of 'the speaking voice, engaged in the telling of a
tale', the 'shared ownership of the told tale' (Brown, op. cit., p.
104). We will discover traces of this DNA much, much further
back in Celtic literature.

Very often the common unit of the Celtic tale is a short story,
an anecdote. The original medium in which stories were
transmitted was oral rather than a written. But the voice seems
to break through, even when the form becomes a written one
and the transmitters are Christian clerics. The anecdotal shape
of these early stories may also account for the immense
problems in trying to organise them into groups. Though, of
course, it is only a problem if you see it as one. The bard or poet
would likely have had his own collection, but this would have
been made up of all sorts of pieces, some of them not very long,
for you can only try the patience of a court for a limited time.
And the bards themselves may have wished to put more
aesthetic effort into poems:

> For the Irish, as for many other peoples, poetry was the
> medium of inspiration and the vehicle par excellence of

sacred tradition ... prose was poetry's poor relation ... However, if it did not enjoy the same social prestige as poetry, it had, nonetheless, a functional importance denied it in other major literatures in that it was the normal medium of storytelling (Mac Cana, 1980, p. 21).

Now, of course, Mac Cana is speaking here mainly about the Gaelic bards, and in a short book such as *His Literature in Irish*, fairly drastic foreshortening inevitably occurs. In the previous chapter, Mac Cana had drawn attention to the complex impact of Christianity and, specifically, to the role of the Christian clerics in preserving, modulating and even challenging the forms and cultural structures which underpinned the old order. It is likely that there were, in reality, aspects of the relationship between the old order and the new Christian order that were at times fraught, at times harmonious, at times melded and mingled and, at times, stubbornly separate. And given that it was clerics as well as the older order of *fili* and bards who, from about the eighth century onwards, began to write down prose tales, we can hardly expect to find seamlessness in this genre any more than in poetry.

But, as Mac Cana rightly recognises, the prose tale is, by definition, more subject to redaction and change than poetry. To complicate the picture, it would seem that the oral tales often contained a mix of poetry and prose. It is much easier for us to remember a poem intact than a story. And one of the reasons for this is the formal properties of poetry written before the twentieth century; its regular rhythm and rhyme. But if any of us were asked to retell a story we had heard, the 'cribs', if I may put it, are no longer there. And I use the word 'cribs' in both senses: as the upright edges of a cart, the planks that contain the load and, in the more English sense of 'cribs', as aids to memorising pieces. We may be able to remember 'The Blackbird Over Belfast Lough' and other short lyrics composed by clerics in syllabic verse, denuded of accentual rhythm, because they are short; written forms, devoid of rhythm or rhyme are very hard to memorise. That is why most people cannot quote more than a line or two of a modern poem like 'The Wasteland'.

Thus it is that when we come to prose, the risk of departing from any kind of oral original is, as Mac Cana argues, much greater. This is, of course, not necessarily a bad thing at all, for what you will get as a result, is considerable variation in the telling of any particular tale.

There is another factor: the proliferation of stories is legion, and yet certain features or events or characters seem to recur. Let us imagine how a cleric or a bard faced with the writing down of prose tales in the eighth century would approach this task. A cleric, by training, rather disposed towards a single version of the truth, might be inclined to either conflate different versions of a story into one 'authorised' version. But a bard, by training, would be perhaps much more content to simply record the best version of the story to his ear, while simply allowing that there are many other versions, and indeed being perfectly relaxed about that fact. In the same way, a traditional musician might learn to play 'Tripping up the Stairs' or 'St Anne's Reel', being conscious, in the first instance, of getting all the notes right and the technique, by listening intently to a range of players handling the tune and then producing a version that might follow very closely a particular player of renown, or borrow different little techniques from a number of players. And we must also remember that the bardic artist is likely to be influenced very intensely by what is local to him, for he is, after all, at this stage, a key stakeholder in his *tuath* or small kingdom. He will hear new stories at big gatherings, but it is vital that the way he tells his story makes meaning for his local community. But the bardic training was not merely focused upon the local and the wider world of, for example, the classics, would have been known in the bardic schools (Davies, 1995).

With the coming of Christianity, the gathering together of stories by bards and *fili* to create a repertoire was augmented and subjected to greater formalisation by the Christian clerics. There emerged a new kind of approach which was focused upon classifying tales in new ways. The older tradition organised tales thematically – for example, there were tales of cattle raids, battles, feasts, adventures, elopements, visions and voyages, to name but a few. This kind of classification would have made considerable sense when the function of the poet was to recite, at court, tales appropriate as it were, to local events. So, as Robert Welch tells us, the poet would have likely recited a tale from his cattle raid catalogue if the local king was about to muster his men to go a-rustling. And it is not unlikely that he might have conflated more than one story or even worked in a reference to the lineage of his king or some such local tie to give the story more traction in his own *tuath* or district. Modern storytellers, like John Campbell from south Armagh, would likewise adapt certain details of a story to create a local connection. For all that was about to befall Ireland in the intervening centuries, the Celtic Spirit lived on, as demonstrated in the extraordinary tenacity of those old bardic storytelling practices.

It seems to me that the Christian clerical sensibility was, perhaps not surprisingly, given the immersion in biblical narrative, focused on a chronological story, beginning with creation (Genesis), moving to the Fall of Man, then following the history of the Jewish people and subsequently, the story of Christ himself and ending with the end of this world (Apocalypse, Judgement). The Christian world view is historical, chronological, because without a sense of historical development, conceptions of spiritual growth, salvation and redemption are meaningless. In the light of this, then, we can maybe begin to understand why the clerics began to organise the oral pagan stories, into a more discernible chronological pattern, so that they begin to represent the first attempts to create a history of Ireland. This change of emphasis from the fragmentary pieces organised thematically and socially, was of course not confined to Ireland and we can discern the start of history elsewhere, for example in *Holinshed's Chronicles* across the sea.

There was another impetus, dating back maybe to the twelfth century, and that is the urge towards a national con-sciousness throughout Europe, and maybe with the 'nation states' in Italy. We use the word 'national' very advisedly, for it is very different in conception and practice from nineteenth-century expressions of Gaelic or Celtic nationalism. We simply mean to suggest that in Ireland, as elsewhere, efforts were being made to attest the value of a nation through its cultural products. Thus, the creation of a corpus, a canon, began to become important. A nation needed not only a chronological story (a history) but a literature that would reflect its glory. And if this were to be intelligible to audiences, and more important-ly readers, outside Ireland, it needed to be gathered together in some way. So, there grew a demand for compendia, for collections of tales that could be put in a satchel and carried across Europe so that the prestige of Irish learning could be properly appreciated. The first of these compendia was, as noted earlier, the *Book of Invasions*.

Mac Cana offers another, or additional, explanation. In the eleventh century the Church embarked upon a reform programme which diminished the predominance of the old abbot-led monasteries and placed greater emphasis on episcopal direction. Continental orders such as the Cistercians started to establish monastic foundations in Ireland. Such orders had a strong penchant for centralisation and indeed for organisational control under the authority of a bishop. It is hardly surprising, then, that this zeitgeist also manifested itself in a view of culture that made the idea of collecting diverse materials into a central coherent whole a kind of natural imperative.

In the second half of the twelfth century the Normans came. The safeguarding, gathering and regrouping of existing literary resources may have stemmed then from a presage that profound changes were coming, and that the centralising impulse, of which the new religious orders were the harbingers, was to expand into many areas of political and economic life (Mac Cana, 1980, p. 33). At any rate, it is in this period that we are to see the first of the great manuscript collections, encompassing material stretching back five centuries. So we owe to these medieval clerics a very huge debt, for without their work, the rich and substantial literature would not have survived. That it became better known on the Continent, where many of the manuscripts were lodged and many, after the Reformation, were compiled, is one of the prettier ironies of our history. Thus, while Continental influences within Ireland might not always have been welcome, it is the Continent that saved a huge amount of Celtic literature. We will come back to that a bit later.

At this stage, let us look at the clerical classifications and give some examples of each; but just before we do this, here is Mac Cana:

> Perhaps what is most impressive in [the tales] is the depth and variety of the tradition which they embody ... They abound in archaisms of theme, ritual and diction which bring us as close and sometimes closer than the Mahabharata to the well-springs of primitive Indo-European theology, and they constantly reveal in rich lodes and outcrops the presence of a sensuous theology of the earth's divinity that is more deep-rooted than the patrimony of Celt or Indo-European (Mac Cana, 1980, p. 21).

Approaching Chronology: The Three (or Four) Cycles of Tales
Some scholars have used a classification which groups the tales
into three phases; others make a four-stage division:

- Mythological Tales (to do with gods and goddesses)
- The Heroic or Ulster Cycle
- (The King or Historical Cycle)
- The Fenian Cycle or Cycle of Fionn MacCumhaill and the
  Fianna.

Mythological Tales
Mac Cana is surely on the right track in assuming that myth
comes before history (though it could be argued that in Ireland
it also comes with it and after it). The mythological tales, then,
deal specifically with the gods and with the otherworld of the
pagan Irish. Muireann Ní Bhrolcháin argues that the Irish sagas
are the most popular areas of study and of most interest to the
general public (Ní Bhrolcháin, 2009, p. 5). Mac Cana adjudges
the most important of these to be *The Battle of Mag Tured*. This
tale tells of the gods of the Irish, the Tuatha Dé Danann (the
people of the goddess Danu). The story relates the victory of
the rather spiritual Tuatha Dé Danann over the Formóiri –
earthy, somewhat lumbering types. This demonic horde is, of
course, defeated. And, not surprisingly, the business has to be
done through a battle between the gods. Within the story, the
youthful god Lugh slays the Cyclopian, Balor. We cannot fail
to note that spirit claims victory over matter, the mind/soul
conquers the physical, the bodily; thus good is signified by
spirit while evil is assigned to the realm of the physical. We can
see a distinctly Christian teleology operating here – but, of
course, in the Celtic world, the distinction between the physical
and the supernatural, matter and spirit, is rarely adamantine.

NESTING SWAN

Interchanging forms: Nesting swan, Tyrone-Armagh border.

We have noted early European attempts to develop history, and two of the learned compilations produced by the Irish were the *dinnseanchas* (The Lore of Places) and the *Lebor Gabála* (*Book of Invasions*). These collections contain much mythological lore. Mac Cana does not think highly of the literary merit of these massive compendia and directs us rather to *Aislinge Oengusa* (*The Dream of Oengus/Angus*). Oengus, the son of Dagda, the father-god, falls ill through love of a girl who appears to him in a dream or *aisling*, a word – a device more precisely – we will come across in a later chapter. The divine

163

elders then mount a prolonged search for her. After a long time, at the feast of Samhain (1 November), Oengus comes upon the girl in the form of a swan at a lake in Connacht. Obligingly, he changes his form to match hers (perhaps the gods were a little wiser than mere mortal men) and together they fly off to his palace, singing such music to make all who heard them fall asleep for three days and three nights.

The style, comments Mac Cana, is simple and terse. Most interestingly, he says that 'like some of the best modern short stories, it achieves its effect by suggestive economy rather than by elaboration' (Mac Cana, 1980, p. 24). We cannot help but think of Joyce here. Mac Cana does not spare his contempt for the later misty romanticism of Celtic literature by people like MacPherson. And, of course, it is hard not to hear about this story without also thinking of that famous poem by W. B. Yeats, 'The Song of Wandering Aengus'. Maybe just a wee shade dewy, but, of course freighted with symbolic produce. The golden apples of the sun, the silver apples of the moon – not items to be got locally, but to be brought, as a matter of archaeological fact, from more exotic climes than Emain Macha. But it might be also worth noting that Yeats was also, as Eamonn Hughes has pointed out (Hughes, 2012), a great man for collecting, for creating a canon.

The Heroic Cycle

Perhaps the most famous of the heroic tales is *The Cattle Raid of Cooley (Táin Bó Cúailnge)*, and the most famous hero is Cúchulainn. The heroic tales are often, though by no means always, centred in Ulaidh (part of modern Ulster) and, specifically, in Emain Macha – now known as Navan Fort and situated about two miles from the current ecclesiastical sites in Armagh. Many will be familiar with the rough outlines of the story of *The Cattle Raid of Cooley*. Queen Maeve, with her husband, leads a raid into Ulster to capture a famous bull called Donn Cúailnge (The Brown One of Cooley). The men of Ulster were affected by a strange weakness which made their defence of their prize bull a mite tricky, for warriors are not really supposed to have physical weakness. But Cúchulainn is immune from this weakness, and so it is left to him to defend the bull and the territory. The Brown Bull also features and he faces the great White-horned Connacht Bull. After, as Mac Cana gleefully expresses it, 'a conflict of cosmic proportions' (p. 30), the Cooley Brown One destroys the White-horned Connacht Bull utterly. After, the heart of the Brown Bull bursts within him, but not before he makes it home to Ulster.

As Mac Cana observes, these are divine bulls, just as Maeve bears the trace of a goddess. The characters and animals in fact all operate in a strange, fluid world, at times somewhat of this world, at times seeming to belong to a purely mythological world. Maeve is

> a mixture of vamp and virago, who brazenly cuckolds her husband with Fergus MacRioch, the Ulster hero whose prodigious virility ranks him among the super-human, if not the super-natural. She passes many partners through her hands, which is only as it should be considering that she is in fact the goddess of the land and its sovereignty, whose sacred function is to mate with those who merit kingship and cast aside those who do not (Mac Cana, 1980, p. 28).

Equally, Cúchulainn transcends the merely human. And like nearly all ancient heroes – Beowulf, Odysseus – he is alone. And like all ancient heroes, he represents a wider code, valorising physical prowess, bravado, a noble disregard for his own safety and a tendency to vaunt, and a predilection for glory over conquest or material reward. The bulls are really an extension of this heroic, epic code. The choice of animal is perfectly logical and practical, given that cattle were the most prized possession in ancient Ireland as many a place elsewhere (hence John Bull).

The Táin is a very large tale and is, according to Mac Cana, the most complete portrait of a heroic age in Irish (Mac Cana, 1980, p. 30). There are other remarkable tales, for example, *Fled Bricrenn* (*The Feast of Bricriu*). Here a different side of the heroic life can be glimpsed. Bricriu is a bit of a rascal, a trickster. For fun, he invites all the Ulster heroes to a great feast and then goads three of them, including Cúchulainn, to compete for the champion's portion. It ends with a beheading game. The champion's portion motif is very old and, again, logical in a society where heroes needed their sustenance, their fill of meat and drink. Food is vital both at a pragmatic and at a symbolic level and, of course, in structural terms, a feast or dance is a great way to get all your characters into one room for a nice dramatic set piece – think of the Christmas dinner in *A Portrait of the Artist as a Young Man* or Netherfield Ball in *Pride and Prejudice*.

But perhaps the most tragic of the heroic tales is *The Death of Aife's Only Son*, in which Cúchulainn is brought to slay his own son, a motif also present in classical literature. For Mac Cana, the tale which has had the most impact is *Deirdre and the Sons of Uisneach*, and certainly many later writers were to create their own versions: Lady Gregory, Synge, Yeats and James Stephens.

The King Cycle

These are tales mostly concerned with delineating the virtues of the ideal king, but as in other cultures, these categorisations fail to acknowledge that there are often heroic and mytho-logical elements in the same tale. Limitations of space do not permit more than a cursory glance at these stories, but perhaps the most famous king was Cormac Mac Airt. But, as *The*

Destruction of the Hostel of Da Derga demonstrates, with tragic irony, even the wisest and most generous of kings can err. Cormac tempers justice with excessive mercy and the ironic result is 'a welter of violence' (Mac Cana, 1980, p. 27) in which Cormac loses his own life. The king tales have a social orientation and, as Christianity begins to impress itself upon the older pagan material, the good king is of course one endowed not only with Christian beliefs but Christian virtues – rather at odds with the heroic code. Wisdom, justice and hospitality are emphasised over the warrior values.

The Fenian Cycle

Fionn himself was probably a deity and his band of warrior heroes are not confined to any *tuath*, giving them a sort of capaciousness. In the Fenian Cycle there is, thus, perhaps a greater sense of adventure, of journey, and also a strong sense of the land not so much as a place to which people belong, but as a semi-sacral context through which the heroes move, in a harmonious relationship with nature. Many of the stories are poems from the twelfth century using the form of lays. It is not unlikely, especially given the close contacts between the Irish and their Continental comrades, that the form was influenced by the popularity of European balladry about this same time. We may note that with the ballad form, we make a return to accentual verse. This may help to explain why so many of these tales survived long after the collapse of the Gaelic order – they were more easily remembered.

Mac Cana advances the case for *The Converse of the Old Men* (*Acallam na Senórach*) as the most aesthetically pleasing of these tales. This is really an anthology, comprising a frame story and containing over two hundred separate stories, interspersed with many lyric poems. This feature alone would tend to underscore the close relationship with nature noted earlier.

And, indeed, the way the frame operates further encourages a close identification with nature and indeed particular places. For the frame narrative has Caoilte mac Ronain accompany Patrick on his Christianising mission, and in response to his courteous enquiries, Caoilte relates stories associated with the hills, rivers, plains and other notable features of the country they are travelling through.

Now there are three things of especial interest here. One is that sense of the history belonging to place. Henry Glassie, the American anthropologist, has remarked with some acuity that in Ireland space is temporal (Glassie, 1982). And we all know this to be true. Dungannon was the fort of Gannon O'Neill, Brockagh was once Mountjoy and before that it was Brockagh, and Shankhill in Belfast once declared its loyalties to an old Catholic Church. And, more specifically, that sense of space and place being temporal is a layered and often contradictory business. Place is a kind of palimpsest upon which our sometimes contended history is marked by a succession of nominations, namings. In a curious sort of way, we live not just in our own world but in the otherworlds of history and myth, and it is not possible to walk ground in this country without being aware of its resonance; the closeness of worlds so different to our own. The Aboriginal Australians have a similar sense of this palimpsest in their songlines, though perhaps reaching back far more directly to mythic origins, there being less invasions and settlings, however traumatic they proved to be.

The second thing is that some of the places are named because of their topography – so, for example, if St Patrick were to take another trip around these arts and parts, we would be telling him that the townland of Annaghbeg conforms topographically with its name, a small watery place, just as the Moy (An Maigh) is a plain (near the Blackwater and Lough Neagh). John Hewitt was to echo that Celtic Spirit many centuries later in a poem called 'Ulster Names':

The names of a land show the heart of a race;
They move on the tongue like the lilt of a song.
You say the name and I see the place –
Drumbo, Dungannon, or Annalong
Barony, townland, we cannot go wrong (John Hewitt,
1991, p. 386).

Now these two things are related to the third thing, which
is about how we get to know a country. Ireland is the most
mapped country in Europe, because so many different sets of
settlers / planters / invaders / reformers / adventurers came
here. The Ordnance Survey was undertaken here, as elsewhere,
by the Royal Engineers. The mapping here is about laying
claim to territory. St Patrick, it could be said, was also, more
subtly, laying claim, but he seems to have been much interested
in getting to know the country for its own sake – as an
otherworld. And indeed Friel's play *Translations* suggests that
there was at least one Sapper who rather fell for the music of
the places (Friel, 1981). Eamonn Hughes has spoken about Van
Morrison's cognitive maps of Belfast in his songs: 'the blues
rolling down Royal Avenue' (Hughes, 2012). I think this
application of cultural geography is an intriguing and useful
concept. For what we get here is a set of conjunctions: the local
street (never named in blues songs), the imperial underlay of
that street name and the 'invasion' of black American blues.
So, place, space is not stable, but subject to change, to
influences from outside. And these influences sometimes have
the curious effect of causing the indigenous dwellers (who
once were alien here too, to borrow from John Hewitt), to feel
displaced, to feel as if they are living in an otherworld. But this
predicament can also give rise to a further irony; if outside
influences are over-restricted, if the culture of a place imprisons
those dwelling there in a kind of inner exile, then there can
arise a feeling that the individual is inhabiting an otherworld

– one contrary to, clashing with, his own imaginative construction of what the world could be. In his song 'Astral Weeks' (Morrison, 1968), Morrison himself lamented, using the very lexis and cadence of the oppressed inner exiles who write the blues: 'I ain't nothing but a stranger in this world.'

Behind Morrison's threnody is not only some reflex that is Irish in the broadest sense of that term, but a reflex that is apparently quite un-Irish: an identification with, a near inhabitance of, the situation of the black blues men. But of course behind that is the Bible and Morrison's immersion in – note it – gospel music. No escaping Christianity, in one form or another. And what is the most important aspect of this Christianity? Transcendence; a lifting up of the soul to another place; an Elysium. And so powerful is 'this lonely impulse of delight' (to quote again from Yeats, 'An Irish Airman Forsees his Death'), that the physical world is transformed in the process. The cognitive map is superimposed upon the commercial; Imperial Street and Royal Avenue are suddenly an otherworld. There is an eruption of the marvellous as the blues come rolling down, like a biblical cloud. This otherworlding is a feature of many Belfast writers, notably David Park and Glenn Patterson; the luminous, numinous moment, an epiphany to which the soundtrack is the dramatic sound of angels' trumpets (a blues instrument if ever there was one), presaging the Last Judgement, and justice. No harps here.

We have travelled, like some late Yeats spectre, 'far out of this world'. And so many of those late Yeats figures are in the wilderness, or yearning for a transformation which will take them to a Byzantium utterly unlike the Ireland they are condemned to live in, a society so inimical that the artist figure will seek the margins, the wild places, if he has not already been sent west. But we have done so to demonstrate how Irish writers and bards have, over so many centuries, responded to the many exigencies that history has thrown upon their path with an imaginative capaciousness that is astonishing. The tension between an immense love of the local place to which we belong, along with the sense of that place as itself unstable, otherworldly, and a need to wander, to move, to be out of there to an other otherworld, seems to reach very far back in Irish literature. Perhaps the coming of Christianity itself was the first crystallisation of these conflicting forces. Alternatively, maybe the paradoxically countermanding appeal for comfort of the familiar and the yearning for the unknown was there long before, for it is, maybe, deep in the heart's core. So it is that the tales of the Fianna embody both a devotion to a local place, an honouring and celebration of it, and a sense of the country as a space, a place of wandering.

Now sometimes this wandering is great fun altogether. And the merry band has superlative antics in this essentially Arcadian construction. Mac Cana continually draws attention to the fluidity of the boundary between the natural and supernatural, the material world and the otherworld. The Fianna are 'in close association with nature, animate and inanimate ... there is the same unaffected intimacy with the creatures of the wilderness that we find in some of the lives of the ascetic saints' (Mac Cana, 1980, p. 35). These tales would have been originally classified as echtra or adventure tales. But, as Mac Cana perceptively notes, the Fianna are a 'rootless and restless fraternity of men who have severed their tribal affiliations and given themselves up to the hazardous freedom of the great no-man's land beyond the borders of organized society' (Mac Cana, 1980, p. 35).

It is thus hardly surprising that we have also many tales which extend the possibilities of adventure – and the ramifications of exile. There are, for example, loads of stories about journeys to the otherworld. Perhaps the most famous of these is the story of Oisín and Tír na nÓg. At one level, the story is a complex dramatisation of the tension between the desire for this world and the desire for an otherworld. Oisín voyages to the otherworld of Tír na nÓg – the land of eternal youth, but misses his own local place. He is warned that if he sets foot in Ireland age will wither him (and perhaps also 'custom stale', to borrow from *Antony and Cleopatra*). But the exile's yearning for the lost places that he belonged to prevails. The material world, the real world, is by definition subject to mortality, but the otherworld Elysium paradoxically palls because of the very endlessness of its beauty and bounty. Now you will all recognise that this tension characterises both pagan and Christian belief systems, and there are many parallels for the journey to strange and exotic lands in other literatures.

In the story of Diarmuid and Gráinne the journey is presented as being primarily an exile tale, full of loss and yearning for homeland. This motif was to be echoed for centuries as the people from this island, whatever their religious background, found themselves in the condition of migration and exile. Very often, significantly, the ballad form is the medium. We hear it in 'Carrickfergus' and in the Ulster Scots ballad 'Slieve Gallion's Braes'. But not all these ballads of migration are sad. There is, for example, a song about the leaving of 'Enniskillen Town', with its much more hopeful message about the potential of the land of promise, or, if you will, the New Jerusalem.

And speaking of New Jerusalems, there are also many tales about voyages with a missionary purpose. The most famous is probably the Latin *Navigatio Brendani*. Brendan sets out in quest of the 'land of promise of the saints'. Mac Cana is most fulsome in his praise of this story as 'the chief single contribution of Ireland to the general literature of medieval Europe' (Mac Cana, 1980, p. 26). Doubtless, because it was in Latin it became better known, as Latin was the international language. But, of course, there is a wealth of stories based on the voyage plot. The voyage story is known as the immram (rowing about, circumnavigation). Many of these tales mix pagan and Christian elements, like *The Voyage of Bran*, and the *Voyage of Máele Dúin* (rendered satirically in the twentieth century by Brian O'Nolan (Flann O'Brien) in *An Béal Bocht*).

Some of the stories may have enjoyed popularity in the fifteenth and sixteenth century because of what was happening in Europe at the time: the voyages of discovery. Technology had made possible what had only been imagined, but because of the imaginative freight attaching to stories of journeys to otherworlds, expectations may have been a mite on the side. In reality, few ended up like that Cortez, so fantastically imagined by Keats in his 'On First Looking into Chapman's Homer':

Then felt I like some watcher of the skies
When a new planet swims into his ken;
Or like stout Cortez when with eagle eyes
He star'd at the Pacific – and all his men
Look'd at each other with a wild surmise –
Silent, upon a peak in Darien (Keats, 1816; rpt 1988, p. 72).

The allusion to Homer implies stories are nearly always better than the real thing. And indeed, this period saw a great florescence in adventure stories such as Thomas Nashe's *The Unfortunate Traveller* and, a bit later, Daniel Defoe's *Robinson Crusoe*.

Stories about voyages are, however, not always happy and full of exotic promise. We may think here of tales like *Buile Suibhne*, with its almost unbearable sense of anguish. Sweeney has madness put on him for defying a Christian saint and is condemned to wander the land. But not only are his senses put astray; he is turned, with a malevolence worthy of a Druid, and of course, expropriated from the Druid, into a creature half bird, half man; a huddle between earth and heaven, as Flann O'Brien puts it in *At Swim-Two-Birds*. And this tale suggests something, not just about the grim potentiality of the adventure or voyage tale to darken into a tale of fugal isolation, but a nature portrayed not as bounteous but as elemental. Yeats was to focus on these aspects to furnish his late Romantic chiliasm, while Beckett and Flann O'Brien were to fuse these aspects into their own postmodernist comic nightmares.

In the next chapter, we will discuss two other important literary forms, aisling and satire, and we will try to explain how these ancient forms responded to the particular historical circumstances of much later times. We see a hint of this in the references above in what I think is a tribute to the richness of the Celtic Spirit and the literary forms which embodied it. It announces itself, articulates itself over many centuries, long after the social and political reality of the old orders had gone, rewiring itself, reconnecting and retransmitting that spirit through conjunction with new forces in new worlds. But certain it is that the recursive motif in Celtic art, the recursive serpent's tail, endlessly circling back on itself, has long influenced how we tell our tales. What this reveals about our psyche is that, perhaps, at worst, there is no getting away from ourselves (the Joycean cracked looking glass, the nightmare of history) or, at best, we recognise that nature is cyclical and we must needs move within its rhythms. For every springtime land of promise, there is the inevitable confrontation with our own mortality, the sere and yellow leaf; for every winter of discontent there is a summer of bliss, a time of fulfilment. For which we may offer thanks, having seen and heard all these notes in Celtic literature, when we could not always manage them ourselves.

CHAPTER NINE

After the Normans: The Great Change
Tess Maginess

The Aisling as a Glimpse into History

It may seem a mite peculiar to begin this chapter not with an account of the huge changes that affected Ireland, and that Ireland affected, after the Normans, but rather with a consideration of a very particular literary genre, the aisling. We may plead two mitigations. The first is that this book does not make any claims to be a comprehensive historical account over several centuries – others have accomplished that task with far more authority. The second is that by tracing some versions of the aisling, we may, odd as it may seem, be able to gain a glimpse of the changing political, economic and cultural landscape between roughly the 1600s and the early 1800s. And the question we will try to answer in the process is what happened to the Celtic Spirit in this epoch?

After the Normans, one of the most important genres was the aisling or dream/vision. This is closely related to the French reverdie tradition, again calling to attention influence of secular high art from the Continent on Celtic literature. The aisling was composed in both poetic and prose forms. The basic format is that the speaker/poet is perhaps sitting under a tree or in some solitary place and falls asleep. A dream comes to him in which he – and we – are transported into some idyllic realm. The aisling incorporates elements of early Irish lyrical verse: the connection with nature, and that ability to be, as it were, transported by nature into a lyric reverie; as well as wonder tales and the immram tradition, where the speaker journeys from this world into an otherworld, either physical and/or metaphysical.

There are many variations from this basic format. For example in *The Vision of Mac Con Ginne*, which is an early medieval tale, the hero is a poor clerical student who throws over the books for the arguably more attractive (if equally precarious) alternative of tramping the roads and making poems. The frame narrative then gives way to a series of adventures which, according to Mac Cana, embodies a splendid version of the 'Land of Cockaigne' (Mac Cana, 1980, p. 39). We will come back to this a little later in the chapter.

Aisling and Satire

There are also, in this tale, merciless satires on monastic charity, superb parodies of established literary genres and even a forthright burlesque of the Crucifixion. So the Monty Python team did not invent this kind of parody in our day with their *Life of Brian*. It must be acknowledged that many people of faith will find the very idea of a burlesque on such a sacral subject deeply offensive. In other contexts, some Muslims are vexed to the core by any depiction of the prophet Muhammad in terms that are less than reverential. All we can do here, and all we must do here, is to register the fact that writers back in a far more conformist time than the one we now live in as Western Europeans (and we will not even get into the far trickier facts of existence, never mind literature, for those living in places where schools to educate girls are burned or the fate of those who try to challenge the wisdom and justice of such policies) did write literature which held up the distorting mirror of comedy to reveal a few home truths. The truths, of course, were about humans, mostly anyhow.

The Land of Cockaigne is a medieval mythical land of plenty, an imaginary place of extreme luxury and ease, where pleasure is always at hand. Though recognisably a version of paradise, Cockaigne is, as it were, not patrolled by Christian values, harking back to more pagan sources. Indeed, it is frankly amoral. Abbots can be beaten by their monks, sexual liberty is all the Dionysian rage and there is always plenty of excellent food – skies rain cheeses. This concept, if we may so call it, was incredibly common across medieval Europe, with local versions in Italy, Spain and France – and much later in London, hence, perhaps, the word 'Cockney' (Pleij, 2001). Pieter Bruegel the Elder also produced a painting on the subject. The concept may well have classical antecedents (Bonner, undated). It may well be that Cockaigne was constructed as a sort of fantasy island because medieval life was, for a lot of people, bound very tightly; an escape valve of some sort was perhaps as much a necessity as a desire.

Very many people endured a life of poverty. Society was also rigidified at many levels. Christian values taught all to be obedient, to obey the Church no matter what its representatives did. Chastity, poverty and charity were preached, but at the same time the Church (that is to say, the Catholic Church, since there was no other) was becoming a major player in international politics, gathering into itself a great deal of earthly as well as spiritual power. In that context, it is not altogether surprising that such a genre – subversive, escapist, comedic – should emerge, especially within a broader literary tradition that favoured fantasy over what we now call realism, mainly because until the Renaissance realism had not actually been quite invented.

The Irish, it seems, were not slow to offer their own contributions to the ludic, satirical aisling tradition. Mac Cana praises 'The Vision of Mac Con Ginne' as 'a remarkable tour de force of wit and learning and a convincing proof that Irish prose was far from dead' (Mac Cana, 1980, p. 39). Nor, we might add, has any force been able yet to extinguish it, though astonishingly determined efforts have been made so to do. We will return to that a little later in this chapter.

What is also remarkable to us, now conditioned as we have been in various ways by history, is that a poem like this belongs to – and maybe even informs – international literature. This Irish aisling is a fully working part of a European tradition, not some marginal scrap from an uncivilised people. And yet, of course, it is remarkable that a country like Ireland, so geographically peripheral, so marginal, is producing writing that is at the top of the European bent.

There are two or three other things of relevance here. Vivien Mercier, in a really fine book called *The Irish Comic Tradition* (1962), makes a very convincing case for the deep roots of a comedic perspective in Irish literature and draws particular attention to the fondness for fantasy, the ribald and the grotesque. I may point out that this was also part of a European sensibility, though it does seem to have had a certain tenacity in Ireland. Perhaps, ironically, because the country did become marginalised in so many senses and, thus, cut off from Europe, it retained, conservatively, its radically critical sensibility.

There may also be something afoot here in this poem to do with a growing European tendency towards anticlericalism. Let us recall that the speaker of the poem abandons his clerical studies for the older – or newer – life of the déclassé poet, out there on the road. The poem may be read as a kind of coded critique of the centralising and reforming agenda of the Continental Catholic Church. The little detail that he is a poor clerical student seems irrelevant and maybe is, but the practice of dowry-giving, a transactional, commercial nexus may have been a matter of considerable concern to a would-be cleric. If he were from a poor family, his lot, by implication, might be much less comfortable and prestigious than a student whose people could pay, by endowing, perhaps, the new and splendid monastery for which he was bound. It was not the first or last time that learning and money got a bit mixed up. But if this is taken in conjunction with the actual targets of the satire in the poem – so-called monastic charity, and even extremely, a critique that bites right down to the very core of Christian belief – we begin to apprehend the slowly building but corrosive dissatisfaction that was to erupt with the Reformation. We see it as early as Chaucer.

In Ireland there may well have been some who, like the man who composed this poem – perhaps a cleric, fantasising about not being a cleric, or a cleric gone out from the new order – did not think well of what they viewed as the autocratic dictates of the Cistercians, preferring the more organic cellular organisation of the old Irish Church. But we must also remember that this clerical student himself, historically speaking, invaded a more ancient order, or came to rescue it, to take it from its benighted state into the light of Christianity, depending on your point of view. We may recall Mad Sweeney, a much earlier *refusenik*.

The Great Change: Representations of History in Literature

By the seventeenth century, a raven or two has come to roost. For a great deal has changed in Europe and in England and in Ireland. A lot of big things happened. Maybe the biggest of them is the Reformation. That was a rather dramatic 'game changer'. Nobody can pretend that this process was not a long and winding skein. But, it is the integument of that religious struggle with politics (inevitable, given the earthly position of the Catholic Church by Luther's time), combined with another European-wide phenomenon, the impulse towards geographical discovery, which was to have so profound an effect upon the nature of literature in Ireland.

Ironically, perhaps one of the impulses behind the voyages of discovery was that people had read a lot of stories about lands of Cockaigne, where milk, honey, cakes, cheeses, sex and gold flowed. And why would you not, given all the new technology and cartography and cosmology (for a ship steers by the stars) want to go on a bit of an immram? Then there is the small matter of the riches that could not just be experienced in these exotic but possibly chartable places, but brought back to plump the coffers of warring states and nations.

In no time at all, you have, articulated by the best minds in the country, elegant justifications for conquering territories and spreading civilisation. And given that the Reformation and before long the Counter-Reformation has occurred, spreading the true religion (depending on your denomination) as well as the customs and language of the conquering Western European forces were prime missions.

In Ireland, the way that worked out was that we had Edmund Spenser, who wrote a most beautiful poem about his marriage down about Cork, and quite a lot of other documents in his capacity as English official about the exciting project of civilising and reforming the Irish. The Irish had, he claimed, become barbarians, savages; as they would have to become to justify their suborning (Spenser, 1596).

The colonising project was nothing if not determined; the customs, laws and language of the 'mere' Irish were replaced with those of the coloniser. An Act of 1537, for example, forbade the wearing of Irish-style garments and the speaking of Irish. The Catholic religion was to be repressed as politically seditious, given the establishment of the Protestant succession in an atmosphere of threat from Catholic Europe, and theologically unsound. Wherever possible, the native savages were to be parted from their land, to allow the proper management and cultivation of it.

It is a story with two sides and it is a story not confined to Ireland, though we are enormously eloquent about presenting ourselves always as the 'special case', which, of course, we are, but then we are not the only special case, and arguably not the worst. Thus, Ireland was to be created as it had been created in more ancient times. In an earlier era, the *fili* and Christian clerics told us, we had Firbolgs and Fomorians and Tuatha Dé Danann, slugging it out. Then the Milesians came, as we hear in 'The Song of Amorgen', emerging as the good guys, *writing* themselves up as benevolent discoverers. Then we had Patrick and the Christians, proclaiming they had chosen the Irish, perhaps precisely because we were such hard cases, kidnapping the noble Patrick and enslaving him in Antrim, with precious little about him but sheep and shamrocks. But what a wonderful job the Christians made of us, converting us to their mission of enlightenment (except for Mad Sweeney). Then, following the pattern, in come the Vikings who were perhaps a little overzealous in the arts of plunder but did, apparently, introduce us to trade. As the Vikings did not seem to do any favours to either the *fili* or the clerics, who were in charge of the telling of all tales, the Vikings have had what we might now call a bad press. The recursive trope is of fear, of burnings and raiding and the destruction of sacred sites (with a lot of valuable metal inside them). And after the Vikings, we hosted the Normans, specifically invited by certain parties. They built towns and introduced some notion of fine dining, fine manners, fine courting (such *amour propre*, resulting in dynastic intermarriage with the old Gaelic families), fine words and fine laws, not altogether in harmony with the ancient Brehon system. The Normans morphed into the Old English and further changes were considered necessary as the shape of the political, social and economic map began to change. And they were succeeded by the New English and a more radical shift towards a policy of conquest by plantation and colonisation.

The spirit of that 'enterprise of great pith and moment', to quote Hamlet, was wholeheartedly reformist and impelled by a desire no less sincere than that of Patrick's to bring enlightenment to what was perceived as a dark place. There is only one problem, and that is what appears to have been a near total insouciance about what was already there in Ireland by way of culture. And what was there was a hybrid and complex culture, full of idealism and satiric twists, a culture already invaded or hospitable to a long line of visitors and also open to international Continental influences. But, militarily speaking, Ireland was weak.

Still, Ireland was not exactly El Dorado. It was not hugely rich in the commercial items that could fetch a high price in London. Nor was it the Land of Cockagine – at least at first sight. There was not even a potato; that iconic luxury had yet to be introduced from the New World. The colonisation of Ireland was, one suspects, much more to do with its dangerous geographical location as a back door for the invasion of England. It may also have served as a kind of near-to-home seedbed for models of colonisation that could be tried in much more extensive (and presumably profitable) territories.

Anglo-Irish Writing

To narrow again to the specific literary and cultural impact of these policies, we have a range of literary work being produced. That range – and this perhaps allows us to glimpse the sheer scale of the change – encompasses radical decisions in terms of language, subject and point of view. So we begin to get, in time, the production of literary work from people who were connected, directly or indirectly, with the New English. Thus, we have Spenser, and even Walter Raleigh staying in Ireland for a while and, later, in the eighteenth century, we have Swift and Goldsmith. While we do not have space, regrettably, to dwell upon these writers in any detail here, it could be argued that in authors like Goldsmith and Swift, we do have a certain kind of Celtic Spirit, in terms of a certain defence of the place. For while these men were most definitely part of the Anglo-Irish order, they did seek common cause, if not with the native Irish, then with Ireland's claims for justice. Goldsmith's harrowing dystopian pastoral 'The Deserted Village' could, of course, have been written about many an abandoned English village, but it is not improbable that, at the least, he drew the details of the poem from what he saw around him in Ireland. Swift's *The Drapier's Letters* and *A Modest Proposal* are satiric excoriations upon the woeful state of Irish trade due to English taxes. Swift was certainly familiar with Hibernio-English (Fabricant, 2003, p. 65) and the sheer grotesquerie of his writing may well owe something to the bardic tradition. Furthermore, like Dryden, Swift would have at least been aware of the fabled power of the satirist who could, as Dryden averred, rhyme you to death. Nuala Ní Dhomnaill, speaking of the confraternity of Gaelic poets in Dublin in Swift's time, notes that Swift profited from this community of scholars and poets, evidencing this by his version of 'O'Rourke's Ructions' (Ní Dhomnaill, 2008, p. 58). Without doubt, Swift was a complex figure in terms of his attitudes, and it is also true, as Robert Mahony has argued, that he has been recruited for a variety of cultural and political camps after his time (Mahony, 1995). Perhaps, like the old bardic satirists, he was possessed of very considerable largesse when it came to denunciation – that there would be more than one target for his satire is hardly surprising. And, as we will see shortly with a figure like Peadar Ó Dornín, the allegiances and identities of the writer are not to be so easily pinned down.

Bardic Poetry after the Great Change
But, the focus of this chapter bids us to narrow further here and return to writing that is more directly and indeed avowedly Celtic and Gaelic in spirit. Perhaps in another book the complex story of how the Celtic instilled itself in the New

English and the Anglo-Irish may be properly told. And, equally there is that Spenserian story that might bear retelling, of how that Celtic Spirit was, for many, simply of no interest, or a wicked force to be extirpated. For many historians, 1601 (The Battle of Kinsale) and 1607 (The Flight of the Earls) are the seminal dates. And while the decline of the old Gaelic order was, in reality, somewhat more gradual, the dramatic events of the opening years of the seventeenth century were to have profound effects. According to Mac Cana, the schools of the *fili* gradually perished in the aftermath of the wars of 1641–50 (Mac Cana, 1980, p. 47).

The break-up of the Gaelic clan estates in that violent period left the bards in a very tricky position. According to Jane Ohlmeyer, a later leg of the 1537 Act sponsored the removal of 'tympanours, poets, story-tellers, babblers, rymours, harpers or any other Irish minstrels who served as symbols of the feasting and fighting culture' (Ohlmeyer, 2012, p. 30–31). And, she notes, some of the bardic poets, guardians of the aristocratic tradition, acknowledged the nobles (a mixture of Irish chieftans after Surrender and Regrant, and New English peers) as the true and legitimate leaders of Irish society (Ohlmeyer, op. cit., p. 66).

It must have been a mite difficult to write great literature with no steady patron, no steady money, no steady status and the country in a 'state of chassis' in the words of Sean O'Casey – and with no story to tell, but a story of loss or making do and mending. We might compare the very different spirit that permeates the 'expansive' literature of that period when Ireland sent out its learned men, by popular demand, to the farthest corners of Europe and beyond. Perhaps the decline of the whole Gaelic order – a cultural nexus – might have been a bit like, in a rather different context, the radical decline of the shipbuilding industry in Belfast. Here too, was a jealously guarded and often hereditary skilled profession. Within twenty years the world had changed utterly. Men who were prized, valued, who could call on the pride of their fathers and grandfathers and uncles and cousins and call forth the pride of their sons, and their kin, were suddenly redundant, displaced. The new order broke up their communities, their learning forums, their dwelling places.

Commenting upon the cataclysmic nature of the Great Change, J. E. Caerwyn Williams cites Lughaidh O Celerigh: '[T]he authority and sovereignty of Gaelic Ireland has been lost till the end of time' (Caerwyn Williams, 1958; rpt 1992, p. 193). That there was elitism, protectionism and prejudice in these old orders is also undeniable, as Declan Kiberd points out (Kiberd, 2000, p. 20–21). But certain it is that the art and craft they had was dispersed, diluted, scattered and devalued, and that order, for the most part, descended, some remaining in various guises; awkward jags in the finely drawn plan of progress. As Alan Harrison argues, some lamented the imminent catastrophe, while others tried to ignore it and stubbornly maintained their old ways (Harrison, 1991, p. 274). Some became itinerant schoolmasters and scribes; some became farmers; some became artisans and labourers (Connolly and Holmes, 2013, p. 107). Some took the boat and left the shamrock shore.

Among those who left was Geoffrey Keating (Seathrún Céitinn), 1580–1644, who went with his Gaelic masters and spent the rest of his life in exile on the Continent. Others 'widened their portfolio' and narrowed their ideals, becoming general scribes and teachers as well as poets to scrape together a living, and others made an accommodation with the new 'settlers', the new masters. One thing is for certain: all the writers of the period from the early 1600s right through to the 1800s viewed their situation and the situation of Ireland as calamitous and the dominant tones are lamentation, elegy and satire. That is not to say that there are not many moments of wit and passion and tender lyricism. But it is, mainly, the poetry of the dispossessed. This was, by the way, the title of a fine anthology edited by Thomas Kinsella and Seán Ó Tuama (Kinsella and Ó Tuama, 1981). The personal and collective fate of the bards perhaps reflected and inscribed a more general anguish among the native Irish. This was to resurface in the nationalist movements of the nineteenth century, which saw also many translations of these earlier Renaissance poets. Perhaps, because we need to be wary to be fair, life for an ordinary Irish person may not have been a bed of roses under the clan system, but the attempt to violently sweep away land, religion, culture might not have been entirely welcome either among the so-called 'native Irish'.

Chief among the exiles, along with Geoffrey Keating, were Pádraigín Haicéad (Patrick Hackett), Eoghan Rua (Owen Roe) and Fearghal Óg Mac an Bhaird (Young Fergal Ward). Eoghan Rua was the hereditary *ollamh* (chief poet) of the O'Donnels and accompanied them into exile. These poets, perhaps not surprisingly, wrote many elegies, made all the more plangent by their physical separation from their homeland. Very often that love of their lost place was expressed directly, but also indirectly through the creation of a trope that was to prove immensely enduring – the identification of Ireland with a woman. Sometimes in this metaphorical identification of Ireland with a female lover, the woman is given a name – Kathleen Ní Houlihan, Roisin Dubh. The woman/ Ireland is depicted in a variety of impossible positions. She is the deserted lover, hoping for the return of her noble espoused – an allegory, in the mid-1700s, for the hopes placed in a Jacobite overthrow of the Protestant succession in England, and indeed in Ireland. But, of course, there may have been, for some, a guilt behind that trope too, maybe a sense that the noblest have abandoned their love. And there is a candour in that admission too.

Some of the poets who went into exile entered the Church and became actively involved in the Counter-Reformation. This was understandable, given the broader agenda of countering Protestantism in Ireland and, with it, the entire cultural, economic and political assault upon the old order. As J. E. Caerwyn Williams points out, 'the Continent was nearer to Gaelic Ireland than England or London' (Caerwyn Williams, 1958; rpt 1992, p. 198). And, we may add, not for the first or last time. We look back to the cleric scholars satchelling their learning across Europe and forward to George Moore, Joyce and Beckett. And as Williams points out, the beginning of the seventeenth century was a period of extraordinary literary activity among the exiled Irish on the Continent (Caerwyn Williams, op. cit., p. 205).

Geoffrey Keating was, for example, an important figure in the founding of the Irish College in Louvain. Pádraigín Haicéad became a Dominican. Haicéad deployed the woman trope in another way, colouring it with a deeply moral complexion; having exercised his venom against the perfidy of Albion, he castigates the Irish for entering into a sluttish collusion with the English, and, as a consequence, 'nurturing the litter of every alien sow'.

The displaced poets also adverted to the aisling form, adapting it to reflect their own contemporary concerns. Indeed, the aisling becomes a kind of mors(e) code, often lamenting the loss of the old order. The vision of a beautiful woman (the *speirbean* – the sky woman, or fairy woman) morphs into a political allegory in which the dream transmutes from personal romantic fulfilment to a political magic that breaks the bonds of English oppression. This genre reached its peak, according to some commentators, ironically with the collapse of Jacobite hopes after 1745 (O Buachalla, 1996; Nic Eoin, 2002). And perhaps the most eloquent scribe of that hopeless excitement was Eoghan Rua Ó Súilleabháin (Owen Roe O'Sullivan). As

Charles Dillon poignantly comments, the aisling poems were framed also against the poets' own loneliness and solitude (Dillon, 2012, p. 143).

But before turning to Eoghan Rua, let us look for a moment at a poem by Keating that is not about culture and politics, but about a woman who is not anything but a woman. The traumatic events in the wider world could not but inflect what these poets wrote about – after all, their function, as the old Gaelic society would have expected it to be, was to be public, to voice, indeed to shape a collective response to the politics of the day. Yet, we can discern in the Gaelic poets an urge also towards a different kind of function for poetry – to express a more personal, private domain. Now, of course, we must be careful not to make lavish claims for the Gaelic poets in anticipating the poetic concerns of the Romantic poets, and indeed the Modernists. The realm of personal love was one well and truly worked over in English and Continental poetry of the *amour courtois*, the highly stylised genre wherein the woman is always unattainable and the lover alternately burns and freezes with desire. The Gaelic poets would, doubtlessly, have been familiar with this literary representation of love, but what is interesting is the subversion of the conventions by Keating. He appeals, of course, to an older folk tradition, which has its origins in the classical figure of the senex or old man, but Keating dramatises, in the most frankly sensual terms, the plight of the older lover. The old man is no longer a stereotypical figure of ridicule, but a man caught in a dilemma that is strangely postmodern, which might be the same thing as saying that it is perennial. And, in stark contrast to the representation of the woman as a stiff, almost hieratical figure debarred from being sexually active or even assertive, we have as the title of the poem 'A Woman Hot with Zeal'. Now, it might seem that, in the temper of the times, the subject is religious zeal, but not one bit of it. This poem is told from the perspective of an older man who, it would appear, is making a bad job of satisfying sexually his young lover. It is a great poem because the point of view is so self-deprecating, because it is technically well wrought, and also because it is so modern in its frank sensuality. The poem, also, of course, reflects that older Celtic Spirit, which is by no means averse to a bit of ribaldry. And indeed, it might be argued that the Christian remodelling of women, combined with the encroachment of post-Reformation legal dispensations limiting the role of women to chattels is challenged in this poem by an older Brehon order in which women, it appears, had rather more by way of rights and rather more by way of understanding.

It may be argued that the woman-Ireland trope became a shade too pure in the nineteenth century and lost a great deal of the open vitality and raw passion which characterised it in the seventeenth and eighteenth centuries. And, it might be said, that the Irish poets were far less constrained than their English counterparts. Spenser's *Faerie Queene*, with its almost neurotic emphasis on a public, political, virginity, might be said to betoken a myth of lifetime restraint which strains credulity to its limits.

The Irish poets, perhaps harking back to the Brehon Laws where a woman could divorce her husband for sexual inadequacy, were not unduly bound to a desiccated Romance code in which woman is untouchable, interested only in sending men out upon crusades that keep them at a safe distance. These poets, though doubtless aware of this code of courtly love so ubiquitous in Elizabethan English poetry, know how to convey to a woman, with just a little bit of mockery, the effect she could have. In 'Lovely Lady Drop your Arms', Paras Feiritear (Pearse Ferriter), left his lady in no doubt of her charms – her dazzling breast, her, we may note, *Elizabethan* bust. Was Ferriter poking fun at the 'Virgin Queen' so rhapsodised by Spenser, who might not have been, well, all that virginal (Welch, 1994)? Or, was he more broadly ridiculing the emergent alien cult of women as disembodied figures, frozen in symbol as virgin queens, sky women, Gaelic Ireland? Ferriter was hanged as a rebel by the English Parliamentarians in 1653. According to Mac Cana, he was in the great tradition of aristocratic amateur poets; a nobleman, a soldier and a man of considerable learning, who could describe with restraint as well as profound tragedy the fate of the Gaelic order (Mac Cana, 1980, p. 47).

And what of those who stayed? Dáibhí Ó Bruadair (1625–1698) rode the tide for a while, but then history caught up with him. He died in poverty. 'O it's Best to be a Total Boor' and 'Pity the Man who Didn't Tie Up Some Worldly Goods' fair drip with venom. The philistines who do not appreciate the art and worth of the poet is a theme addressed also in a poem by Pádraigín Haicéad, 'You Learned Shower'. Ó Bruadair's tirade against the boor also reveals some interesting glimpses of the art of the bardic poet and the changing conditions in which he was forced to operate. Not only has the bard now to write down his 'well-tongued' oral verse, he must needs also master how to cope with the very modern invention of print. The original Gaelic court is no longer there by way of audience. He must write in accentual metres, a form despised by the poets, who had forgotten that it was the clerics who constrained them to write in syllabic verse, because stressed or accentual metres are viewed as the measure of the mere balladeer. Now the poet has to gain a living by demeaning himself to have his work printed up for all sorts of undiscriminating people with whom he has no kinship or allegiance. He is reduced to hawking his poems on printed sheets – to the lowly status of the ballad singer. Yet, as Charles Dillon reminds us, the Gaelic bards understood that to survive they must adapt, and not just in terms of their literary forms (Dillon, 2012, p. 145).

In 'Pity the Man' we also get an insight into the specific linguistic situation for the Gaelic writer. The Gaelic bard would have studied Latin and Greek and would have been familiar with the classics, but also had to learn another language: English. The poet is, clearly, a man of great skill and learning – his Latin is not merely adequate but 'clever' and his English no pidgin bluster but 'tricky'. Charles Dillon is, again, illuminating. While the focus of his essay is Peadar Ó Doirnín, with whom we will shortly become acquainted, the same exigency is present in both Ó Bruadair and Ó Doirnín, the necessity of not only learning English, but learning to the extent that the poet can master it at a sophisticated literary level (Dillon, 2012, p. 145). This may be merely a pragmatic reflex, an acknowledgement of the necessity of surviving in a drastically altered world where the audience, keen also to survive, wants English, the language becoming dominant as the currency of commerce, realpolitik. But it may also be something more deeply embedded in the psyche of the writer in any era and any culture: the imperative of understanding the new, of negotiating with contemporary reality. And, of course, we must recall that the Gaelic bards were conditioned by many years of hard training; and part of that training was mastery of languages as well as literatures. So, to be a poet worthy of talking about, the new language, English, must also be now included in the arts of the poet. It is a matter of professional pride, even though that language was associated with a political and economic calculus – ill devised to provide protection to the old order of Gaelic poets. And, as Dillon delicately reminds us, the Gaelic poets had also to think of patrons. While the invention of print made possible popular versions of Gaelic lore, the poets still yearned for a cognoscenti who could more fully appreciate their art. But where might this be found? Well, we will come back to that shortly.

And, of course, that poem also reveals two features of the Celtic Spirit. The first is the central importance of generosity – the clan chief would bestow patronage liberally and this, in turn, would be reflected by the largesse of the *fili* or bard himself. We see the same association between alcoholic input and poetic output in a poem by Cathal Buí Mac Giolla Ghunna (1680–1705), 'The Yellow Bittern'. So we see reflected Celtic Spirit in another sense also! Even a late song like 'Carrickfergus' still couples this association of performance and hospitality, symbolised by a plentiful supply of lubrication: 'I'll sing no more now, till I get a drink.'

Aside from feasting and the wee dribble of drink, there is, for example in MacCuarta, a more poignant lament upon the Great Change in terms of the 'cold house' the poet encounters. 'Where has my welcome gone?' asks MacCuarta's speaker, returning to the place where ownership and language have changed, shutting him out from what he had perceived as his own place (Dillon, 2012, p. 148).

That tone of personal anguish, connecting itself with the wider fate of the Gaelic order that was noted earlier, can be heard too in Seamas Dal MacCuarta (1650–1733). His 'Welcome Sweetest Bird' follows the long tradition of the Gaelic lyric poem, one of the earliest examples of which is the well-known 'Blackbird Over Belfast Lough'. Here the poet's anguish derives from the loss of his sight (*dall* means 'blind'), so that he can only remember the beauty of nature.

But the bird motif also begins to take on a symbolic reson-ance for MacCuarta and many other poets. In 'The Drowned Blackbird', we can see a fusion between that older lyric nature poetry tradition and political allegory – a form especially popular among English Renaissance writers like Spenser and Shakespeare. It is clear that the Gaelic poets were quite aware of current English and Continental literary modes. Here the drowning of the blackbird symbolises the drowning of Gaelic hopes with the Flight of the Earls. And, added to the bird trope, is the familiar personification of Ireland as a woman – specifically, 'the fair daughter of Conn O'Neill'. The last stanza of the poem is remarkable for the depth of its symbolic meaning, the stark clarity of its rendering of the natural world and a dignified grief expressed in the most spare of language:

> Fair beauty who comes of Ulster's royal line,
> Rest as you are: 'tis better than running wild.
> Your small bird, loveliest singer of the treetops,
> Is not your concern, though he be washed with lime
> (Trans. S. Ó Tuama and T. Kinsella, 1981, p. 129).

Aogán Ó Rathaille (Owen O'Rahilly) c 1675–1729, is also an important poet of this period. Though he lived mostly around Kerry, he still takes fire from the exile poems of his earlier masters. In a poem like 'Valentine Brown', Ó Rathaille's speaker undertakes an imaginary voyage to find Valentine Brown (again, recalling the immram tradition in early Celtic literature). But the immram serves as the impetus for his lament over the loss of the old order in specific political terms. O'Rahilly was a Jacobite and Brown's father had been a sympathiser. When his son inherited, the O'Rahilly family were only given a very small part of their land back. So this is also a revenge poem; but the complex intricacies of loyalties in this period is not evident in Ó Rathaille's magisterial elegy:

> Demish ravaged in the west, her good lord gone as well,
> Some foreign city has become our refuge and our hell.
> Wounds that hurt a poet's soul can rob him of renown:
> I have travelled far to meet you, Valentine Brown (Trans. Kennelly, 1992, p. 36).

Ó Rathaille was also a master of the aisling form and his justly famous 'Brightness of Brightness' also deploys the Ireland as woman personification and the opposition of plenty and poverty we saw in Ó Bruadair. Mac Cana comments that the poem runs like a stream of limpid sound, citing Frank O'Connor's praise of it as 'pure music'. Mac Cana concedes that the deft flitting movement and light and sparkle are virtually impossible to capture in translation, though he reckons O'Connor made a 'middling good shot at it':

Brightness of brightness lonely met me where I wandered,
Crystal of crystal only by her eyes were splendid,
Sweetness of sweetness lightly in her speech she
squandered,
Rose-red and lily-glow brightly in her cheeks contended
(Mac Cana, 1980, p. 50).

More vitriolic in its condemnation of the inhospitable newcomers is a poem by Seán Clárach Mac Dónaill (1691–1754), 'Lock Up, O Rocks'. Here the reputation of the bards for the satiric curse poem is well illustrated in the extravagant eloquence of this vatic fusillade.

As Dillon informs us, there was also emerging a new Gaelic, noted by Art Mac Cumhaigh, which was, we may presume, adulterated and contemptuously viewed by the Gaelic poets as an unliterary poetic expression (Dillon, 2012, p, 144). This was probably not unconnected with the degeneration of form from strict syllabic metre to the more popular accentual ballad rhymes. More accessible, more easily remembered, but of course not 'the real deal', though as we have seen, it was the Latin Christian influence which drove Irish verse towards syllabic metre. The question of what is authentic and what is not becomes a mite vexed. At any rate, what seems to be also a target for the Gaelic poets is a 'new Gaelic' which lacks the recondite, archaic authority of the traditional forms. Mac Cumhaigh inveighs against the hospitality afforded to the new men, the *arrivistes*, writing in this new Gaelic, while proper poets are denied honour and hospitality. For modern readers, this is a hard concept to understand, accustomed as we are to valuing originality and poets who break with tradition. But we have only learned to think that way since the Renaissance. For the Gaelic poets, breaking with tradition (a tradition however, ultimately open to question), must have seemed like a terrible betrayal. And yet, these poets, tuned to English and Continental verse too, in the period of the European Renaissance must have seen that the old model, the old reliance on authority, the idea that great poetry must be built upon what has gone before, was open to fundamental questioning. Nonetheless, the aesthetic potential and challenge could not but have been immensely complicated and problematised by the particular historical circumstances in which the Gaelic poets found themselves. The urge towards defence, towards protection of an entire culture and way of life and economic security threatened must have been immense. That these poets offered what seem to us in our enlightened times, where decisions about the past seem so often simple, an ambiguous and even contradictory response perhaps serves to remind us that we can all live out the past of others more easily than our own present. What would we do, how would we write, had we lived in that time?

For some, like the anonymous poet who dedicated his poem to Arthur Magennis of Iveagh, writing of any sort was now impossible:

One must not spin the threads of lore;
one must not follow up the branches of kinship;
one must not weave artistry or lyrics;
poetry should not be spoken of (Trans. Donal Ó Baoill,
undated, p. 5).

And it must be said that, as S.J. Connolly and Andrew Holmes have argued, the poems can be read in very different ways – and indeed have been read in very different ways, as we will see a little later. Connolly and Holmes warn us against an overly simplistic interpretation, arguing that the work of these déclassé Gaelic poets can be read as 'evidence of real and widespread disaffection, as largely rhetorical exercises on a traditional theme, or as a reflection of nostalgia on the part of a specific group, the poets, for a lost world in which they had enjoyed a position of privilege and esteem' (Connolly and Holmes, 2013, p. 108).

195

While all of these interpretations can be contested and even harmonised, there seems no doubt that the Gaelic bards were faced with a set of circumstances that were far from congenial. Yet, some managed to continue some form of their craft well into the eighteenth and even nineteenth century. But it was, inevitably, a rearguard action. They were partly able to survive through a certain informal sodality – there were coteries in Munster, in south-east Ulster and even in Dublin. Charles Dillon tells us that there existed 'a sophisticated community of literati still attached to the systems and modes of Gaelic Ireland, but reacting to and evolving in the rapidly changing and increasingly Anglophone society in which they found themselves' (C. Dillon, 2012, p. 143). J. E. Caerwyn Williams and Nuala Ní Dhomhnaill, among others, remind us that there were thriving, if marginalised communities of scholar poets during the Great Change. Caerwyn Williams recounts a contention of the bards in the early seventeenth century in which nearly seven thousand lines were paraded before the public (Ní Domhnaill, 2008, p. 58; Caerwyn Williams, 1958; rpt 1992, p. 211). This parade of learning was to be observed by Carleton two centuries on, in the contest of those remnants of the Gaelic order, the hedge schoolmasters (Carleton, 1830).

We will conclude with a word or two about the south Armagh poets, and within that we must limit ourselves to a brief discussion of two of them: Peadar Ó Doirnin and Art Mac Cumhaigh. Ó Doirnin was born around about 1700 and died in 1769. He had a very colourful life, including a spell as tutor with the English settler, Arthur Brownlow, near Lurgan. He died at his desk at his hedge school in Forkhill (Kieran, undated). His poems evince an interesting blend of formal diction, influenced by classical allusions and closely observed local detail, thus fusing the rather baroque literary style of the English poets of the time and calling upon the older traditions of Irish lyric nature poetry. Perhaps his most famous poem is

'Mná na hÉireann' (The Women of Erin) a paean to the ladies of Ireland. This poem was set to music in the 1960s by Seán Ó Riada.

Ó Doirnin, as Charles Dillon convincingly argues, was by no means straightforward in his allegiances or his attitude to language. Intercultural and interlinguistic contact was, Dillon argues, ongoing. The south Ulster poets perceived competence in English as not only a matter of cultural and social otherness, but as a sign of erudition. Dillon cites Fearghas Mac Bheattha's elegy on Mac a Liondain in which he refers to his excellence in English (Dillon, 2012, p. 149). Ó Doirnin, in a love poem, descries the fact that the woman he loved is with a man who is without English (Dillon, 2012, p. 149).

The lack of English indicates, for Ó Doirnin, a boorishness and want of sophistication. As Caerwyn Williams attests, Daithi Ó Bruadair similarly mocked those who could not speak English (Caerwyn Williams, op. cit. p. 214). That was another kind of boorishness. Dillon (2012, op. cit.) recounts an oft-told tale in the lore of hedge school literature in which Ó Doirnin successfully sees off a challenge from a contender for his hedge school. Significantly, he mocks his adversary, Maurice O Gorman, not for his lack of mastery in Irish, but in English, parodically mimicking his poor command of the new tongue. Ó Doirnin's superior mastery of 'tricky English' is the basis for the lampoon of O Gorman. O Gorman is presented as an ignoramus, unable to 'translate' from one language to another, still preserving the syntax and vocabulary of Irish rather than being able to master the very different constructions of English. Of course, it must be said that only a reader fully conversant in both Irish and English could fully savour the inter-lingual ironies – and this tells us something about the audience that Ó Doirnín really wanted to appeal to. That such an audience was small among the general populace, by now becoming illiterate in two languages, and among the patrons, perhaps reflects the grievous foreshortening of vista available to the Gaelic poets.

Dillon's fascinating essay traces Ó Doirnin's relationship with the planter family Brownlow. A few more salient truths emerge. The Brownlows, from grandfather to grandson, evidently offered not only patronage to latter-day bards like Ó Doirnín, but were manuscript collectors in their own right. This may indeed be the first plotting of the graph of what is now called the colonial position. On the one hand, we hear expressed a passionate loyalty to a culture repressed in a tone so elegiac that it admits the irretrievability of the loss; on the other, a kind of determination to master the new language, the new culture, with such skill that the colonised becomes near enough 'the real thing'. And beyond that, the colonised can use that mastery to resist, subversively, at times, the cultural values and 'great tradition' of the coloniser. Or sometimes, as an artist, as a poet, the colonised writer may want to have the freedom to just accept that some of the culture of the coloniser is aesthetically pleasing in its own right.

We have spoken often in this book about that aspect of the Celtic Spirit that has to do with hospitality, with welcome for the stranger. Welcome is not easy if the stranger takes your hospitality and then your house and then your very culture. The house grows cold, a place from which you have been displaced, nothing but a stranger in this world, to quote again Van Morrison. And yet, over history, as we have seen, one race, one religion, one culture, displaces another, as if by some natural law. But in Ireland, matters are never so simple. Older forms, older ways of being, seem to keep presenting themselves at the threshold between the past and the present, sometimes for good and sometimes for evil and sometimes for irony and sometimes for pure joy. Sometimes it may even occur to give us pause between certainty and uncertainty, a moment in which some kind of interchange, some small generous transformation occurs because people allow, what poets allow, imagination. And maybe imagination always must have 'a local habitation and a name', an anchorage in the particular, the vividly sharp image of place, shadowed and deepened by all that has happened there. We may well rejoice in the purity of the early Irish lyricists who simply rendered the place. But we must consider too that they lived in times that cannot have been always free of politics and even history. Maybe they just edited it out; maybe that was their aesthetic. But by the eighteenth century, place has, without doubt, become historical, temporal, political, too. The immanence is less of gods and more of men.

But what of the representation of place? We have seen that in the tales of the Fianna, while Arcadian and placeless in certain ways, there is also a growing loyalty to the local, to the specific place, influenced by the *dinnseanchas*, the lore of places, collected together in the twelfth century. That place, invoked not just in its topographical meaning but in its temporal associations, becomes, over time, ever more palimpsestal, the layers of myth and history accumulating. So in Art Mac Chumaidh (1738–1773) too, we see that strong devotion to local place that characterises so much Irish poetry. 'The Churchyard at Creggan' is, however, freighted with political and historical meaning. The poem is also an example of the aisling tradition and like many other examples, is a political allegory.

The poem reprises the theme of exile and also contrasts the generous patrons of the past with the modern crowd 'sneering at every poem you make'. But there is a defiant note eerily linking Mac Cumhaigh right back to 'The Song of Amorgen':

Don't question me; I do not sleep
On this side of the Boyne.
I'm a changeling; on the step
Side of Grainneog, from the loin
Of faery race, I'm spring (Trans. Deane, 1991,
pp. 293–5).

Mac Cumhaigh is buried at Creggan, near Crossmaglen. His grave lies in what is now the Church of Ireland grounds, which sits inside the Poets' Glen, a place of very considerable magic. There are plaques there too, to many of the other local poets. To sense the Celtic Spirit in all its palimpsestic complexity – pagan, Christian, planter, Anglo-Irish – a visit to Creggan is essential.

These poets produced a distinctive literary form called the *trí rainn*, three verses in syllabic metre and one verse in accentual or song metre – evidence that they had to adapt to a

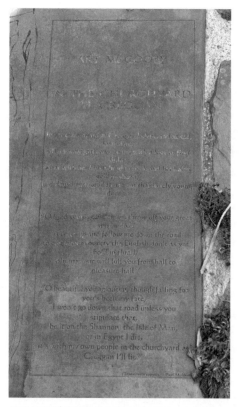

THE POETS' GLEN, PLAQUE TO ART MAC CUMHAIGH

A sacred place. The Poets' Glen, Creggan, South Armagh. In the glen are memorials to a number of the south Ulster poets.

much less literary audience. And while the times were bad, there was opportunity for a bit of badinage too among the coterie, and there was quite a tradition of 'warrant' poems where poets would pretend to warrant or law each other.

The urge for a bit of fun, often satirical, is perhaps brought to its greatest height in a comic aisling, the quite splendidly savage 'Midnight Court', written by Brian Merriman. The idealised woman is burlesqued and the poet comes off badly enough as well. Doubtless, this talent for self-mockery for a comic puncturing of the high ideals that had sustained an increasingly fugal order was, in its own way, annealing and, of course, took its sustenance from the comic version of the aisling that we looked at earlier in 'The Vision of Mac Con Ginne'. We are to see that comic spirit surface with fantastic effect in the nineteenth and twentieth centuries.

Perhaps one of the most famous of all these late Gaelic poems is 'The Lament for Art O'Leary', which, it is argued, is a very powerful poem in Gaelic and in translation. The poem was written by Eibhlín Dubh Ní Chonaill (Dark Ellen or Eileen O'Connell), 1743–1780. The beauty of it derives, I believe, in some part from the dignity and restraint of its tone. This is no squealing match but a tribute full of clear, extremely well-realised detail and governed by a diction that is magisterial in its quiet understatement. But at the end, hope is well and truly gone. There is no delivery for the women of Ireland and they must be brave in the face of despair. A new, tenebrous image of Ireland is inscribed:

> But cease your weeping now,
> Women of the soft, wet eyes
> Till Art O'Leary drink
> Ere he go to the dark school –
> Not to learn music or song
> But to prop the earth and the stone (Trans. Frank
> O'Connor, 1991, p. 311).

It was to be a long wake. But, as we will discover in a later chapter, though the body lies in the dark school, the Celtic Spirit is resurrected, taking on new shapes, recycling in forms welcome to some, contested by others.

CHAPTER TEN

The Celtic Spirit: New Forms
Tess Maginess

A New Trope for Ireland: The Cracked Glass

Towards the end of *A Portrait of the Artist as a Young Man,* James Joyce causes his dubious hero, Stephen Dedalus, to proclaim that he must escape the nightmare of history. We meet him again in the opening pages of *Ulysses,* fallen and back home in Dublin, more despondent than disdainful, but still knocking out the metaphors. As he looks at his reflection in the mirror, a new trope forms: Ireland as the cracked glass.

It seems as if it is not possible in Ireland, whoever is in charge of us, to show a clean pair of heels to history. The bards after all, could not have managed at all without it, for how, between this world and the otherworld, could they have wrought a praise poem or a satire without an energetic and well-informed recourse to history, myth and genealogy? No more could they have written their extraordinary laments had history not wrecked the Gaelic order.

But the metaphor of the cracked glass introduces another dimension, another point of view. We may see ourselves through the long sonata of our dead, our history, but what kind of self-portrait, what kind of reflection of ourselves is it when the mirror is cracked? What does that suggest about the past and what does it suggest about identity? Now, as we have seen in earlier chapters, the coming of the English and later the Scots was by no means the first intercalation of what were regarded as alien forces; we need only recall St Patrick, or even the Milesians. And, as we have seen, there are varying attitudes manifested about this seemingly recursive business of being invaded. Some might have called it 'a splendid, progressive vision, this mission of bringing light into darkness', while

NEW FORMS

Refracting the Celtic Spirit: The Celtic Spirit was to be reflected in many and sometimes disturbing new forms in the nineteenth century.

others, like the Mad Sweeney, were a shade less enthusiastic. But, it is not really until the Great Change, that is to say, the plantations, that we begin to see the articulation of the impact of invasion as a crisis of identity, or if you will, a crisis of representation.

There are a number of reasons why this is the case. One of them is that the very concept of national or individual identity does not really exist in the world until the Renaissance. We may think of Shakespeare's *Hamlet* as perhaps its seminal text. So we now have a sense of individual self and we also have a sense of self as being part of a body politic, frankly, a nation. So, if we map this on to our own dear land (the most mapped country in Europe), the consequences are stupendous and exceedingly complicated. We have only the space here to trace but a few of the main contours of the map and the cartography which designed it. In one of the poems discussed in a previous chapter, we have the poet MacCuarta lamenting that it is he who has become the alien in his own land. So, for the 'native' Irish, the old Gaelic order (itself a compound of Norman, Old English, Gaels, Vikings, Milesians and heaven knows what else) the Great Change has resulted in a state of affairs where the bard is a bit like Oisín returning from Tír na nÓg. And perhaps that ancient tale about Oisín's return had some basis in a political or historical reality too; the poem thus acting as a metaphor for expressing traumatic cultural change many centuries before.

In Elizabethan times, the Gaelic bard (and the culture he stands for, part for the whole) is informed by official proclamation that his language, dress, laws and culture are now banned, being barbarous and dangerous. Over time, while such laws relaxed, the deeper impact begins to register itself and that, it could be argued, included a profound riveness about his identity; he must perforce be officially English, though he still feels, unofficially, Irish. At a personal level, he faces self-betrayal in two directions. Most obviously, he must appear to be English, thus perpetrating a lie about his own historical genesis. Less obviously, he must betray that Irishness (however dreamily or muddily defined, for the concept of nation is also a bit of a new thing) to become what he must now become – part of the new world, where he is as English as possible. And the permutations do not end there. As we saw with poets like Peadar Ó Doirnin, there may be also a pull towards at least certain aspects of the new dispensation; there may be an attraction towards English forms, albeit as proof of the bard's erudition. Identity may be riven, but the writers, like everybody else, tried to make the best of it, adjusting to the new world.

And what about the planters, the colonisers / reformers / new blood? Well, a curious thing happens here too. For within a century of the plantations we have a new formation: the Anglo-Irish. Now, of course, it is not that new, for the Normans and the Old English could also be described as Anglo-Irish. But the deliberate policy of colonisation, with its messianic zeal to extirpate all that is wild and lawless and backward, leaves less room for manoeuvre in the matter of identity and national allegiance. The post-Plantation Anglo-Irish are charged with turning Ireland English; that is their manifest duty and destiny. But whether it be that the Celtic Spirit slipped sometimes somehow under their skin with the rain and the smell of turf, or whether it be a much more banal matter of the consequence of people living in a new country in time taking on a little of its complexion, it is impossible to know. And this consequence is by no means inevitable; for we need only look at South Africa to apprehend how cultures can operate systematic apartheid.

But, the picture is, of course, more complicated than that. On the one hand, we have polarisation, indeed a kind of apartheid, symbolised, for example, by the walling in of the Big House. But on the other, before the ink is dry on the Act of Union (1800), we have literature emerging which posits – even within the very walls of the Big House – various forms of 'hybridism', to use Homi Bhabha's term in relation to personal identity and public/political identity (Bhabha, 1994).

The First Lady of the Big House

In this context, it is condign to offer a discussion of Maria Edgeworth's *Castle Rackrent* (Edgeworth, 1800; rpt 1969). We cannot hope to do justice in so short a space to a book so rich in complex irony and so foundational for any understanding of the literature of the Big House. Like many of her class, Edgeworth spent much of her early life in England. The sub-title of the novel is *A Hibernian Tale*, thus placing it in a curious linguistic and political ether that escapes the contamination of it being 'mere Irish' (to use a Spenserian phrase) and the aloofness of it being exclusively English (a traveller's tale, as it were). So Edgeworth settles for the Latin denomination, doubtless conscious of the curious fact that her adopted island had not, unlike England, been conquered by the Romans. Those great imperialists clearly missed a trick, or maybe shrewdly accounted that the Hibernians would be more bother than they would be worth.

We may note that the first Rackrent is Sir Patrick O'Shaughlin – not an English planter, but a noble from Gaelic stock, who has retained his land (or a part of it) through Surrender and Regrant. Thus, Sir Patrick shifts his political allegiance from Ireland to England, but retains a great deal of his cultural identity as a Gaelic chieftain. Significantly, Sir Patrick is admired by his tenantry for his insistence upon exercising hospitality – a virtue central to the Celtic Spirit. However, Sir Patrick is open and liberal to a disastrous extent. Now, of course we could argue that Edgeworth is legitimising the plantation enterprise while critiquing that version of it in which the native Irish are let be in charge. But, it is not as simple as that, for the subsequent incumbents of Castle

207

Rackrent – some much more Anglo than Irish – all manage to make matters worse for themselves and for their tenantry. So the plot of the novel descends inexorably into chaos and ruination. It is as if Edgeworth has somehow been able to predict the fall of the Anglo-Irish; a fall that begins with their very accession. But, unlike most Big House novels – for *Castle Rackrent* sponsored a whole genre that persisted well into the twentieth century, though the Big Houses themselves were mostly gone by then – *Castle Rackrent* creates a fate perhaps arguably worse than ruin. The Big House does not decay irreparably, a symbol of the fate of its owners. Worse, much worse, it falls into the avaricious and immeasurably vulgar clutches of a gombeen man. This rapacious oaf is, by happy or unhappy coincidence, a scion of the family of Thady Quirk, the native Irish retainer and a faithful servant to the Anglo-Irish masters. Every effort is made by Edgeworth to have us, as readers, like Thady. We are meant to like him because he is an admirer of the best in the fusion of Anglo and Irish. His contempt for his own blood, his own kin, constitutes a satire which embodies that crisis of identity and representation we spoke of earlier: for, while Thady speaks in a voice slightly revealing his roots – that is to say he speaks with a slight Irish accent and a slight aversion to dialect – his loyalty, in Edgeworth's formation of him, is towards the Anglo-Irish, not towards his own people.

Now, we must step very nimbly here and consider to whom Edgeworth is speaking. That is to say, we need to consider the question of who her readers were. And we can safely say that the bulk of them were *not* the Plain People of Ireland (to borrow a phrase from Myles na gCopaleen, who had some very provoking things to say about identity and cracked glasses, or was it jugs?). The bulk of Edgeworth's readers were likely not even the Plain People of England who were, like the Irish, mostly illiterate. They had the blessing or the curse of being illiterate merely in one language. The 'national' school system (how loaded that word is in Ireland) only began to be introduced midway through the nineteenth century. Indeed, Edgeworth was away ahead of her time in advancing the cause of education as a consummation devoutly to be wished. She was in this either more or less prescient than some of her contemporaries, for what was suspected by some and which we all now know is that to educate a people you have conquered is to cut a rod with which your own back might be beaten.

So the people for whom *Castle Rackrent* was intended was the upper and middle class in England and the Anglo-Irish in Ireland, when they were in Ireland, which was not, of course, all the time, since many of them were absentee landlords. And, as an educator, and a strong opponent of absenteeism, Edgeworth was keen to show her readers what Ireland was really like. Now, it may be contended that the portrait she composes is in many respects unflattering and that, as such, the book is a bit of an own goal. However, at the very least, she represents Ireland as place containing amusing characters; albeit in the middle of a desolate bog. And here she anticipates a good deal of literature written in English about Ireland for the rest of the century. But the idea that the Irish and the Anglo-Irish are both good for a laugh in the coffee houses of London must have been a mite discomforting for the Anglo-Irish themselves – placing them on the same footing as the roistering MacMorris of Shakespeare – and in danger of candidacy for the callous caricaturing of *Punch* some decades later. It is as if she has made the Anglo-Irish a great deal more Irish than she or they would wish them to be. Objects of ridicule. A cracked glass indeed. Of course, Edgeworth writes within a long tradition of satire in which Anglo-Irish writers have occupied an especially significant space – from Goldsmith and Swift to Sheridan to Wilde and Beckett. That tradition goes back both to Gaelic and Continental satire.

Edgeworth was also the mother of a tradition – the Big House novel. Interestingly, many of them were written by women, Sommerville and Ross and Lady Morgan, for example. In *The Wild Irish Girl* (1806; rpt 1999), Lady Morgan is keen to propose a breaking down of the divisions and separations in Irish society, between Gaelic and planter. But, of course, it is also reflective of class, as we would expect in a nineteenth-century novel. The wild Irish girl is no scullery maid in the Big House, but the scion of an ancient Irish 'noble' family, albeit much reduced in circumstance. Somerville and Ross follow Edgeworth in many respects in choosing to offer a tone that is meant to be comic. However, they are writing near the end of the century and in a novel like *The Real Charlotte* (Somerville and Ross, 1894; rpt 1999) the subtlety of the gradations from Irish to Anglo-Irish to English become much more pronounced.

DRISHANE HOUSE, CASTLETOWNSHEND, CO. CORK

Sometimes making light of tricky plights: Drishane House, Castletownshend, Co. Cork was the birthplace of Edith Somerville. Here, she and Martin Ross (Violet Florence Martin) contrived their complex reflection of life in Ireland in the enclosing last years of the nineteenth century.

In that sense, the novel operates more like a Jane Austen work, but the lines, so very finely drawn, are here not so much across class as race and creed, though class comes into it too. Charlotte herself is a kind of parodic Lizzy Bennet from *Pride and Prejudice*; not quite Anglo-Irish enough, not quite rich enough, not quite Irish enough either. She is addressed by a pleading tenant as, significantly, 'Honourable Madman'. Charlotte is mad, but no madder than many in her situation: unmarried, faced with a very small pool of 'suitable' men, impoverished, unlovely, and caught in a riven and blundering identity that seeks, betimes, identification with the Anglo-Irish and at times with the natives. Her hyphenation is not a source of anything but deep chagrin, but, of course, she is also an easy butt for the comic contempt of the coarser reader on either island. Another character, Pamela Dysart, represents, as Julian Moynahan has argued, the same hyphenation and hybridism at a slightly higher level in terms of suitability: 'She had spoken "in a soft voice that was just Irish enough for Saxons of the more ignorant sort to fail to distinguish, save in degree, between it and Mrs Lambert's Dublin brogue"' (Moynahan, 1995, p. 7). Pamela's aspirations are higher in class terms and, concomitantly, in racial terms: she must not choose below her, she must choose above her and, geographically, beyond her. As if she actually had any choice.

Rare Collectors' Items

Van Morrison once referred to a masked man living with a gun as a 'rare collector's item' (Morrison, 1974). *Veedon Fleece*, the album on which this lyric appears, has been described as one of Morrison's most Celtic albums. Perhaps he took his cue not just from the Troubles raging around him as he returned on vacation to Ireland, but also from the Antiquarians, collecting, preserving, interpreting and translating a lost past. The

Antiquarians operated also in times of political upheaval, of repeating upheavals and contentions between the imperial order and the natives. It may well have been in response to such clear and present dangers, wherein the proper separation between the Anglo-Irish and the barbarous natives was reasserted, that we have in the nineteenth century the emergence of the Antiquarians, questing for some other definition of a long-vexed matter of identity. These men were not given to a satiric turn of mind, and their enthusiasm for Celtic culture and the discovery of it of was unequivocal. At the same time, many of the Antiquarians were mostly firmly unionist in their politics; that is to say, they believed trenchantly in the maintenance of the arrangement which saw Ireland as a sister kingdom (albeit a sister with the track of soot up the side of her face), part of not so much an English but a British and indeed imperial culture. That political and personal allegiance would tend to enforce a polarity between English and Irish, between rulers and ruled, coloniser and colonised, master and servant.

And yet, the Antiquarians were bent, with immense seriousness of purpose, upon the enterprise of discovering the lost Celtic Spirit, which had evidently gotten lost. Who managed to lose it? It would be quite egregious, but tempting, to suggest that this quest for the lost Celtic Spirit was a kind of atonement for the rigorous suppression of it by their ancestors. Others might demur at the Antiquarians and the literary men who followed them placing themselves in charge of and taking the credit for bringing to the light of civilisation a civilisation they had dismissed as brutish and lacking anything remotely resembling culture. It may well be that the Antiquarians did not think about the matter in these ways at all and rather, being part of an international imperial *Weltanschauung*, they did what people of their class in England and France and Germany did: they started to take a great interest in medieval history.

Other Days Around Me

Now, of course, this new interest (we hesitate to call it fashion, for it was much more than that), was manifest among the Gothic novelists towards the end of the eighteenth century, and Anglo-Irish writers applied successfully for positions in this pantheon, including Bram Stoker. With the Romantics, a little later, this medieval otherworld becomes the stuff of the new English aisling. Here is Shelley's 'Ode to the West Wind':

> Old palaces and towers
> Quivering within the wave's intenser day
> All overgrown with azure moss and flowers
> So sweet, the sense faints picturing them (Shelley, 1820; rpt 1994, p. 401).

The palaces and towers quiver not within the intenser day or time of the wave, but 'within the wave's intenser day', so that the palaces and towers seem to be a kind of Atlantis, a lost romantic city under the sea.

And the idea is not new, for we hear it in Thomas Moore's 'Let Erin Remember', where the fisherman sees 'the round towers of other days in the waves beneath him shining':

> On Lough Neagh's bank as the fisherman strays
> When the clear cold eve's declining,
> He sees the round towers of other days
> In the wave beneath him shining (Moore, 1854, pp. 20–21).

Shelley had come to Dublin in 1811. He might have had read Moore's song or heard it, for it was published in 1808. Moore was not, strictly speaking, Anglo-Irish, but in his choice of theme and subject was, one may suspect, guided by the discoveries of the Antiquarians. The Celtic Spirit and Celtic culture were becoming not only authorised but approbated. Moore, with his charming settings of ancient Irish melodies with lyrics in English, evoking a gentle yearning for the past quite deracinated and cleansed of the malcontent political undertones of the remnantal Gaelic bards (to say nothing of the radical Presbyterians of the 1798 rebellion), was a popular figure in the fashionable salons of London. Shelley was a radical and a revolutionary and indeed, ironically, wrote a pamphlet in support of Irish 'freedom' and proclaimed his solidarity from an upstairs window in Sackville Street. A bit late, for the radical ideals of the French revolution and the rebellion of the United Irishmen in 1798 had been more or less effectively snuffed out. Whether the image in Shelley's poem, so remarkably similar in its architecture to Moore's, was a kind of homage, or a brazen bit of theft, it might be churlish to decide. However that may be, we cannot but be in awe of Shelley's fantastic, near hallucinogenic rendering of it. That hint of *nostalgie,* the yearning of dream and desire, and that sense of an overpowering, almost narcotic state of heightened perception. Well, it will not be long before we will hear a voice not unlike that of Shelley and yet, so unlike him, when we come to young Yeats.

Later in the nineteenth century we have another revival of interest in the medieval with the pre-Raphaelites in painting and with poets like Tennyson and Arnold. By this stage, the fondness for the medieval has acquired a more exotic dimension. This is not surprising, given that artefacts were beginning to be brought back from outposts of Empire like India and Africa, which were viewed as representing a simpler, older world than the hectic urban industrialised world of London or Paris. And there was at this time, running alongside this rather nostalgic late Romanticism also a rigorous scientific movement, keen on classifying and collecting the treasures of the empires.

So it is within these contexts, as Mac Cana suggests (Mac Cana, 1980 p. 53), as well as the specific and problematic context of Ireland itself, that antiquarianism began to flourish. The Antiquarians were mostly drawn from the ranks of the Anglo-Irish; they, of course, had the educational resources and the time. Some of them were keen on what we might call a Celtic Revival from an impulse of scientific interest. Some, maybe, were second or third sons who did not inherit (and most of them were not scions of the great Anglo-Irish power-houses, significantly enough), or did not obtain a commission and go to further flung wormholes of Empire. Some, perhaps reviving that improving and reforming spirit which so animated the architects of plantation, like Spenser, may have thought that they would have to step in and make a proper job of gathering up all this Celtic material to classify it and interpret it. Some just liked the sound of it perhaps, and the look of the old manuscripts. Some may have seen a richness that they genuinely had no idea had existed before they came. Some may have wished to identify more closely with the people of the place – or at least their lost great poets, nobles in their own right. And some may have seen the revival of this material as an eloquent testimony to the cultural greatness of a people who should therefore not be subjugated and should be entitled to their independence as a freestanding nation. And some, like the Brownlow family from Lurgan, had an ancestry which mixed Gaelic and planter (Dillon, 2012, p. 154).

Significantly, a department of Irish had been set up in Trinity College (established in 1592) as part of the civilising mission and the bastion of the Anglo-Irish Establishment very early on. The purpose of this may only have been that the Church of Ireland divines could convert the native Irish by having access to their language. However that may be, the Anglo-Irish Antiquarians went about the 'discovery' of ancient Irish/Celtic artefacts with some considerable fervour and rigour. Now, it must be said that there was an interest in antiquities as far back as 1700 and many societies were actually first established in the late seventeenth and early eighteenth centuries, such as the Dublin Philosophical Society and the Royal Dublin Society and, of course, the Belfast Society for

Promoting Knowledge, otherwise known as the Linen Hall Library. And we have seen that there were landlords like the Brownlow family who were patrons of Gaelic literature.

But it is really in the late eighteenth century and in the nineteenth century that the passion for antiquities begins to spread more extensively across the land. The survey which follows is by no means exhaustive but, hopefully, will serve to indicate the range and scale of the Antiquarian enterprise. Edward Bunting, born in Armagh, was hugely influential in writing down Irish music and his *A General Collection of the Ancient Music of Ireland* (1796, 1809) was a major contribution. Thomas Moore, already mentioned, published his *Irish Melodies*, the first collection appearing in the 1790s. Denis Coffey produced the first modern Irish primer John O'Donovan also produced a grammar of the Irish language and worked closely with the Ordnance Survey Project, as did the self-taught Eugene O'Curry, who also did a lot of work on Irish manuscripts. George Petrie published his *Round Towers of Ireland* in 1833, and *The Music of Ireland* in 1855. Samuel Ferguson, a Belfast man, wrote on archaeology and published *The Lays of the Western Gael* in 1865 and a long poem, *Congal*, in 1872. Sir William Wilde, father of Oscar, and his wife 'Speranza' were also key figures in the collection of oral tales and folklore.

Andrew Carpenter offers an intriguing comment on the poetry of Charlotte Brooke, whose *Reliques of Irish Poetry* (1789), he argues, is the first extended translation of 'polite literature' from Irish to English (Carpenter, 1991, p. 980). Carpenter asserts that Brooke's translations of Gaelic poetry are not in accord with the tone and style of the originals, but that, like Moore, she made the Gaelic note available in English. It may be, he argues, that 'this note was more akin to the pseudo-Celticism of James MacPherson in Scotland than to the living Gaelic tradition of the 1780s in Ireland ... but Gaelic could survive in English only in a 'Celtic' form (Carpenter, op. cit., p. 962).

And, of course, in the middle of the nineteenth century we also had the Young Irelanders. As Carpenter argues, the Celtic Spirit of this group was allied to the increasingly urgent claims of the Irish Catholics for full civic status. This interest in the past, then, could be viewed in some quarters as 'positively revolutionary' (Carpenter, op. cit., p. 962).

James Clarence Mangan, coming from Gaelic stock, did some fine translations of bardic poetry, most memorably, 'Roisin Dubh' (Dark Rosaleen). This was chosen, doubtless, for its fairly explicit political allegory of the delivery of Ireland from what the Young Irelanders perceived as the British yoke. John Mitchell's wife Jenny, who had connections with a major landlord family, the Verners of Armagh, was also an active force. Thomas Davis praised Antiquarians like Ferguson for their contribution to conferring a 'dreamy renown' to ancient Ireland and for his pedigree to nationhood. Though, as Thomas Flanagan points out, Ferguson was a hard-headed Antiquarian and was likely to be distrustful of 'dreamy renown' with all its Shelleyesque and radical undertones, and he was not likely, as a unionist, to declare any allegiance to Irish nationhood (Flanagan, 1989, p. 72).

All of these complex affinities formed the compound chemistry of the cultural crucible of the late 1890s – the period of the so-called Celtic Twilight or Irish Renaissance. And, as we hope to demonstrate, there was an inevitability about the tensions and even contradictions inherent in reviving the Celtic Spirit in literature.

Going Native with the Celtic Spirit: Voice and Print
But before we get to that celebrated nadir, I would like to mention, however briefly, some nineteenth-century writers in whom the vexed questions of personal and political identity are, quite literally, voiced. I can but mention Lever, Lover, the

Banims and George Moore as novelists attempting to register, from a non-Anglo-Irish perspective, that terra incognita that was Ireland. These middle-class Catholic writers were as keen as Edgeworth and the Anglo-Irish Antiquarians and were embarked upon a not entirely dissimilar mission. Their message, tinged with Romanticism, is, basically, that Ireland is not full of savages. Perhaps a salient feature of the Celtic Spirit in literature is a certain tendency towards a messianic impulse – and this, it seems, long before colonialism. Very often these novels are marked, as is Edgeworth's *Castle Rackrent*, by the co-presence of two voices; one colloquial, the other authorial, Latinate and educated, speaking, as it were, in RP English (or a slightly overdetermined form of it). Now, the effect of this – and we are simplifying horribly – is to articulate two Irelands: the rural tenant unauthorised, or at least unregistered, speaking voice and the Anglo-Irish authorial and writerly voice. Again, we see inscribed a particular combination which we have drawn attention to in literature that long predates what we now term 'colonial'; that distinctive business of co-presence of the spoken and the written which goes right back to the early Celtic literature. Back then, the nexus was the encounter between an oral Celtic culture and the incoming writerly Christian clerics. In the twentieth century, Flann O'Brien dramatised it in *At Swim-Two-Birds* as a policy of opposing voice to print (Hurson, 1984, p. 94–5). But, of course, O'Brien's novel both supports and challenges that aesthetic. And here, in the nineteenth century, we see the same dramatic tension between voice ('native', authentic) and print (authorial, interpretative, translating). Is this a less discussed aspect of the Celtic Spirit in literature? Was identity always, in some sense riven between the internal and the external, alien and native, the past and the present, the private and the public/political, defence and acceptance, the spoken word and the written word? And is the Celtic solution to a Celtic problem to inscribe/voice (write and speak) *both* ways of being? Is this some kind of essential, irreducible and indefatigable part of the Celtic Spirit?

Let us return to the nineteenth-century 'native' novelists. Though these writers are much more sympathetic and understand a good deal more about what life is like for the Plain People of Ireland, they still consider it necessary to interpret that reality and, paradoxically, also to distance themselves somewhat from it (as if they *were* Anglo-Irish) through the deployment of this authorial voice. Now of course, as it was for Edgeworth, there is the crucial matter of readership too. For there is still no real chance of most ordinary people reading these novels, since the population is illiterate in two languages. There was also, as the nineteenth century wore on, an increasing tendency in the British media to demonise the Irish, as simians, as 'roarin boys', as fighters and wild men. This perspective was no doubt fuelled by the rebellious and disloyal activities of the Young Irelanders and the Fenians, as well as the increasing numbers of actual Irish coming into England as a result of general poverty and, most pressingly, in the 1840s, as a result of the Famine (Wade, 2011). The share of responsibility for a particular recurring phenomenon that, conceivably, should have been borne by British politicians, was not always closely interrogated in the English press. The Irish were, in one way or another, 'trouble'. These writers are, as it were, on their best behaviour, acting as liminal figures attempting to interpret positively – sell, if you will – the culture of the native Irish to the English and Anglo-Irish middle and upper classes. With dramatists like Boucicault, they had their work cut out; *The Colleen Bawn* is, on the surface, about as stage-Irish as you can get, but there are more subtle messages beneath its roistering surface.

But it is with Carleton that the full messianic impulse declares itself: 'I found them [the country people, tenant farmers, labourers, cobblers, hedge schoolmasters] a class unknown in literature' (Carleton, 1834, p. x). And it is Carleton who takes upon himself the vocation of bringing his people to the very centre of literature – both in Ireland and beyond it. That he achieved a very considerable measure of success, especially in his shorter tales and sketches, cannot be disputed and this is really the first time that we begin to have that world told, as it were, spoken forth, by a writer who grew up within that hidden Ireland. And you might reasonably expect that Carleton would be, thus, gloriously untroubled by issues of identity. Not one bit of it. Indeed, if anything, he is the extreme case of riven identity. Rejected for the priesthood, he went to Dublin and fell in love with a young Protestant lady whose near relation just happened to be an extremely vigorous evangelical by the name of Cesar Otway. Carleton became a Protestant and started to write for Otway's publication, *The Christian Examiner*. Now whatever the motivations of both men, it remains the case that this was the organ through which Carleton first revealed his 'class unknown in literature'. God works in mysterious ways, his wonders to perform. The intention may well have been, at least partly, to paint a true enough picture of the native Irish as to create a platform from which their priest-ridden predilections and superstition could the better be exposed. However, Carleton is sometimes seriously 'off message' and also attacks with a degree of temerity never before seen the evils of the landlord system – not of course the institution of landlordism itself. He sailed mighty close to the wind, in terms of alienating the Establishment, but Otway did not, it seems, censor him. In the 1840s Carleton wrote also for *The Nation*, the magazine of the virulently Nationalist Young Ireland movement. What Carleton did was to anatomise the condition of Ireland in such a way as to expose the limitations of all classes and creeds. In that sense, he most closely prefigures Joyce, whose Ireland was no less comfortable for Romantics than for bigots.

Carleton forces us to see the extraordinary vitality of the life of ordinary people, and he also forces us to see what is foolish and what is sectarian. And, in a novel like *The Black Prophet,* he refuses the convenient official view of the famines – for they recurred – as an act of God, citing in the footnotes report after report testifying to the tragic human consequences and warning about neglect by the authorities both within Ireland and in London, and the landlords. That the novel is a Gothic mystery tale of outlandish improbabilities reinforces Carleton's argument that Ireland is a country deprived of meaning, a place of chaos, a phantasmagoria. And that this could have been prevented. Carleton published *The Black Prophet* in 1846, but he draws on a previous famine of 1829 for his material. The nightmare of history is that it repeats itself. And repeating, recycling 'reflection' is a cracked glass, seen through the cracked glass of the writer's political and cultural optics.

Before moving on to talk about the Celtic Twilight or the Irish Renaissance, we should say a word about George Moore, for Moore in many respects is an interestingly hybrid figure among the middle class 'native' writers. He came from a mixed heritage landlord family who had made their money in trade and was a literary man across a number of genres. Moore spent many years out of Ireland, in London and on the Continent, where he came under the influence of the French naturalists, especially Zola. In *A Drama in Muslin*, Moore, according to John Cronin, in that 'plum cake of a book' holds to exquisite ridicule the degenerate Anglo-Irish ascendancy and dramatises the increasing tension with a restless peasantry (Cronin, 1980, p. 120). But, as Cronin argues, in *The Untilled Field* Moore sets out to ridicule the Gaelic past, but becomes seduced by the lonely beauty of the country and the quiet gentleness of some of its people (Cronin, op. cit., p. 132). Moore returned to Ireland during the Literary Revival, but he remained an ambiguous figure among ambiguous figures, asserting the necessity of condemning the cultural philistinism of Ireland and the need to escape it, but even his artist analogue, Alice Barton, does not quite make it to Paris. We can see how Moore, in his own hybrid identity and outlook, influenced both Yeats and Joyce. For both writers, so dissimilar in so many ways, were intent upon reconnecting Ireland and Europe, in reasserting that older Celtic Continental flow. That Paris happened to be the centre of the cultural world in the late nineteenth century, the locus of the intellectual and aesthetic avant garde, was not lost on either of them. And hyphenation, ambivalence, was to be the making of them both.

Through a Glass Darkly: The Celtic Light or Twilight
Notions of repetition and recycling and reinterpretation or even reappropriation abound in the rhetoric surrounding the cultural florescence of the 1890s. Various appellations have been invented, then and since, to attempt to define what it was that people were doing: the Irish Renaissance, the Celtic Revival, the Celtic Twilight. Indeed, as Norman Vance has suggested, the 'Renaissance' was a complex of different movements, cultural, political, social and spiritual, intermittently intersecting and reinforcing or aggravating each other (Vance, 2002, p. 101). Of course, some of those involved regarded the notion of repetition or revival with a more baleful eye, as Vance acknowledges, it was 'problematic for Irish Ireland extremists' (Vance, 2002, p. 100). And for certain literary men, among them James Joyce, or rather Joyce's creation, Stephen Dedalus, the Revival was a business to be scorned, especially in its more Gaelic avatars (Joyce, 1916, p. 197). And yet there is no doubt in most people's minds nowadays that a great deal of fine work was produced in the space of thirty years. That this period was a high watermark in Irish culture has been, since the *animateurs* themselves told us this was the case, an accepted fact, a *recu* not to be questioned. What will we think about it in another fifty years?

Now, in the context of this book, we need to concentrate as specifically as we can on words like 'Celtic' and 'spirit'. The phrase 'Celtic Twilight' came down, possibly, from Matthew Arnold, who delivered a series of four highly influential lectures on Celtic literature, later published as a book in 1867 (Arnold, 1867; rpt 2008). The lectures formed Arnold's successful case for getting a Chair in Celtic literature in Oxford. Arnold, like the French commentator Ernest Renan, saw the essence of the Celtic Spirit as residing in ecstatic natural description, emotionalism and magic. Bruce Stewart, on his excellent *Ricorso* website, offers an impressive set of inter-pretations of Arnold's work, especially by writers of the Revival (Stewart, undated). However, Arnold went on to argue that the Celts were impractical and wilful and feminine and thus it was only right that Celtic literature remained a tributary of English literature and the Celts themselves a tributary (in the more Roman sense), continuing to be governed by the Anglo-Saxon rationalists as was only sensible and right. This British hegemonic view of the Irish (Stewart, op. cit.) and of those marginal people, who had been taken under the protection of empires, as childlike, ungovernable and female, was very common among the ruling classes in Europe at this time. That it provided a justification for rejecting pleas for greater 'national' independence was perhaps merely co-incidental.

The young Yeats was very influenced by Arnold, but, according to Bruce Stewart, his riposte, 'The Celtic Element in Literature' (1897), parted from Arnold by asserting that, far from being a tributary, Celtic literature is the original form which provides the gateway to mystery and beauty for the Anglo-Saxons (Stewart, op. cit.). It was an arch move. Yeats's sleight of hand appears to decolonise Ireland, asserting the pre-eminence of the Celtic Spirit. Perhaps he should have called his lecture 'The Celtic Reversal'. But as far as Yeats was con-cerned, twilight it certainly was not about to be, with all the

223

implications of a safe disappearance of that very Celtic Spirit which could then be invested with a shimmering *nostalgie*, like a first and foolish love, but the dawn of a cultural renaissance, built upon the rediscovery of the Celtic Spirit. Or was the very appeal of the Celtic Spirit precisely that it was a culture upon the verge of extinction, as Declan Kiberd and Eamon Maher have argued (Kiberd and Maher, 2002, p. 87), a beautifully doomed enterprise, unlikely to really threaten the shaky political foundations of Anglo-Irish governance and in tune with the hunger of the great London and Paris imperial markets for the exotic, the innocent, the pure? We can dare such a question only perhaps because of our proximity to this period and because, since that time, the whole perspective of postcolonial thinking has created a sometimes sheer and, some would say, strident and unfair critique – itself a reflex of our own time. Questions have to be asked of all periods, all phases of the cultural expression of the Celtic Spirit; and asked from all sides.

Recalling the events of the last decades of the nineteenth century, Yeats declared that Ireland was, after the fall of Parnell, 'like soft wax' (Yeats, 1922, p. 83). And it was upon this soft wax that he was determined to stamp his own imprimatur. And Yeats was maybe happy enough to have the authority of Arnold for his own, rather more subversive, enterprise. Joyce accused Yeats of that 'treacherous instinct of adaptability', perhaps because he felt that Yeats blew rather with the wind, politically speaking. Well, we must allow for two things here. The first is the turbulence of the times themselves and the second is that even great poets, and maybe especially great poets, are not always politically right-on. If Yeats, in the finish up, rejected his earlier politically nationalistic fervour – as expressed in a poem like 'Kathleen Ní Houlihan' and in early plays on this symbolic figure starring Maud Gonne – it must also be remembered that, as we have seen, Joyce's Stephen Dedalus contemptuously dismissed the ardent nationalism of his fellow students. We do not know what Joyce himself felt, but we know that, unlike Yeats, he took the boat. Whether Yeats should have gone with him is, well, another story.

Many of the main 'actors' and *animateurs* in the Celtic Revival were from Anglo-Irish backgrounds. At the one end of any axis that existed between cultural and political nationalism, and, often that axis did not, we suspect, exist, there is a further difficult choice to be made and that is between what might be termed Redmondite constitutional nationalism and what might be termed Republican physical force nationalism. It is clear that at least at one point, Yeats had travelled a very long way. And, for some, maybe in entirely the wrong direction. Certainly, Yeats himself was to so modify his attitude, especially after Independence, so as to become almost the opposite of that early self – or one of them. For there is a swooning, symbolic tincture to many of his early poems too, for example his collection *The Rose,* reflecting the international aesthetic moment of the *fin de siècle* and his profound connection both with the sensibility and, also, as is the case in every age, with the audience, the taste, the saleability of ideas within an international cultural market. And, as we have seen, Ireland was something of a hard sell for a very long time. Yeats was not alone in either his messianic impulse or his adjustment amid the forces of politics and history.

And we also need to bear in mind that the Celtic Revival (encompassing Welsh and Scottish elements) was itself a European movement, profoundly motivated by a reaction against urbanisation and industrialisation. The Celtic was appealing precisely because it was an otherworld, a romanticised medievalism glimpsed against the 'filthy modern tide', to quote a later Yeats poem 'The Statues' (Yeats, 1949; rpt 2008, p. 282). For some, at the time, it was an opiate against the crass materialism and mass-produced tawdriness of the virulently enterprising Western world. It was also a glorious chance, especially for Yeats and Synge, to align themselves with the international avant garde of the civilised world and offer their own exemplum of alterity.

For the Celtic Spirit could be both à la mode and, crucially, a powerful ordinance in a long-standing relationship characterised by a discomforting admixture of wounded standoff and 'kiss me quick' between the English and the Anglo-Irish. As Edgeworth, in the more nuanced and also critically sharper novel that she wrote after *Castle Rackrent*, *Ormond*, revealed, the absentee Anglo-Irish landlords, by virtue of their absence, might be English in Ireland, but in England they were unfathomably and thus unforgivably Irish. This colonial riveness about identity was by no means confined to the Anglo-Irish, as we have tried to demonstrate. So, I think, in that sense, what Yeats and his Anglo-Irish confrères were about was not to create, as if by magic, Irish literature, but to assert, as they had never before asserted, a sense of themselves, not so much as national but as local and not so much as national as international. The vexed issue of nationalism is, for all concerned, a vexed issue because it mutates, just as the crisis of identity seems to have resolved itself through an uncharacteristic ferocity of energy and self-realisation into a crisis about power. Seamus Deane is sharp enough: 'Irish culture became the new property of those who were losing their grip on Irish land [which constituted] a strategic retreat from political to cultural supremacy' (cited by Stewart, undated).

And all this, just as the Anglo-Irish know who they are and begin to exult in their very hybridism and their very polarity. No *mere* English they, but the guardians of the Celtic Spirit, if you please, and the most thoroughly modern enunciators of that modish Celtic Spirit in the chiliastic Western world, desperate for escape from the consequences of Empire and their jaded knowingness. Well, Ireland, carefully managed, could not but be a hit.

And if, as was inevitable, that culture upon the point of extinction, as Kiberd has called it, died, they who tried to revive it were on the right side. It did not prevent the burning out of them, and, less dramatically, the collapse of estates from death duties accruing from a lifestyle that somewhat mismatched a high rate of spend against a decreasing rate of income from the old investment, land. In the end, the 'land' they had been invested with, by fair means or foul, did for them, not just because of the Land League, but because land, not invested in, became an increasingly historical and thus obsolete currency.

We are in no way suggesting that any of this occurred to the fervent champions of the Irish Literary Revival. They were, of course, artists. But no artist has ever come out of Ireland until the latter end of the twentieth century who could escape the nightmare of history, to say nothing of the cracked glass of his own reflection – to himself, to the people of the place, images rarely matching. But that is not to say that artists did not attempt escape, only to find that their most fecund imaginative ground was precisely a drama of polarity and hybridism.

But Yeats favoured always a drama of polarity, though, paradoxically, the basis of it and the impulse behind it was hybridism. A syncretic and ersatz mix of *fin de siècle* aestheticism and a ferociously cold enthusiasm for certain elements of the Celtic Spirit, an inner and an outer sort of dedication. Yeats collapses, with sublime insouciance, beneath his slim, orchestrating hand, any notion of historicity, deferring, distancing, after his early nationalist gaucheries, the objectionable, vulgarities of the new reality, framing a sensibility determinedly heroic in its outcastedness. The Anglo-Irish were victims. And the Anglo-Irish were, in the Yeats canon, increasingly, the artists. So enormous was the influence of Yeats that this stance was to become the gold-standard attitude for writers from this island for a generation and a half.

THE LAKE ISLE OF INNISFREE
The call of the Celtic wild: The Lake Isle of Innisfree, Co. Sligo.

Yeats was, first and foremost, interested in literature and culture and he seized the moment after the fall of Parnell when politics seemed to have stagnated. With Lady Gregory and others he put a huge effort into setting up the Irish Literary Theatre (called in somewhat medieval dreamy style, the Abbey Theatre). He published collections of stories, he published poems, he set up, with his sisters, the Cuala Press. Certain of Yeats' early poems are especially worthy of mention in the context of this book. There is the aisling like 'The Song of Wandering Aengus' with its blend of Irish rural, elemental local, symbolism influenced by the occult and a strong sense of an otherworld just out of his grasp. We see also the emergence of what is to become a typical Yeats figure – the outcast, the man who rejects the vulgarities of common existence (the Plain People of Ireland and recently thrusting

People of Ireland), Catholic piety and gombeen materialism. Is it possible that Yeats drew to some extent on Gaelic material like *Buile Suibhne* (*The Frenzy of Sweeney*) or some crib of it, as well as chorically 'mad' characters from Carleton like Raymond Na-Hattha? He certainly was familiar with Carleton and produced an edition of his work (Yeats, 1889). But while his early praise for Carleton was for his Catholic authenticity, he tends to drop out of the pantheon of the later Yeats (Howes, 2006, p. 27). There is 'The Lake Isle of Innisfree', a version of the English Pastoral fused with early Irish hermetic lyric poetry. And he 'revives' and of course reinterprets Gaelic literature through his plays, *Cúchulain* and *Deirdre of the Sorrows*.

Another very important figure at the time was Douglas Hyde, also from an Anglo-Irish background, who set up the Gaelic League in 1893. Hyde advocated that the only way that Ireland can truly revive its Celtic Spirit is to de-Anglicise; that is to say, that the reality is that most of the people can no longer speak Irish never mind read it, so all the rediscovered and wonderfully elucidated manuscripts in the world, so lovingly pored over by antiquarian and scholar, are incomprehensible to the marginal few who still speak Irish.

The Gaeltacht dwellers, for Hyde, belonged to a threatened species, living on the margins of the margin, on the remote western seaboards of Kerry and Donegal and Aran. If a revival of a Celtic Spirit was ever realistically going to happen, then the living speech of these people needed to be nourished and grown. This new impetus for reviving the spoken, oral language was to result in a number of dictated auto-biographies, the most famous of which is probably Tomas Ó Criomthain's *An t-Oileánach*, translated by the English Gaelic scholar Robin Flower, whose translation was, a generation later, the target of the coruscating satire that is *An Béal Bocht* (*The Poor Mouth*) by Myles na gCopaleen. Other notable auto-biographies included Maurice O'Sullivan's *Fiche Blain ag Fás*

(*Twenty Years A-Growing*) and *Peig* by Peig Sayers. We may note here too, the underlying dialectic between speech and written material, even given the immense efforts of the Antiquarians to make available, in one form or another, the 'lost' Gaelic written corpus, to say nothing of the English versions rendered by Yeats, Synge, Lady Gregory and others. Of course, Hyde realised that the written material was not readily available to many people, either because many still could not read or because what had been discovered was viewed as too remote in every sense – linguistic, cultural, educational. A huge gap existed between what was left of spoken Irish and the scholarly and artistic resources now available.

To some extent, John Synge subscribed to this project of reviving the living spoken language. Having studied Irish in Trinity College Dublin, just as his clerical family forebears did, that they might spread the Good Word, Synge went out to Aran not to preach but to listen, between the chinks of the floorboards, to the language of the people. This suggests a curious kind of eavesdropping which casts Synge in the role of spy rather than confidante, and while his plays were received with enormous critical acclaim by Yeats and other leading luminaries of the Revival, they were not always greeted with complete gratitude and appreciation by the less enlightened sections of the Dublin theatre-going public. Indeed, as is now well known, Synge's *Playboy of the Western World* caused a riot. Yeats, never slow to seize a dramatic moment, strode up on to the stage and denounced the audience. Poor Synge presumably listened from some cramped eyrie, there and not there. The Dublin public, we may presume, was mainly Catholic and 'native' Irish (though we know how glib and lacking in subtlety, never mind authenticity, such terms are) and apparently took particular exception to the mention of the word 'shift'. In the light – or dark – of an increasingly influential Catholic Church, reasserting its long-lost authority but heavily freighted with British Victorian concepts of modesty (small ironies on a small island), 'shift' was portrayed by Yeats as a kind of gombeen prurience – a graceless erasure of the immense and spectacular enterprise of the Revival project. Of course, the central protagonist, Christy Mahon, is really an artist analogue outcast by a pietistic and unimaginative society. But, whether this got through or got through only too well, many Dublin theatregoers did not like to see themselves portrayed as the villains of the piece. That Yeats and Synge failed to grasp this little sensitivity is another irony of the situation. Ireland in colonial times was hardly ready for art, never mind artists. A further irony, surely, given the corpus of Irish literature still extant, thanks in part to the Antiquarians, never mind what was lost, about which the Plain People of Ireland knew precious little, since history had connived to divest them of any sense that they had a culture. Would they have been proud of culture had not the Plantation project taken place? Can pride in culture only come from conquest of another culture?

People may have been, at the time, touchy about yet more negative representations of themselves. And perhaps the fact that they, the people, were being cast as the villains of the piece by artists, artists from backgrounds perceived to be, to some extent, alien (the Anglo in Anglo-Irish) tended to reinforce, however unintentionally, colonial attitudes, or at least a mortification among people that these artists were as contemptuous of them as their landlords and 'superiors' were. And, after all, it had been a very long time indeed since the elite order of bards had strode the land, all that most people would have known of them was a tattered echo through street balladeers and travelling teachers scraping a living. So, it must have been difficult indeed to appreciate that there could be such a thing as an artist coming out of this country.

On the other side of the business, the artists had to deal with an audience who were largely uneducated (though through no fault of their own mostly) and accustomed to the high jinks of melodrama and not the finely crafted and much quieter plays of Yeats and Synge. Perhaps also, ironically, as city people they were not always highly tuned to the version of rural dialect (itself dramatically heightened) presented in Synge's plays and were thus out of the loop a bit here too. Nonetheless, there were many who did appreciate what they were doing.

The Inheritance of Loss

So, the architects of the Celtic Revival has their work cut out for them. If they hoped, as certainly Yeats – and in a more modest way Synge – did, that not only literature but the makers of it would become the modern-day bards, would enjoy some of the prestige that writers enjoyed on the Continent and even in London, they were to be sadly mistaken. They had to fight for every inch of cultural territory. That some of the leaders of the Easter Rising – Pearse, Thomas Mac Donagh, Erskine Childers – were literary men might have helped a bit, but by then, more than one 'terrible beauty' had been born. And Ireland was to be divided on more ways than one. The fragile idealism which perhaps betokened, at least in retrospect, some commonality of purpose, tragically dissipated with 1916. Ireland, or part of it, gained her freedom. Ulster gained freedom too by remaining within the Union. Or at least some people in each jurisdiction gained freedom. Southern unionists were left marooned in a state in which they were marginalised; Northern nationalists were left marooned in a state in which they were marginalised. Whatever had been gained by way of cultural commonality, albeit through certain versions of the Celtic Spirit that were new forms or ersatz flummeries, depending on your point of view, started to get lost in the cacophony of recriminations. The irony was, presumably, not lost on any side. One consequence was that post-Partition Ireland and the new state of Northern Ireland were to allot a very thin and proscribed ground for art and artists.

The legacy of the Revival writers is still a matter about which there is considerable debate. What nobody can deny was that this was a period of literary and cultural activity of outstanding range and volume. As Shakir Mustafa points out, the Revival did provide a subjugated people with an alternative history, or perhaps more accurately, a set of myths through which could be constructed out of the ruins some kind of Celtic heritage. Mythmaking may not be all bad (Mustafa, 2002, p. 71). That the Celtic Spirit was defined in so many ways, some of them contradictory, testifies not just to the pro-blematics of identity, to the more baleful ironies and paradoxes involved in transacting, in real life, what the Celtic Spirit could or couldn't mean, but to some deeply shared impulse of delight.

That, as Yeats put it in 'An Irish Airman Forsees His Death', a lonely impulse of delight' (Yeats, 1949; rpt 2011, p. 111), exposes the immense difficulty of any individual's particular struggle with identity on this island is an inheritance both seductive and risky, elevating and confining the artist to the position of martyred outcast inveighing against the sleazy or wrong-headed political reality from era to era. And the writing of the Revival posited many different definitions when it came to identity. Though always somehow, implicitly if not expli-citly, personal, individual identity was entangled with cultural, political, racial and religious identity. The identity of the *artist* was to become, in this nexus, increasingly that of the outsider and, to make matters worse or better, a Steppenwolf with a shard of broken glass in his shapely, wounded paw.

We may remind ourselves that this crisis of representation was not at all simply an issue for writers from an Anglo-Irish background, or if not an issue for them, an issue for their readers and their audiences. While some may have rejected or accepted Yeats and Synge and Hyde as just another version of the Protestant Boys, loyal and true, keeping the natives in their place while hijacking their very literature, the reality is that the problem of identity runs through the writers coming from the Catholic tradition – most notably Joyce (though George Moore had his bothers too).

Whatever about what Stephen Dedalus says, archly dismissing the Catholic Church and nationalism (though, of course, ironically, happy enough to appropriate – or reappropriate the central sacral function and high political status to the artist as it was in bardic pre-Christian times and as it is in the aesthetic paradise of Paris in the nineties), it is not insignificant that Joyce calls over the heads of the nationalists and the Catholic Church in having as the real hero of *Ulysses* a Jewish man called Leopold Bloom, who avers that Ireland is his nation (Joyce, 1922; rpt 2010). For a race forced to wander the earth, that is indeed a poignant statement. And if the well-brushed and top-hatted citizens of Dublin keep Bloom politely to their margin, Joyce welcomes him and takes him in – a sort of Celtic Spirit, betokening a welcome for the stranger. And though Joyce disavows explicitly any identification with the Celtic Spirit, there is surely, in *A Portrait,* that old Celtic motif of the serpent eating its own tail, echoed also in *Ulysses*, but broadened out to become a more affirmative embrace of the cyclical, drawing also on Continental sources such as Vico. And even more strikingly in *Finnegans Wake* (Joyce, 1939; rpt 2000) we have inscribed the immanence of the river, and the sacral significance of the river, going right back to early myths about the river goddess, Bóinn, rinsed maybe with a Hercletian optimism. That there is optimism is surely in itself a source of optimism. And *Finnegans Wake* might be read, even more fully than *Ulysses*, as a 'signature of all things we read'. For both novels are, whatever else they are not, palimpsestal; they build

THE CELTIC SPIRIT: NEW FORMS

and build their extraordinary layers of association of places and the lore of places and can thus be read as a modern day *dinnseanchas*. The associations are, by the twentieth century, longer, broader, more complex, involving the reading that any colonial writer would have been subject to – the classics, the great texts of the English canon, the religious texts of Catholicism. But the note is also determinedly, modern, forward-looking, not the *nostalgie* of the later Yeats. Joyce, though perhaps an unlikely and even unwilling recruit to the corps of the Celtic Spirit, may nonetheless prove to be one of its most enduring scribes, because, like the *fili* and the clerics and the déclassé bards, his outlook insists on the future as well as the past.

And then there is O'Casey: a marginal Protestant at the margins of the Revival, a defender of the urban working class, a purveyor of Dublin speech – in English; and really a little bit de trop for the Abbey board. Still, fair play to them, they did let him do some stuff, but not quite enough to topple their balance, their emphasis on the past, on the rural. So O'Casey left, as Joyce left, to undertake their own immrams, as so many had done before them.

The threat of one kind of betrayal or another is ever-present, the threat of inauthenticity is ever-present, the threat of authenticity is ever-present. Well, it seems that, from very far back, a living in more than one world is central to the Celtic Spirit. And the recourse to the otherworld of Gaelic literature and artefacts and music and speech may be a reflex that we all sometimes yearn for; and, equally, reject. We see ourselves, right enough betimes, in a cracked glass. Just as, at other times, we see in the mirror an image which insists that we are the fairest of them all. The others, the polarised other, cannot begin to compare. And sometimes we achieve moments, just as the writers of the Revival did, when we revive not just our jagged differences, but some image which sees the crack, is the crack, and which laughs at the spectacle, a spectacle of disjunction and brokenness which, paradoxically, we all recognise as being, somehow, a common reflection. But that is only in our tower, or in our cabin.

Yeats, the towering figure of the Renaissance in every sense, made a great performance about his retirement into the private. Small blame to him, maybe, but the coldness of that retreat – and his arch dismissal of the Plain People of Ireland as gombeen men, vulgar, uncivilised, priest-ridden and un-imaginative objects of contempt – contains unfortunate echoes of the unquestioning messianic thrust of the Plantation project. That such a messianic impulse was, thereafter, to be so marked a feature of the 'write backs' to that project suggests that a questioning and complex and messianic attitude shared, if nothing else was shared, by both Anglo-Irish and Irish was to become a central dynamic of the literature that this island produced. Whether this be an inherent indigenous facet of the Celtic Spirit (and there is, as we have seen, some evidence for that, and some evidence against it) or whether it be the outcome of the encounter between the Anglo-Saxon and the Celtic Spirit we must leave the gentle reader to decide. All we can say is that to observe some hospitality towards the stranger, towards the other, encompasses a recognition that the other is our worst nightmare *and* our projection of our fantasy selves. So amidst polarisation, hostility, fears of suppression and conquest of the personal and political self, perhaps there is also a rueful recognition of our complex selves; tainted, invaded, refreshed, challenged. But the changing sky is there for all of us, the common blackbird over Belfast Lough, and the man observing it that sees not himself but the bird; the other, the thing not yet seen, but glanced at, missed.

CHAPTER ELEVEN

Celtic Spirit in the Twentieth Century
Tess Maginess

Narrowed Ground

From the middle of the nineteenth century, as the current tale would have it, the tail of the Celtic Spirit curled itself into a Gaelic and then, after Independence, an Irish Catholic spirit that stiffened into an insular and defensive Free State (no irony where none intended, as Beckett would have it), spikily repelling invaders. The tale, propagated first by writers from both parts of the island, has settled into comfortable cliché. The Free State, as articulated by its more official and officious praetorian guard, in the forty or fifty years after Partition, cannot but have been, to the new Northern State, a very distinctly unappetising breakfast of champions. That the breakfast was a dish a dog might shy his loyal head from may have had to be beneath the notice of the aspiring architects of the new Ireland. But, of course, it is fashionable to portray this period as repressive, defensive and a terribly wasted opportunity. And there is no doubt that the era from Partition to the mid-1960s was, culturally speaking, a difficult time, even a dark age. Revisionist historians have, as Shakir Mustafa argues, tended to be dismissive of the positive effects that mythologising may have, valuing only the Modernist spirit at the expense of what recycling of the past may have to teach us (Mustafa, 2002, p. 70). It must also be acknowledged that the task facing the two states was immense. It must have been extremely difficult to continue the idealist spirit which sponsored the Celtic Revival, which sponsored also – and not the same thing – the political movement for independence and, equally, the political movement against independence in Ulster, but not confined to Ulster, both characterised by a willingness to resort to arms. And, in that context, lest we forget, there were thousands of men from this island who gave their lives in a world war that had become, for many, increasingly entrenched and futile – though we were only to fully know that in the 1960s, when all wars were seen as a particularly bad idea. The Troubles, doubtless, enforced this belief.

For many, the new dispensation yielded benefits, on both sides of the border. Small farmers were able to buy out their family farms; there were better provisions for health and education, especially after 1948 in Northern Ireland. Would these changes have come anyway, in a world where the influence of the British Empire was receding? Perhaps, but the genie was out of the bottle all over the world. Everything had changed. To confine ourselves to the cultural ramifications, it may be argued that there are to be observed, in the island after Partition, two contending impulses: one towards the creation of new states, new orders, embracing the Modernist spirit of radical change; the other an impulse to conserve, to return to an island before colonialism. But we must qualify this: for the majority of denizens north of the border, no such impulse was present. Indeed, the very definition of themselves as 'colonial' may even yet constitute a great insult to the Ulster unionists who formed that majority and defended it by all means. As Stephen Howe argues, such terms as 'colonial' and 'colonised' may be most unhelpful (Howe, 2000, p. 4). Howe is right, along with other commentators like Liam Kennedy, to question the use of such terms. He is right also in pointing out that the academic arguments about this subject, which reached their heyday in the 1980s, not accidentally in the middle of the Troubles, perceive, from all sides, the world 'colonial' as loaded with pejorative meaning (Kennedy, 1996). But, it may be said that others are also entitled to view the experience of the last five hundred years or so with greater equivocation or even asperity and even to deploy, with integrity, such terms as 'colonialism'. While Kennedy's argument that Ireland does not qualify in economic and social criteria for colonial status, by comparison with the Third World (and, indeed, he is quite right to rebuke those who use the term as if their position was anywhere near as grievous as that of the population in India or Africa), may we not legitimately question the narrowing of the definition to an equation of colonialism with Third World countries without an implicit accusation of crassness? The riven identity manifested so often in Irish literature, regardless of who is writing it, from Joyce to Hewitt, can arguably be compared to similar expressions of cultural self-division and polyphony in writers such as Derek Walcott and Kiran Desai, to say nothing of Andrea Levy. Colonialism need not be either promiscuous in its claims, or lacking in generosity towards the other.

At any rate, some there were, at official level, who sincerely followed Hyde in the project of trying to de-Anglicise Ireland, not just by making the learning of Irish a requirement for a job in the new civil service, but in a wider cultural mission which had the sincere intention, doubtless, of fulfilling the ideals of the Revival in restoring Gaelic and Celtic culture, of repossessing a dispossessed cultural inheritance. De Valera's vision of the comely maidens dancing at the crossroads has become a target for more or less undisguised ridicule, but we must remember too that De Valera was appealing, if a shade too literally, to the essentially recreative project of the revivalists – many of whom were, ironically, scions of the Anglo-Irish order which was, at its highest levels, indisputably associated with maintaining the political and economic machinery of the 'sister kingdom'.

After Independence, Yeats composed figures like Crazy Jane and Michael Robartes who were outsiders who inhabited a kind of timeless, elemental landscape, but who were implicitly critical of the new Ireland. While these figures owed much to earlier noble madmen from Celtic literature, especially the frenzied Sweeney and Carleton's holy fools (as well as Shakespeare), his operation of the Celtic Spirit was not confined to imaginative sympathy and self-identification with those who were likely to be viewed as 'astray'. Yeats also drew upon the satiric tradition in Celtic literature with some asperity, and his excoriations of the new gombeen oligarchy were not infrequent. So Robartes and Crazy Jane and the whole architecture of the Yeatsian Tower betokens a private, retreated, imaginative space, sacral in its way. Though, of course, this is a theology that supplants Christianity, harking back in some sense to a pagan world, and so very distinctly anti-clerical in its orientation that Yeats seems more a disciple of the Protestant evangelical Caesar Otway than Carleton does. Significantly, Yeats, like Joyce's Stephen Dedalus but much more implicitly, replaces theology with the new religion of art. And there are also many poems who addressed directly the public issues of his time. Thus, for example, he berates the State for its philistinism in relation to the establishment of a gallery of modern art. But matters are never simple and Yeats, though undoubtedly conservative in his chagrined elegy for the lost 'wild' Celtic-Spirited Ireland, was, in the context of the Catholic-Church-dominated 'Free State', also a Progressive in his plea for a galley of modern rather than ancient art and, as a member of the Senate (Seanad), he eloquently and bitterly opposed the State's interdiction on divorce.

For Joyce as well as for Yeats, the new Ireland could only compare ironically with the great dreams that were to be had about a new dawn in Irish culture as well as in politics. But for both Joyce and Yeats, the disillusionment also had to do with an international mood of despondency and bitterness. Yeats, like T.S. Eliot, lamented the loss of what was seen as a unifying culture (though was it ever?). Eliot, in a not dissimilar vein, bleakly suggests that the task of the writer is to shore up fragments against our ruin. But there is, it could be argued, one crucial difference between Eliot and Yeats and that is that Eliot is more prepared to make the best of a bad job. With figures like Prufrock he turns, however sadly, to the new modern world, whereas Yeats, by and large – but by no means entirely – turned away from it, turned back to the past (or a past he had fashioned).

And Joyce takes his cue, it could be argued, more from Eliot than Yeats. In *Ulysses*, near everything is subject to irony, except for the searingly sharp descriptions of Dublin (really a character now) – a city in movement, albeit paralysed – and except also for Bloom. And Bloom is modern, owing nothing to any Celtic Spirit. Or so it would seem. But it is Bloom, with his receptivity, his acute observation – not of nature but of a city – who reminds us, ironically, of the early Irish nature poets. His respect for place and his great pride in being from this place also mark him as one filled with that Celtic Spirit. The wandering Jew is far more at home in Dublin than the arch and remote Stephen. And Joyce surely welcomes Bloom, offering a sort of Celtic hospitality through his compassionate and nuanced portrayal of the stranger.

Now there is also in *Ulysses* the famous or infamous Citizen episode and it is here that Joyce most lays siege, not so much to the Celtic world as to the romanticised nationalist Ireland that seemed to have been invented by certain elements in the Celtic Revival and pursued without question by the new state, appropriating certain elements of the Celtic Revival. For Joyce, what is wrong with the Citizen's view is that it is mushy, sentimental, a boy in a pub 'givin' out of him'. This maudlin muddiness is, for Joyce, a kind of fake Celticism; ersatz, backward-looking; a cracked glass in which the nightmare of history endlessly, recursively, reflects itself. Where is the real world; where is the modern world? Nowhere to be heard or seen.

Celtic Ironic

And such a critical, ironising angle of vision is also evident in the generation of writers who came after Joyce: Flann O'Brien/ Myles na gCopaleen, Frank O'Connor, Sean O'Faolain, Patrick Kavanagh, Austin Clarke and Louis MacNeice.

Austin Clarke, who wrote many poems inspired by the older Celtic literature, generally preserved his satiric arsenal for attacks on censorship and the powerful position of the Catholic Church in the new 'Free State'. Now, it seems, ironically, it is the Irish themselves who are inventing and imposing Penal Law. Clarke's anti-clericalism is evident even more directly in 'Burial of a President' (Douglas Hyde), an astringent castigation of the new Establishment who will not break the Catholic Church taboo attending Protestant services. Clarke's outrage is directed at the lack of generosity. And largesse is so central a Celtic virtue, to say nothing of welcome for the stranger. The irony is truly terrible, for it was Hyde who called most vigorously (from his planter, Anglo-Irish perch) for the de-Anglicisation of Ireland. Not that anything like that would ever happen now. Ah no. Sure don't we all go to services in other churches?

Well, in case there is any hint here that criticism might be directed northwards (heaven forfend) here is Paddy Kavanagh praising the Ulstermen in 'The Twelfth of July':

The Twelfth of July, the voice of Ulster speaking,
Tart as week-old buttermilk from a churn,
Surprising the tired palates of the south.
I said to myself: From them we have much to learn –

... The pageantry of Scarva
Recalled the Greek idea of dramatic art.
The horse dealers from the Moy or Banbridge,
The Biblical farmers from Richhill or Coleraine
All that was sharp, precise, and pungent flavoured
(Kavanagh, 2003, unpaged).

But, of course, both Clarke (who is to be the subject of some very tart satire in Beckett's *Murphy*) and Kavanagh had a whole other side to them. While the function of the poet was to be a scourge, a satirist, just as the ancient bards occupied a public, choric and indeed vatic function, each in their very different ways also inscribed a lyric, even mystical outlook in other poems, which connects them in another way to the Celtic Spirit. Clarke reprises the legend of Diarmuid and Gráinne and Kavanagh reprises that immanence we spoke of earlier, that sense of the land as sacral, as transcendent, in poems like 'Shancoduff' and 'Tarry Flynn'. But these poems also reflect that insider knowledge that came from writers like Carleton – the positioning is not pastoral but an insider view:

The sleety winds fondle the rushy beards of Shancoduff
While the cattle-drovers sheltering in the Featherna Bush
Look up and say: 'Who owns them hungry hills
That the water-hen and snipe must have forsaken?
(Kavanagh, 1964; rpt 1973, p. 30).

And there is the direct identification with the older Celtic, Pre-Christian world:

O Pagan poet you
And I are one
In this – we lose our god
At set of sun.

And we are kindred when
The hill wind shakes
Sweet song like blossoms on
The calm green lakes (Kavanagh, op. cit., p. 3).

And what about Louis MacNeice? He is perhaps primarily viewed as a public poet, connecting both with Kavanagh and Clarke, but also with Auden and Spenser. In *Autumn Journal*, Ireland and Ulster receive this accolade:

the voodoo of the Orange bands
Drawing an iron net through darkest Ulster ...

Up the Rebels, To Hell with the Pope.
And God Save – as you prefer – the King or
Ireland.
The land of scholars and saints:
Scholars and saints my eye, the land of ambush
Purblind manifestoes, never-ending complaints,
The born martyr and the gallant ninny (MacNeice 1966;
rpt 1979, p. 50).

We can 'scarce scape calumny' – any of us. Well it must be
also said, though it might offer little comfort, that the 1930s and
1940s was, internationally, a period in which writers were very
much aware of their role as, to borrow from Stephen Dedalus,
'the uncreated conscience of their race'. So Auden and Spender
share the acrid note we hear in MacNeice and Clarke. Part of
this outlook is distinctly local; a mood of disillusionment
perhaps inevitable after the high-rise visions of the Celtic
Revival. Part of it is also related to the sense of cultural
depression which set in during the Great Depression of the
1930s all over Europe. Writers were not only articulating this
sombre and enervated atmosphere, but also warning of the
dangers arising from the spread of fascism. Writers took on a
kind of public duty and if their imprecations were baleful, they
could see what perhaps the politicians were a wee mite slower
to see: how the world could once again fall prey to dictator-
ships – of one kind or another. Ireland, north and south,
seemed to many of its writers to be following not the path of
freedom so gloriously imagined, but the rutted track of an
inauthentic, backward-looking governance.

At the explicitly cultural level, what they were objecting to
was that one false image of Ireland, of the Celtic Spirit, had
been replaced by another, which was conspicuously lacking in
spiritedness, in accomplishment and in internationally
renowned achievement. The new Ireland and the arts? 'Land
of scholars and saints, my eye.'

But there was something else, maybe, too. Harold Bloom has coined the term 'the anxiety of influence' (Bloom, 1973). What I think he means by this is that state of affairs where, inevitably and, to use a Joycean word, ineluctably (without light), the writers following a generation of artists of huge accomplishment and international cachet cannot but feel that they are but shadows. The influence of Joyce himself, as well as Yeats and as well as Eliot, was massive. How could the next generation not feel the anxiety of that influence?

So what to do? For writers like Frank O'Connor and Sean O'Faolain the main response was to turn resolutely away from the path of that shadow. They forged an art that was public – in reaction to the seeming introspection and inaccessibility of the Modernists. They moved away from experimentation, they moved away from art which left ordinary people totally in the dark and they moved towards an art that engaged with the issues of the times in a form that was accessible: realism. Perhaps the seminal text here is O'Connor's 'Guests of the Nation', where the harrowed, lonely voice of the narrator/ protagonist cries out against the zero-sum game that political, public identity has descended into. The relationship between England and Ireland, the consequences of centuries of conflict, are distilled into that terrible and powerful tale of ordinary people, little men, forced into choices that never can escape one kind of betrayal or another (the nightmare of history, indeed). And how desolate it must have been to live in a place where the nightmare is never put to an end; where the past recycles itself, not as tragedy, but as irony and farce, a darkness echoing.

For Flann O'Brien/Myles na gCopaleen and Beckett, the answer to the current condition of Ireland might have been, if you don't laugh you will scream. Under the pseudonym Flann O'Brien, Brian O'Nolan published his first novel *At Swim-Two-Birds*, in 1939 (O'Brien, 1939; rpt 1975). And if we are looking for Celtic Spirit, we will certainly find it here, after a very particular fashion of ambiguity. It is a novel of extraordinary brio, and O'Brien's comic achievement is all the more remarkable given the dark atmosphere of those years in Ireland, and indeed in Europe. Early critics were quick to compare O'Brien with Joyce and it is easy to see that O'Brien has learnt certain techniques and ways of working from the Modernist 'father'. There is, as there is in *Ulysses*, a predilection and prodigious talent for mimicry. But while Joyce contains, within the literary imperium that is *Ulysses*, satiric send-ups, ironic renditions of almost every style in the history of the great canon of English literature, O'Brien's codology is less concerned with writing back to the (British) Empire as writing back to Gaelic and Celtic literature – and indeed, to Joyce himself.

There is no doubt that the book exhibits an anxiety of influence, but O'Brien is spry and agile enough to skip out from the shadow and to create a work that is startlingly original from fragments of what are to be called in *An Béal Bocht*, the 'guid books'. And, he goes further than Joyce in forging a bricolage that features both high art and popular art. You get everything in this wee 'manuscript': comic book escapades, extracts from reference books, lumps out of *Buile Suibhne* (O'Brien lifting and recycling staves from the MA thesis of one Brian O'Nolan), pastiches of the new 'aesthetic' novels, racing tips, catalogues of outrageous plenitude recycled from Fenian literature and stunning reproductions of Dublin dialect. There is just about every class of a character in this novel from Finn MacCool to the Ringsend Cowboys, from a debonair devil called the Pooka McPhellimey to an uncle who works in the Guinness Brewery, from the denizens of Dublin digs to a cow who ends up in court. Ah yes, and loads and loads of authors and storytellers. Does this bricolage work, or is it another ersatz dog's breakfast? Of course it works. And why? Well, there are a number of reasons. One is that O'Brien is not only an enormously talented mimic, able to exaggerate his references to the point of comic absurdity. And this talent for mimicry is, as Homi Bhabha points out, a feature of the experience of people in a colonial situation (Bhabha, 1994). The colonised will strive, in order to survive, to learn the language, the culture and the mores of those who are in control. At the same time, the potential for the mimicry to be subversive is apparent. We have seen this already in the Gaelic poets of post-Plantation Ireland and indeed in Joyce. This is not confined to a colonial paradigm – just consider any 'office' in the modern world. Perhaps it is simply the defence of those who feel powerless, an impulse to mimic the language (especially official jargon) and mores of those in power, but also a mischievous impulse to send it up, to think against what you are saying, pleasingly, reassuringly reflecting the values of those in power, but, so to speak, from the teeth out.

Another reason the book works is that there is a kind of Celtic largesse about the range of O'Brien's satiric victims. If we have entered the Age of Irony, then its spirit is truly Catholic. And, almost until the end, it is bright, playful, hugely energetic; Promethean. Celtic shape-changing has nothing on this, though it is built, of course, on a Celtic comic tradition where exaggeration and grotesquerie and fantasy are the absolute order of the day. And so, another reason why the book works is that O'Brien simply unmoors himself from any prevailing requirement for realism. While *At Swim* is built on Irish cultural history, it is by no means untrammelled by its more nightmarish determinism. The very experimentalism of the book enables it to fight free of constraint. A good book should have as many as three openings. An author should grant his characters freedom; they have the right to self-determination and a decent standard of living – perhaps like Ireland itself.

The narrator announces early on that all novels are shams, wherein the reader is expected to believe in a set of wholly insubstantial 'people'. However, if we accept that the novel should be a self-evident sham, then that liberates both writer and reader into a world where, knowing that everything is only pretend, anything can happen. If Ireland cannot or will not be free, then her imagination can. So, ironically, the *licensed premises* of the novel (the assertion that characters really do not have any freedom because they are not real people), opens the bar, so to speak, for the creation of a set of characters who spend their time contriving to keep their authors asleep or distracted so that they can get on with their ordinary or extraordinary lives. For the author is despotic – a dictator – whose aim is to control his characters. Now, of course, ironically, it cannot be otherwise for the author must be so a god, hovering above his handiwork, as Joyce has it.

But O'Brien, like many writers of his generation, was deeply suspicious of the godlike artist, detached, remote. So O'Brien becomes a kind of satanic force, challenging by satire and irony the dangerous apostasy of the artist. And O'Brien also emphasises in this novel what many of his own generation highlighted too – the sense of post-Partition Ireland culture as itself being a sham, a fake, a dog's breakfast. So, paradoxically, his sham novel actually challenges that fakery, that post-colonial tendency to mimic the old regime, just as in times of colonisation, the individual is often forced into a double betrayal – trying to mimic the new and dominant culture so as to be accepted by it and at the same time, subversively mocking it. Riveness may produce its own quite extraordinary imaginative harvest. So, O'Brien's irony, like Swift's and Carleton's and like the snow at the end of Joyce's 'The Dead', spreads over all. But that irony is also, paradoxically, often unironic as it embodies itself in the characters themselves. While Finn MacCool may be reduced to Mr Storybook, he nonetheless commands sympathy, not only for the diminution of his canonical status, but for the tales he is fit to tell. From

MacCool we get to Sweeney and who could not but be moved by his anguished staves. On the other hand, we cannot help but cheer the ballads of Jem-by-God-Casey, the working man's poet, with their stoic cheerfulness. And, do we not, just a wee bit, feel our own arm stretching to lasso a 'baste' in the middle of Dublin with the Ringsend Cowboys; an hilarious ironic recycling of *The Cattle Raid of Cooley*. And this was the era of the cowboy movies – and also, it might be remembered, an era when the majority of people lived on farms, where the actual difficulties of 'capping' cattle would have been only too well known. If the readership was mainly urban, it contained many living in digs up from the country, farmer's sons, who would have relished both the modern cowboy movies and the delicious spectacle of the rural intruding anarchically into the urban, with the city boys wholly unable to manage cattle. Old world, new world; rural Ireland and the new urban Ireland in comic confrontation. Notably, the least sympathetic characters are the authors.

And there is something else here. It may be that O'Brien rather nudges us towards identification with characters over authors, and more specifically, exponents of the tradition of storytelling and ballad-making. What is going on there? Jem-by-god-Casey offers as good a proclamation as any when he asserts that the voice is number one. Now, when we look back over our shoulder to what we have discussed in previous chapters, we may hear a certain familiar note here. O'Brien fits perfectly, and fundamentally, with the Celtic Spirit in literature, because he makes a policy of opposing voice to print; and the voice for him is always superior; or rather, to be precise (in that Ulster manner recommended by Kavanagh) voices.

We talked about what happened in the 'encounter' between the Celtic Druidic and bardic order and the Christian clerics. The Christians brought writing, and with that, privacy, introspection and maybe even the beginnings of that cast of

BRONZE STATUE OF SWEENEY

Changing forms: The bronze statue of Sweeney made by Holger C. Lönze which stands in the Visitor Centre at Oxford island near Lurgan, County Armagh. Sweeney, King of Dál nAriadne in Ulster, insulted St Ronan who turned him into an outcasted figure, caught between human and bird form. He also put madness upon him. The area around Lurgan is associated with St Ronan and Sweeney.

mind which led to the Reformation itself, with its central emphasis on individual conscience. But, the greatest works of literature to come out of Ireland as a result of the arrival of writing, manage, somehow, to retain an oral quality. Whether this be that the clerics increasingly understood that they were dealing between contrasting and maybe even oppositional modes of apprehension and modes of expression, we will never know. That there was conflict and competition as well as harmony between the old order and the new, there can be no doubt, and if we are looking for a symbol of the opposition of voice to print, we will likely do well enough with Mad Sweeney. Let us not forget that his act of defiance was to hurl St Moling's psalter into the river. It is surely no accident that O'Brien recycles Sweeney, not just because he was handy (O'Nolan's MA thesis to hand), but because he is the artist outcast on the one hand (and thus part of an international tradition) but also an oral composer, who will run up a stave no matter how unpromising and undignified his milieu may be. Far from the court where he would have been central and comfortable, he valiantly cries out his songs in the arctic desolation of winter, blackthorn pricking through his feathers. But, he removes himself from the world and retires into his imagination (a Proustian artist, ironically too), only to frame a set of melodious staves with which to entertain the company. He does not always manage to entertain them, and his voice must give way, secede, to the perfect banality of Dublin Digs dialect. For Lamont and Furriskey and Shanahan are storytellers too. And, for all their espousal and defence of the ordinary, they cannot resist pretending to be cowboys. They too are 'arrested', took up for 'horseplay'. And yes, a cow lands up in court also, her honour in danger of besmirchment. Comely maidens, how are ye.

And yet, of course, we are reading, in the dubiously rendered 'privacy of the bedroom'. The only way we can access this pantheon is through a *written* form. And *At Swim* is also an intensely, outrageously *literary* book too. It is not simply a collection of fragments shored up against the ruin of Celtic civilisation and every alien onslaught upon it, or a set of stupendously copied, mimicked voices, but a complex literary edifice, held together with a vice-like authorial grip. And, in that regard, it is an avant garde, experimental literary artefact, advancing and developing the experimentation of Modernism. That the novel ends in despair, is perhaps inevitable, for such satanic verses cannot be sustained by a modest man.

'All things come together and stand apart.' Either/or and both either and or is a feature of the Celtic Spirit as it negotiates its way through invasions, cultural conquests, more invasions, hyphenation, hybridism, acculturation, difference. How are we perceived outside of this island? Who is it that knows the difference, let us say, between an Ulster Protestant and an Ulster Catholic in Rio or the Gaza Strip?

Complexity of identity, contradiction of identity is a prime concern for another of Brian O'Nolan's masterpieces. Perhaps a small bit of background might be useful. After completing his MA, the young O'Nolan got a job in the civil service, for he had his family to support, his father Michael having died relatively young. He also had a sideline writing a column ('The Cruiskeen Lawn' [The Full Jug]) for *The Irish Times* under the pseudonym, Myles Na gCopaleen (Myles of the Little Ponies). The paper was considered by many of the Plain People of Ireland as a rather West-Brit, Anglo-Irish sort of newspaper. It fell to him, or he fell to reviewing Robin Flower's transcription and translation into English of the oral account of Gaeltacht life got from Tomas Ó Criomthain. Flower was an English scholar of Gaelic. Myles detested Flower's 'opulent' translation and, in double quick time, produced his counter-translation. It was a satiric boutade which translated Flower's translation back into Irish but in so overly literal a fashion as to render

Flower's rendition totally ridiculous. The result was *An Béal Bocht* (Na gCopaleen, 1941). Now, of course, this was most definitely a case of Free State Ireland 'writing back' to the whole Anglo-Irish and foreign influence on the Gaelic Revival. Myles was, of course, fluent in Irish not because he was from the Gaelteacht, but because his father was a member of the Gaelic League as well as a customs officer – and hence part of the ruling elite.

But while the satire may be directed at the fake urban Gaels, emanating from Anglo-Irish and foreign quarters, it is also, with equal if not greater vehemence, directed against the Gaeltacht Gaels. While the Gaels and the 'foreigners' may stand forever apart, they are also involved in a fatal collusion. The Gaels play to the stage-Irish type, courting the gold coins from the gallery. Even the wee pigs can be dressed up to pass as true Gaels for the right money.

The foreigners pay their way into a culture and the gaelgoirs from Dublin cannot wait to organise everybody, conscript them into a new version of colonisation and appropriation. The Mylesian satire is more Swiftean than Horatian; invective replaces the ludic high jinks of *At Swim*. But, when all is said and done, this book is about the tragedy of an identity robbed and the impossibility of ever again achieving any sense of authenticity. For people only reflect on authenticity when they have lost it. At the end of *An Béal Bocht* – a novel also hilarious – the narrator meets his father coming out of the 'jug' as he goes into it. Do they recognise one another? Probably not, for every Gael is dictatorially nominated by the English-speaking, oar-wielding schoolmaster as Jams O'Donnell. One is the same as another. For Myles, the inevitable result is a recursive nightmare of history, where a culture ends up eating its own tail and tale. The inference to be drawn from the book is that the new state, far from presenting a future to counter that history, merely repeats the nightmare

with another fake Gaelic identity. It is another form of con-
scription and oppression in which the individual is condemned
to be always blurred out of the equation, his voice so
compromised by the demands of one hegemony or another
that it becomes either rote mimicry or incomprehensible
gibberish, spirit quashed, job done.

The book also contains a terrific satire on immram literature. As with *At Swim*, Gaelic and Celtic literature are subjected
to an ironic recycling. Yet the further irony is that, while
O'Nolan seems to imply that a corpus of literature once
deemed to be of high value is now, in the new dispensation,
debased, ridiculous, in his recycling of that material he is also,
of course, keeping it alive, countermanding the damage done
to that literature by all sides, historically and in the present.

Another more straightforwardly ironic recycling of Celtic
and Gaelic material is present in Beckett's *Murphy* (Beckett,
1938; rpt 1973). Beckett, like O'Brien, is an experimenter in an
age of realism. He is also, by the ironic by, greatly indebted to
Yeats for the stripping of the stage to bare elements and
marginal figures. *Murphy*, on the face of it, is a realist story, but
it soon moves, in the face of its central protagonist into more
or less florid madness. The more Murphy becomes Murphy,
the less is Celia allowed to be. But it is Celia who remains,
survives, at the end of the novel, when all is 'all out'. Celia is,
arguably, the greatest heroine of twentieth-century literature,
except maybe Toni Morrison's Beloved.

Murphy's attitude to Ireland is supremely disinterested.
This is most refreshing after so much 'Party feeling'. However,
he is pursued by an often staggeringly articulate motley of
tympanours from his native land, about whose presence and
intentions he is supremely unaware, being as he is a seedy
solipsist. Nonetheless, his locutions are distinctly, if subtly,
Irish: 'look is there a clean shirt' (S. Beckett, 1938; rpt 1957, p.
41). The tympanours find themselves rebellious, after a few

jars, and flown with insolence and drink, converge to mount an attack on the statue of Cúchulainn in the GPO:

'Howlt on there youze,' said the CG [Civic Guard].
Wylie turned back, tapped his forehead and said, as one sane man to another:
'John o Gods. Hundred per cent harmless.' [a mental asylum in Dublin]
'Come back here owthat,' said the CG.
They drew up behind the statue. The CG leaned forward and scrutinised the pillar and draperies.
'Not a feather out of her,' said Wylie (Beckett, 1938; rpt 1957, pp. 28–9).

So we have voice and print again; the oral and the literary, juxtaposed. And, of course, the demolition of gods, authorities, as the case might suit. And the inescapability of the awkward, frayed and endlessly inscribing palimpsest of this island; a manuscript heard as well as read, voices, offstage, off-mission, marginal and curiously universal.

The Great Change
All are agreed, if they are agreed on nothing else, that the 1960s heralded another Great Change. Whether it was for the better or the worse, readers must decide. We have not space here to chart the literature of what we might call contemporary Ireland, never mind account historically for what happened. But, something happened. Like all such somethings, the Great Change of the 1960s was, for most people, pretty gradual, and for a few, pretty radical. But our question is: did the Celtic Spirit survive in some sense? It seems to us, that the answer to that is yes. While it can be argued that literature from this island in the latter half of the twentieth century both continued the nineteenth-century preoccupation with identity as both a personal and a public, political matter, before and during the

CELTIC SPIRIT IN THE TWENTIETH CENTURY
Tuning In: The runes of our time.

Troubles, there is also a kind of reaction to that nexus which returns the literature to a more international plane, and there is also a continuing fascination with place, or, if you will, space.

In poets like Michael Hartnett and John Montague, the Gaelic past is presented as a lost, irretrievable cultural ghost, haunting townlands and familiar places. Here are a few lines from Montague's 'A Lost Tradition':

All around, shards of a lost tradition:
From the Rough Field I went to school
In the Glen of the Hazels. Close by
Was the bishopric of the Golden Stone;
The cairn of Carleton's homesick poem.
Scattered over the hills, tribal
And placenames, uncultivated pearls (Montague, 1972; rpt 1991, p. 1354).

Montague was, of course, literally an internationalist, having been American-born and having lived a life across many countries, and his work has always also engaged with the avant gardes of Europe and America.

In novels written in the 1960s and 1970s we often have the trope of the marginalised artist outcast struggling against a repressive rural or small-town world. We may recall the novels of Edna O'Brien, the short stories of William Trevor, John McGahern's *The Dark*, or Brian Moore's *The Lonely Passion of Judith Hearne* or Patrick McCabe's *Breakfast on Pluto* or Sam Hanna Bell's *December Bride*. Such prose fictions take their cue really from poems like Kavanagh's 'The Great Hunger'. And while, in these novels, there are occasional glimpses of lyrical beauty, the characters are more often than not aliens in their small, enclaved places. Many of the protagonists are artist analogues, or in some obvious way, different and are taken a dim view of by the locals. We have seen one version of this situation before, in our discussion of the situation of the remnantal Gaelic poets. But there are differences: these modern artist analogues are not at all interested in preserving the Celtic Spirit, nor even any model of nationalism. Nor are they, it seems, greatly interested in celebrating the quiet glories of their townlands and parishes and market towns. Generally, they look outwards, desiring escape to the metropolitan, even cosmopolitan world. To put this another way, they conceive of themselves as modern, radical even, and opposed to what they see as a backward-looking and strangulating provincialism. Even in William Trevor's short stories, most starkly 'The Ballroom of Romance', the central character has her dreams of escape.

Yet, there is also, in this period, a revival of the Big House novel. The tone ranges from the elegiac in novels like William Trevor's *Fools of Fortune*, J.G. Farrell's *Troubles* and Jennifer Johnston's *How Many Miles to Babylon?*, to the wryly ironic in John Banville's *The Newton Letter*, to the broadly comic as in Molly Keane's *Good Behaviour*. There were many other forms of writing in this period, with different concerns, but it is a curious irony that the Big House novel was, from its very inception, preoccupied with its own destruction. An interestingly quixotic note is struck by Paul Muldoon in his early poem 'The Big House', in which the Big House is very much alive, that being the point; a chilling insouciance about what happens both inside and outside its walls (Muldoon, 1986, pp. 22–3).

Drama too starts to be inflected with the more experimental, radical spirit of the 1960s, blowing over even the smallest farm from America and London and Paris. We have, most notably, Brian Friel's classic, *Philadephia, Here I Come* (Friel, 1975). While the play's central dramatic tension arises from the conflict in the protagonist between the pull of home and the ache for escape, it is clear that the young man will go, unable to communicate with his father. For since teenagers have now been invented, intergenerational communication has now become important, even in Ireland! Tom Murphy is another playwright who charts the emergence of a new generation, critical of 'the old brigade'. In an excellent article, Paul Murphy, argues convincingly that Tom Murphy occupies a kind of 'post-revisionist position' in recognising that history is always told from a contemporary perspective; the past and the present are thus 'imbricated' (Murphy, 2010, pp. 68–9).

For writers from Northern Ireland, the limitations of a narrow rural world were exacerbated by, for those brought up as Catholic, a sense of inferiority. This is the deeply bruising experience reflected, for example, in Polly Devlin's *All Of Us There*. For Heaney, life in County Derry was marked by a sense of division. The very names of the townlands inscribed territoriality; the language of place itself a sign of political and economic frigidity (Heaney, 1980, p. 20). But, it seems, that Heaney was keen also to confront, in his own way, this division, admiring the work of John Hewitt in his bid for kinship with Ulster Scots poets and an openness to the other (Heaney, 2002, p. 79).

John Hewitt's work bestrides many decades and in this Northern poet we see a very strong preoccupation with cultural and political identity. Hewitt was part of a quiet movement towards regionalism, which attempted to acknowledge the differences between planter and Gael in Northern Ireland, but to seek a kind of rapprochement. His mood is, therefore, much more sanguine than that of MacNeice. He is perhaps also more assertive in his claims of belonging, most notably in 'Once Alien Here'(Hewitt, 1991, p. 386). But there is a generosity, an open-heartedness in Hewitt's tight, circumspect verse. Such a stance of reaching out to 'the other side' was not welcome in all quarters. And while Hewitt's articulation was matched by symbolic political gestures such as the famous meeting of Terence O'Neill and Seán Lemass, respective leaders of the two partitioned states, peace and love did not exactly break out wholesale in Ulster. The young Heaney, following Hewitt, though coming from the 'other side' also wrote poems in the 1960s which betokened a new spirit of thoughtfulness, of a willingness to consider the other, to welcome what was different. The Celtic Spirit had reared its head (or tail) again. Perhaps the island was capable of being, yet again, recreated. If we did not have Amorgen, we had some lads and lasses capable of using their imagination.

And permission seemed to have been granted, if only by a few, for poets to talk about all manner of subjects and to take their own attitude to Ireland. In the work of Michael Longley, for example, we see combined among other things a fealty to classical literature and a rather delicately pastoral conception of the west of Ireland, as evidenced in poems like 'The West' and 'In Mayo' (Longley, 2007). For Longley, there is undoubtedly affection of his 'second home' in the west of Ireland, but also a depiction of the landscape as essentially a retreat, a place to which he escapes from the city of Belfast. While it is no Yeatsian tower, place is thus represented, as it has been for many urban writers of the Celtic Revival, as space. There is no *dinnseanchas* here, no interest in townland names or in the history of the place or the work or culture of the people who live there. Longley walks through that space, observing closely, delicately, the details of nature. Longley is also a naturalist, bringing into poetry from this island the scientific observational techniques of English poets like Ted Hughes. The space could be anywhere. And his poetry exhibits a very wide range of themes, encompassing jazz, other poets and classical themes.

The young Heaney, *incertus*, almost to the last, follows the promptings of those alienated young artist analogues, but cannot ignore, either, the deep claim of his townland. His first collection is titled *Death of a Naturalist*. It is perhaps overly theatrical for a young poet to draw up death in his first annunciation. But perhaps the 'death' is of a gentler or more playful variety. Is Heaney declaring the death in his own work of an impulse towards writing like a naturalist? There is a poem in that collection entitled 'Personal Helicon', dedicated to Michael Longley, which concludes: 'I rhyme to see myself, to set the darkness echoing' (Heaney, 1966, p. 57).

In the first half of the first line the speaker sees, in the shir of the water, a reflection of himself – not, as might seem at first sight, a Romantic narcissist, but a reflection that has a wee bit of an ironic wrinkle to it. Conscious and self-conscious as he is as a young poet of the grandiose import of that proclamation – here's me renouncing any modest claim to be a mere naturalist, charting faithfully, scientifically, a place, now announcing my immense importance, my art of self-expression – he catches his own (Celtic) swishing tail (and tale) with that word 'rhyme'. With that word he puts a stop to his own gallop. He is a mere rhymer, a boy at a horse fair, as flittered as his flittering sheet song; a boy in a pub rosined up with whiskey, casting out of him his unrelieved verses, sounding maybe an especially pious practitioner of *sean nós*, 'like a bee under a tin'. And, behind that, maybe, the rhymer, the *mere* Irish, targeted by the English laws; one of that degenerate banditti of poets, tympanours and balladeers, otherwise known to the locals as bard or *fili* or *ollamh*. And, before the Great Change, commanding, well pleased with himself. As well he might be, being close to the centre of power in the old Gaelic order, if duffed up a bit by the Christian clerics.

What does the second half of the line portend? 'To set the darkness echoing.' Another business entirely, or somehow intricately related? Might it be that the speaker is saying that the function of poetry has something to do with resonance? With the setting up of some kind of echo between the experience, and the imagination of the poet and his listener. His listener; we are back in an oral plane here. The first half of the line presents us with an oddity, a conundrum, for how could a body rhyme to see themselves? Hearing and sight are yoked together in a peculiar and disorienting metaphor. But maybe not so peculiar; mothers in days gone by were not averse to the exasperated imperative: 'Would you be quiet? I cannot hear myself think.' No wonder, with all they had to contend with. But thinking is, when you think about it, a silent thing, so how could you hear yourself? And yet, we do hear, 'into ourselves' in that unspoken realm. There is, as it were, an interior voice, perhaps not invented by the Protestant Reformation and its emphasis on individual conscience and psychological interiority (think of Hamlet), but greatly drawn upon in post-Reformation 'thinking' among us all.

And the only way of getting that interior process, involving doubt, contradiction, philosophical and sometimes theological complexity about the self, is through writing. That introspection will not do at all for an oral culture, which is all about reflecting the whole culture, not just one individual's self-conscious and conscience, response to it. And what does that entail? Inter alia, it entails a separation from the whole culture, a critical intelligence, and, before we know where we are, irony. Now, we know that irony is not a post-Reformation invention; the *fili* and bards were perfectly capable, indeed lethal, in their deployment of it. But the difference it seems here is that the consequence of the Reformation was, so to speak, to make irony personal. And that demands a written form. Or perhaps it is that a written form demands personal irony. Take your pick. The target of the old bardic irony was public figures. There was nothing personal; if you were a bad king, you might have a lovely face and you might make leaf boats for your child, but your public conduct would be subject, unswervingly, to satiric ridicule, irony included.

So when we look at the second half of that line again and we take in the word 'darkness', just as we took in 'rhyme', for the metrical stress falls heavily on these words, we have to consider what it means. The speaker has already set himself up as a poet in the Romantic sense and has ironised that. Now, and conclusively, for these are the last words of the poem, he wants to set something echoing, to leave a trace, a sound on the page, of his own words, but, equally and maybe more so, for the caesura, the midline break, allows not so much emphasis as contradiction. So, the speaker 'turns' from the personal, from self-regard (even ironic) to a contrasting, maybe even conflicting concept of the purpose of his rhyme. What he wants to set echoing is not himself (his own immortality through his words, his rhymes) but 'the darkness'.

And what is this darkness? Is it merely a young man's fancy turned to thoughts of death? Is it merely a modish postmodern bleakness, an existentialist anomie? Or is it some more public, historical darkness? The speaker looks into the well and sees, as you do in a well, a distorted, grotesque reflection. Perhaps that is the face the English saw, coming into Ireland to civilise it. Another unfathomable well with 'Dark Ages' inscribed upon it. We have no wish to put any words in the mouth of Heaney. All I can say is that at the time when he began to write, the perception of many Catholics/nationalists/native Irish of the 'receiving culture' of 'the Province' was that anything Gaelic or Irish was a bit of a darkness, a nothingness, a well a sensible body could drown in. So, in setting the darkness echoing, is Heaney both acknowledging that Catholic perception of how a dominant unionist and British culture would regard his 'world' (replete with irony and thus all tooled up with Protestant interiority, to say nothing of the Great Tradition of English Literature into which he had been schooled), and declaring, quietly, tentatively, that he wants to register, to inscribe, a hidden Ulster, so far not brought to light? And, it may be said, that Ulster is not his alone; it is the place in which his Protestant neighbours live, 'the other side'.

Throughout his long and distinguished career, Heaney struggled with great integrity to articulate his own ambivalence – pulled between his loyalties to his own people, his need to register the other and his own vocation as a poet. Ironically,

Heaney's greatest influence was, according to Bernard O'Donoghue, Wordsworth – the poet of the everyday, of the forgotten and the hidden (O'Donoghue, 2015). Yet, ironically, Heaney achieved a status not unlike that of the ancient bard: he was at the top table, especially internationally; Harvard Professor of Poetry; entertained royally at Oxford; recipient of the Nobel Prize; his words, 'let hope and history rhyme', became a mantra for the Peace Process. And Heaney sat graciously at the top table when Queen Elizabeth came to the 'Free State' in 2011; he who had refused to be described as a British poet. But Queen Elizabeth made more than one significant gesture during that visit too. The ancient Celtic virtue of hospitality did not go unrewarded.

Heaney, in his later work, expanded hugely his own subject matter and armoury of references. *District and Circle* (Heaney, 2006), his penultimate collection, draws in to the orbit Dante, London and poems about people involved in the Troubles in his native Derry. In his last collection, *Human Chain* (Heaney, 2011), there are a number of poems in which Heaney treats of the early Christian scribes. There is in 'Herbal' a quiet summary which very beautifully describes the intimate relationship between the anchorite and the place around him. We must remember, it is not his place in the sense of him owning it, but neither is he a pastoral visitor to it. Interestingly, the poem is set back from any specific Irish quartering, being an homage to Guillevic's 'Herbier de Bretagne'. Guillevic was a well-known French poet of the twentieth century, keen too on rediscovering or recycling Celtic roots. Thus, across time and space, the foreign and the native are somehow fused through literature:

I had my existence. I was there.
Me in place and the place in me (Heaney, 2011, p. 43).

And there is the magnificent sequence, 'Hermit Songs'. These are poems both private and public, personal and political. The sequence negotiates between two worlds, the oral and the written, between two cultures, but quietly asserts both the worth and the cost of speaking forth and writing forth the past and the present tense. The darkness still echoing, but with, maybe, in the finish, some brief eruption of the marvellous, when all is said and done, here, in this place.

Paul Muldoon, in *A Thousand Things Worth Knowing* (Muldoon, 2015), also adverts directly to the milieu of the early Christian Celtic world. In the opening poem, 'Cuthbert and the Otters' (Muldoon, op. cit., pp. 3–12), Muldoon offers a tribute to Heaney; a bold encomium rising well and truly to the occasion. No less will do, of course. The poem is set, off side, as it were, in a Northumbrian monastery, as Muldoon forms his characteristically sheer metaphorical and metaphysical connections. The plainness of the refrain, set against the esoteric character of the poem, is plangent: 'I cannot thole the thought of Seamus Heaney dead' (Muldoon, op. cit.).

In novels of the past ten years or so we have much return to the past, whether it be the recycling of the world of Synge and Sara Algood in Joseph O'Connor's sensitive, almost mesmeric *Ghost Light* (O'Connor, 2011), or we have Carlo Gebler, exposing another hidden Ireland of the past in *The Cure*, a grim tale in which the practice of ancient Celtic folklore unleashes a ghastly set of consequences (Gebler, 1995). In the novels of Colum McCann, especially in *Zoli* and *Dancer*, we have an Irish writer exploring themes of conflicted identity outside and beyond Ireland. And McCann in *This Side of Brightness* (1998) is concerned with otherworlds as strange and grotesque as any to be found in immram literature. And yet, he is a novelist so full of compassion for the outcasted, for the other. Sebastian Barry in *On Canaan's Side* (2011) and Colm Tóibín in *Brooklyn* (2009) have also furnished us stories about

COLMCILLE DIGITAL, NERVE CENTRE

The Celtic Spirit goes digital: Logo from the Nerve Centre's
Digital Book of Kells.

another largely hidden Ireland – stories of migration, emigration, tales of they who left the Shamrock Shore to find, for their own reasons, an entirely different identity, eschewing, in some cases, their connection with Ireland. Thus we have new versions of the immram, new configurations treating of transatlantic and international themes, deploying often experimental forms and merging, almost, with the postmodern diasporic Grand Narrative.

As for the generation to come, reared on technology and those latest incomers, the new Irish – how, if at all, will they relate to the Celtic Spirit in literature? We have the feeling that the Celtic Spirit, despite many dire proclamations of its demise, is living still and will survive us all, in myriad forms. That we may continue to be generous and warm and tart as buttermilk; outrageous and funny and open to the stranger; myopically focused upon the yellow of a bittern; tuned to hearing voices in our natural schizophrenias and tuned, beyond that anxiety, to the jubilance of wild birds, we humbly pray.

References

INTRODUCTION

B. Cunliffe and J. T. Koch (eds) (2012) *Celtic From The West: Alternative Perspectives From Archaeology, Genetics, Language and Literature*. Series: *Celtic Studies Publications*, vol. 15. Oxford: Oxbow Books.

J. Déchelette (1913) *Archeologie Celtique Premier Âge du Fer*. Paris: Auguste Picard.

S. Heaney (2013) *Human Chain*. London: Faber.

P. Jacobsthal (1944) *Early Celtic Art*. Oxford: Clarendon Press.

R. Megaw and V. Megaw (2005) *Early Celtic Art in Britain and Ireland*. Buckinghamshire: Shire Publications.

P. Muldoon (2013) *One Thousand Things Worth Knowing*. London: Faber.

N. D. O'Donoghue (1993) *The Mountain Behind the Mountain: Aspects of the Celtic Tradition*. Edinburgh: T&T Clark.

E. M. Tillyard (1960) *The Elizabethan World Picture*. London: Chatto.

CHAPTER ONE: THE CELTIC QUEST

D. Adam (1989) *Tides and Seasons: Modern Prayers in the Celtic Tradition*. London: SPCK.

I. Bradley (2003) *The Celtic Way*. London: Dartman, Longman and Todd.

B. Cunliffe (2003) *The Celts: A Very Short Introduction*. Oxford: Oxford University Press.

O. Davies and T. O'Loughlin (eds.) (1999) *The Classics of Western Spirituality: Celtic Spirituality*. New York: Paulist Press.

A. Duncan (1992) *The Elements of Celtic Christianity*. Rockport, Mass.: Element Books.

J. S. Eriugena (1681; 1987) *Periphyseon III*. Translated from Latin by J. O'Meara, in *The Division of Nature*. Montreal: Bellarmin.

H. Exley (ed.) (1997) *In Beauty May I Walk*. New York: Exley Publications.

J. Frisén; K. L. Spalding; R. D. Bhardwaj; B. A. Bucholtz; H. Druid (2005) 'Retrospective Birth Dating of Cells in Humans'. *Cell*, 122 (1) pp. 133–43.

A. Gregory (1902; rpt 1996) *Complete Irish Mythology*. London: Bounty Books.

T. Hartmann (2007) *The Last Hours of Ancient Sunlight*. Available at: www.bodhitree.com/lectures (Accessed: 24 July 2015).

M. Heaney (ed.) (1994) *Over Nine Waves: A Book of Irish Legends*. London: Faber and Faber.

G. M. Hopkins (1918; rpt 1995) 'The Grandeur of God', in R. Bridges (ed.) *Poems of Gerard Manly Hopkins*. London: Humphrey Milford.

M. Bachelor (ed.) *Christian Poetry Collection*. Oxford: Lion Publishing.

S. James (1999) *The Atlantic Celts: Ancient People Or Modern Invention?* London: British Museum Press.

M. Jope (1995) 'The Social Implications of Celtic Art', in M. J. Green (ed.) *The Celtic World*, London: Routledge, pp. 376–410.

J. Koch (2014) 'People called Keltoi, The La Tène Style, and Ancient Celtic Languages: The Threefold Celts in the

Light of Geography', in J. M. Wooding (ed.) *The Otherworld Voyage in Early Irish Literature: An Anthology of Criticism*. Dublin: Four Courts Press.

E. Lhuyd (1707) *Archaelogica Britannica, Glossography, Vol 1*. Oxford: Jesus College Oxford. Available at: https://archive.org/details/archaeologiabri00lhuygoog (Accessed: 8 November 2014).

C. J. Moore (ed.) (1992) *Carmina Gadelica: Hymns And Incantations Collected in The Highlands and Islands of Scotland by Alexander Carmichael*. Edinburgh: Floris Books.

J. Moriarty (1999) *Dreamtime*. Dublin: The Lilliput Press.

J. P. Newell (2008) *Christ of the Celts: The Healing of Creation*. San Francisco: J. Wiley & Sons.

J. O'Donohue (2007) *Benedictus: A Book of Blessings*. London: Bantam Press.

N. D. O'Donoghue (1993) *The Mountain Behind the Mountain: Aspects of the Celtic Tradition*. Edinburgh: T & T Clark.

S. Ó Duinn (2000) *Where Three Streams Meet: Celtic Spirituality*. Dublin: The Columba Press.

Oxford University Press (ed.) (2000) *The Church Hymnal*. Oxford: Oxford University Press.

J. C. Prichard (1831) *The Eastern Origin of the Celtic Nations*. London: Houston, Wright and Quaritch.

L. Reynolds (1981) 'The Irish Literary Revival: Preparation and Personalities', in R. O'Driscoll (ed.) *The Celtic Consciousness*. New York: George Braziller, pp. 383–99.

R. Simpson (2001) *Before We Say Goodbye: Preparing For A Good Death*. London: Harper Collins.

D. Thomas (1972) in J. Reeves (ed.) *The Poets' World: An Anthology of English Poetry*. London: Heinemann Educational Books.

R. Van De Weyer (ed.) (1997) *Celtic Prayers*. Carlisle: Hunt and Thorpe.

J. K. Zeuss (1853) *Grammatica Celtica*. Leipzig: Weidmann.

CHAPTER TWO: THE CELTIC SPIRIT AND NATURE

D. Adam (1989) *Tides and Seasons: Modern Prayers in the Celtic Tradition*. London: SPCK.

J. S. Eriugena (1681; 1987) *Periphyseon III*. Translated from Latin by J. O'Meara, in *The Division of Nature*. Montreal: Bellarmin.

H. Exley (ed.) (1997) *In Beauty May I Walk*. New York: Exley Publications.

J. Frisén; K. L. Spalding; R. D. Bhardwaj; B. A. Bucholtz; H. Druid (2005) 'Retrospective Birth Dating of Cells in Humans'. *Cell*, 122(1) pp. 133–43.

A. Gregory (1902; rpt 1996) *Complete Irish Mythology*. London: Bounty Books.

T. Hartmann (2007) *The Last Hours of Ancient Sunlight*. Available at: www.bodhitree.com/lectures (Accessed: 24 July 2015).

M. Heaney (ed.) (1994) *Over Nine Waves: A Book of Irish Legends*. London: Faber and Faber.

G. M. Hopkins (1918; rpt 1995) 'The Grandeur of God', in R. Bridges (ed.) *Poems of Gerard Manly Hopkins*. London: Humphrey Milford.

M. Bachelor (ed.) *Christian Poetry Collection*. Oxford: Lion Publishing.

C. J. Moore (ed.) (1992) *Carmina Gadelica: Hymns And Incantations Collected in The Highlands and Islands of Scotland by Alexander Carmichael*. Edinburgh: Floris Books.

J. Moriarty (1999) *Dreamtime*. Dublin: The Lilliput Press.

S. Ó Duinn (2000) *Where Three Streams Meet: Celtic Spirituality*. Dublin: The Columba Press.

Oxford University Press (ed.) (2000) *The Church Hymnal*. Oxford: Oxford University Press.

D. Thomas (2000) 'The Force that through the Green Fuse Drives the Flower', in W. Davies and R. Maud (eds.) *Dylan Thomas, Collected Poems, 1943–1953*. London: Phoenix.

R. Van De Weyer (ed.) (1997) *Celtic Prayers*. Carlisle: Hunt and Thorpe.

CHAPTER THREE: THE CELTIC SPIRIT: HOSPITALITY AND HEROES

J. Campbell (1991), in D. K. Osbon (ed.) *Reflections on the Art of Living: A Joseph Campbell Companion*. New York: Harper and Collins.

J. Campbell (1949; rpt 2008) *The Hero with a Thousand Faces*. New York: Pantheon Books; California: New World Library.

Joseph Campbell (2011) *The Power of Myth*. New York: Anchor Doubleday.

R. Ferguson (1998) *Chasing the Wild Goose: The Story of the Iona Community*. Glasgow: Wild Goose Publications.

M. Heaney (ed.) (1994) *Over Nine Waves: A Book of Irish Legends*. London: Faber and Faber.

J. P. Newell (2008) *Christ of the Celts: The Healing of Creation*. San Francisco: J. Wiley & Sons.

H. J. M. Nouwen (1994) *The Wounded Healer*. London: Dartman, Longman & Todd.

S. ÓDuinn (2000) *Where Three Streams Meet*. Dublin: The Columba Press.

J. Ortberg (2012) *Who Is This Man? The Unpredictable Impact of the Inescapable Jesus*. Michigan: Zondervan Books.

R. Van De Weyer (1997) *Celtic Prayers*. Carlisle: Hunt and Thorpe.

C. Vogler (1985; rpt 2007) *A Practical Guide to Joseph Campbell's The Hero with a Thousand Faces*. California: Michael Wiese Productions.

CHAPTER FOUR: THE CELTIC SPIRIT: ART AND CREATIVE LIVING

P. Beresford Ellis (1998) *The Celts*. London: Constable and Robinson Ltd.

M. Brennan (1983) *The Stones of Time*. London: Thames and Hudson.

J. Cameron (1995) *The Artist's Way*. London: Pan Books.

J. Campbell (1988) *The Power of Myth* [TV programme]. PBS, 21 June 1988.

B. Cunliffe (2003) *The Celts: A Very Short Introduction*. Oxford: Oxford University Press.

M. Heaney (1994) *Over Nine Waves: A Book of Irish Legends*. London: Faber and Faber.

C. Matthews (1996) *Celtic Devotional*. London: Gill and Macmillan.

C. Matthews (1994) *The Celtic Tradition*. London: Element Books Ltd.

R. Van De Weyer (ed.) (1977) *Celtic Prayers*. Carlisle: Hunt and Thorpe.

CHAPTER FIVE: THE CELTIC SPIRIT AND JOURNEY

N. Hutchinson (2000) *Walk in My Presence*. Chelmsford: Matthew James Publishing.

M. Heaney (1994) *Over Nine Waves: A Book of Irish Legends*. London: Faber and Faber.

J. J. O'Meara (ed.) (1976; rpt 2006) *The Voyage of St Brendan: Journey to the Promised Land*. Gerrards Cross, Bucks: Colin Smythe Ltd.

E. De Waal (1991) *World Made Whole: Rediscovering the Celtic Tradition*. New York: HarperCollins.

T. O. Clancy (2000) 'Subversion at Sea: Style and Intent in the Immrama', in J. Wooding (ed.) *The Otherworld Voyage in Early Irish Literature*. Dublin: Four Courts Press.

P. Anam-Áire (2007) *Celtic Wisdom and Contemporary Living*. Forres: Findhorn Press.

P. Kavanagh (1977) *By Night Unstarred: An Autobiographical Novel*. The Curragh: Goldsmith Press.

S. Maclaine (2001) *The Camino: A Journey of the Spirit*. New York: Atria Books.

P. Coelho (2005) *The Pilgrimage*. London: Harper Collins.

R. Simpson (2014) *Aidan of Lindisfarne: Irish Flame Warms a New World*. New York: Resource Publications.

J. O'Donohue (2007) *Benedictus: A Book of Blessings*. London: Bantam Press.

C. Matthews (1999) *The Celtic Book of the Dead*. London: Connections Book Publishing Ltd.

CHAPTER SIX: THE CELTIC SPIRIT AND THE OTHERWORLD

B. Cunliffe (2010) *Druids: A Very Short Introduction*. Oxford: Oxford University Press.

A. Gregory (1904; rpt 1994) *Complete Irish Mythology*. London: Murray; London: Octopus Publishing Ltd.

R. Van De Weyer (ed.) (1997) *Celtic Prayers*. Carlisle: Hunt and Thorpe.

J. O'Donohue (1997) *Anamcara: Spiritual Wisdom from the Celtic World*. London: Bantam Press.

W.S. Merwin (2003) 'For the Anniversary of my Death', in R. Housden (ed.) *Ten Poems to Change Your Life*. London: Hodder and Stoughton.

R. Simpson (2001) *Before We Say Goodbye: Preparing For A Good Death*. London: HarperCollins.

The Bible (1995) *Holy Bible: New Revised Standard Version*. Oxford: Oxford University Press.

CHAPTER SEVEN: EARLY LITERATURE: EPIC IMAGININGS

O. Bergin (1970) *Irish Bardic Poetry*. Dublin: Institute for Advanced Studies.

E. Burke (1757; rpt 1968) *A Philosophical Enquiry into the Origin of our Ideas of the Sublime and Beautiful*. Dublin: Graisberry and Campbell; J.T. Boulton (ed.) Notre Dame: University of Notre Dame Press.

J.E. Caerwyn Williams (1958; 1992) *The Irish Literary Tradition*. Translated from Welsh by P.K. Ford. Cardiff: University of Wales Press.

J. Carey (2003) 'The Song of Amorogen', in J. Koch and J. Carey (eds.) *The Celtic Heroic Age* (Celtic Studies Publications). Oxford: Oxbow Books, p. 226–71.

J. Carney (1954) 'The Impact of Christianity', in M. Dillon (ed.) *Early Irish Society*. Dublin: Colm O Lochlainn – At the Sign of the Three Candles, for the Cultural Relations Committee, pp. 66–78.

J. Carney (1969) *Early Irish Poetry*. Cork: Mercier Press.

R. Flower (1947; rpt 1978) *The Irish Tradition*. Oxford: Clarendon Press.

D. Greene (1954) 'Early Irish Literature', in M. Dillon (ed.) *Early Irish Society*, pp. 22–35.

P. L. Henry (1966) *The Early English and Celtic Lyric*. London: George Allen and Unwin.

J. Hewitt (1991) 'Once Alien Here', in F. Ormsby (ed.) *The Collected Poems of John Hewitt*. Belfast: Blackstaff Press, pp. 33–4.

P. Mac Cana (1980) *Literature in Irish*. Dublin: Department of Foreign Affairs.

P. Mac Cana (1991) 'Early and Middle Irish Literature', in S. Deane (ed.) *The Field Day Anthology of Irish Writing*, vol. 1. Derry: Field Day Publications, pp. 1–7.

R. A. S. Macalister (ed.) (1938–1956) *Lebor Gabála Érenn: Book of the Taking of Ireland (Part 1–5)*. Dublin: Irish Texts Society.

G. Murphy (1956; rpt 1998) *Early Irish Lyrics*. Dublin: Four Courts Press.

M. Ní Bhrolcháin (2009) *An Introduction to Early Irish Literature*. Dublin: Four Courts Press.

R. Welch (ed.) (1996) *The Oxford Companion to Irish Literature*. Oxford: Clarendon Press.

W. Wordsworth (1807; rpt 1994) *The Collected Poems of William Wordsworth*. London: Wordsworth.

W. B. Yeats (1892; rpt 1994) *Collected Poems of W B Yeats*. London: Wordsworth.

CHAPTER EIGHT: TALES OF THIS WORLD AND THE OTHERWORLD

C. Davies (1995) *Welsh Literature and the Classical Tradition*. Cardiff: University of Wales Press.

E. Hughes (2012) 'W B Yeats'. Unpublished lecture, The Blackbird Bookclub, Open Learning Programme. Queen's University Belfast, 15 October 2012.

H. Glassie (1982) *Passing the Time in Ballyenone: Culture and History of an Ulster Community*. Philadelphia: University of Pennsylvania Press.

J. Hewitt (1991) 'Ulster Names', in F. Ormsby (ed.) *Collected Poems*. Belfast: Blackstaff Press, pp. 386–8.

J. Keats (1816; rpt 1988), in J. Bernard (ed.) *John Keats: The Complete Poems*. London: Penguin.

T. Kilroy (2010) in T. Brown, *The Literature of Ireland: Culture and Criticism*, Cambridge: Cambridge University Press.

P. Mac Cana (1980) *Literature in Irish*. Dublin: Department of Foreign Affairs.

M. Ní Bhrolcháin (2009) *An Introduction to Early Irish Literature*. Dublin: Four Courts Press.

R. Welch (1996) *The Oxford Companion to Irish Literature*. Oxford: Clarendon Press.

CHAPTER NINE: AFTER THE NORMANS: THE GREAT CHANGE

C. Bonner (Undated) 'Dionysiac magic and the Greek Land of Cocaigne'. *Transactions and Proceedings of the American Philological Association*, vol. 41. Available at: jstor.org/stable/282723 (Accessed: 23 July 2015).

W. Carleton (1830) *Traits and Stories of the Irish Peasantry*. Dublin: Curry.

J. E. Caerwyn Williams (1958) Trans. P. Ford (1992) *The Irish Literary Tradition*. Cardiff: University of Wales Press.

S. J. Connolly and A. R. Holmes (2013) 'Popular Culture. 1600–1914', in L. Kennedy and P. Ollernshaw (eds.) *Ulster Since 1600: Politics, Economy and Society*. Oxford: Oxford University Press, pp. 106–120.

A. Harrison (1991) 'Literature in Irish, 1600–1800', in S. Deane (ed.) *The Field Day Anthology of Irish Writing*. Derry: Field Day Publications, vol. 1, pp. 274–326.

C. Dillon (2012) '*An Ghaelig Nua*: English, Irish and the south Ulster Poets and Scribes in the Late Seventeenth and Eighteenth Centuries', in J. Kelly and C. Mac Murchaidh (eds) *Irish and English: Essays on the Irish Linguistic and Cultural Frontier, 1600–1900*. Dublin: Four Courts Press, pp. 141–61.

C. Fabricant (2003) 'Swift the Irishman', in C. Fox (ed.) *The Cambridge Companion to Jonathan Swift*. Cambridge: Cambridge University Press, pp. 48–72.

B. Kennelly (1992) 'Valentine Brown', in S. McMahon and J. O'Donohue (eds.) *Taisce Duan: Treasury of Irish Poems with Translations in English*. Dublin: Poolbeg Press, p. 36.

D. Kiberd (2000) *Irish Classics*. Harvard: Harvard University Press.

R. S. Kieran, (undated) 'Johnston of the Fews'. Available at: www.bbc.co.uk/northernireland/yourplaceandmine/.../forkhill.shtml (Accessed: 12 June 2015).

D. Ó Baoill (Undated) 'Bardic Poetry'. Available at: www.qub.ac.uk/qol/ (Accessed: 5 October 2014).

T. Kinsella and S. Ó Tuama (eds.) (1980) *Duanaire, 1600–1900: Poems of the Dispossessed*. Mountrath, Portlaoise: Dolmen Press.

P. Mac Cana (1980) *Literature in Irish*. Dublin: Department of Foreign Affairs.

R. Mahony (1995) *Jonathan Swift: The Irish Identity*. New Haven, Connecticut: Yale University Press.

V. Mercier (1962) *The Irish Comic Tradition*. Oxford: Oxford University Press.

N. Ní Dhomhnaill (2008) 'Public Access Denied: or The Unrecognized Literary Landscape in Irish', in *The Poet's Chair: The First Nine Years of the Ireland Chair of Poetry*. Dublin: Lilliput Press, pp. 54–72.

M. Nic Eoin (2002) 'Sovereignty and Politics', in A. Bourke (ed.) *Field Day Anthology: Irish Women's Writing and Traditions*, vol 4. Cork: Cork University Press, pp. 273–276.

B. O Buachalla (1996) *Aisling Ghear Na Stiobhartaigh agus an tAos Leinn, 1603–1788*. Dublin: An Clochomar.

J. Ohlmeyer (2012) *Making Ireland English: The Irish Aristocracy in the Seventeenth Century*. New Haven, Connecticut: Yale University Press.

H. Pleij (2001) *Dreaming of Cockaigne: Medieval Fantasies of the Perfect Life*. New York: Columbia University Press.

E. Spenser (1596; rpt 2010–2015) 'A View of the Present State of Ireland'. *Norton Anthology of English Literature* (web Companion). Available at: wwnorton.com/college/english/nael/16century/topic_4/spenview.htm (Accessed: 19 November 2014).

R. Welch (1994) *The Kilcolman Notebook*. Dingle, Kerry: Brandon.

CHAPTER TEN: THE CELTIC SPIRIT: NEW FORMS

M. Arnold (1867; rpt 2008) *The Study of Celtic Literature*.
London: Smith, Elder & Co; rpt *Culture and Anarchy and
Celtic Literature* (Cambridge Scholars Publishing Classic
Texts). Newcastle upon Tyne: Cambridge Scholars
Publishing.

H. Bhabha (1994) *The Location of Culture*. New York:
Routledge.

W. Carleton (1834) *Tales of Ireland*. Dublin: Curry.

A. Carpenter (1991) 'The Shifting Perspective, 1690–1830', in
S. Deane (ed.) *The Field Day Anthology of Irish Writing*, vol.
1. Derry: Field Day Publications, pp. 961–1010.

C. Dillon (2012) '*An Ghaelig nua*: English, Irish and the South
Ulster Poets and Scribes in the Late Seventeenth and
Eighteenth Centuries', in J. Kelly and C. Mac Murchaidh
(eds) *Irish and English: Essays on the Irish Linguistic and
Cultural Frontier, 1600–1900*. Dublin: Four Courts Press,
pp. 141–61.

M. Edgeworth (1800; rpt 1969) *Castle Rackrent*. London: J.
Johnson; rpt Oxford: Oxford University Press.

T. Flanagan (1989) 'Nationalism and the Literary Tradition',
in T. E. Hachey and L. J. McCaffrey (eds) *Perspectives on
Irish Nationalism*. Lexington, Kentucky: University Press of
Kentucky, pp. 61–78.

M. E. Howes (2006) *Colonial Crossings: Figures in Irish Literary
History*. Derry: Field Day Publications.

T. Hurson (1984) *Fictional Strategies in the Novels of Flann
O'Brien*. Unpublished PhD thesis. York University:
Toronto.

J. Joyce (1916; rpt 1969) *A Portrait of the Artist as a Young Man*.
New York: Ben Heubsch; rpt Harmondsworth, Middlesex:
Penguin Books.

J. Joyce (1922; rpt 2010) *Ulysses*. Paris: The Shakespeare Press; London: Wordsworth.

J. Joyce (1939; rpt 2000) *Finnegans Wake*. London: Faber and Faber; London: Penguin.

D. Kiberd and E. Maher (2002) 'John McGahern: Writer, Stylist, Seeker of a Lost World', *Doctrine and Life*, vol. 52, pp. 82–97. Available at: arrow.dit.ie/ittbus (Accessed: 2 July 2015).

P. Mac Cana (1980) *Literature in Irish*. Dublin: Department of Foreign Affairs.

T. Moore (1854) 'Let Erin remember', in *Irish Melodies by Thomas Moore*. London: Longmans, Breen, and Longmans, pp. 20–21.

V. Morrison (1974) 'Who was that Masked Man?', *Veedon Fleece*. California: Warner Bros.

J. Moynahan (1995) *Anglo-Irish: The Literary Imagination in a Hyphenated Culture*. Princeton, New Jersey: Princeton University Press.

S. Mustafa (2002) 'Demythologizing Ireland: Revisionism and the Irish Colonial experience', in G. Hopper and C. Graham (eds) *Irish and Postcolonial Writing*. Basingstoke, Hampshire: Palgrave Macmillan.

P. B. Shelley (1820; rpt 2002) 'Ode to the West Wind', in B. Woodcock (ed.) *The Selected Poetry and Prose of Shelley*. London: Wordsworth, pp. 401–4.

S. Owenson [Lady Morgan] (1806; rpt 2009) *The Wild Irish Girl: A National Tale*. Oxford: Oxford University Press.

E. Somerville and M. Ross (1894; rpt 1999) *The Real Charlotte*. London: Ward and Downey; rpt Nashville, Tennnessee: J. S. Sanders, in association with A. & A. Farmar, Dublin.

B. Stewart (Undated) 'Matthew Arnold' Available at: at: www.ricorso.net/rx/azdata/authors/a/Arnold_M/life.htm (Accessed: 5 May 2014).

B. Stewart (Undated) 'Seamus Deane'. Available at: www.ricorso.net/rx/az-data/authors/d/Deane_S/quots.htm (Accessed: 14 December 2014).

N. Vance (2002) *Irish Literature since 1800*. Oxford: Routledge.

L. Wade (2011) 'Irish Apes: Tactics of De-humanization', *Sociological Images*. Available at: thesocietypages.org/socimages/2011/01/28/irish-apes-tactics-of-de-humanization/ (Accessed: 15 January 2015).

W. B. Yeats (1889; rpt 2011) *Stories from Carleton, with an Introduction by WB Yeats*. London: Scott; rpt Montana: Kessinger Publishing.

W. B. Yeats (1922) *The Trembling of the Veil*. London: T. Werner Laurie.

W. B. Yeats (1949; rpt 2008) *Collected Poems*. London: Macmillan; London: Wordsworth.

CHAPTER ELEVEN: CELTIC SPIRIT IN THE TWENTIETH CENTURY

S. Barry (2011) *On Canaan's Side*. London: Faber and Faber.

S. Beckett (1938; rpt 1973) *Murphy*. Oxon: Routledge; London: Picador.

H. Bloom (1973) *The Anxiety of Influence: A Theory of Poetry*. Oxon: Oxford University Press.

B. Friel (1975) *Philadelphia, Here I Come*. London: Faber and Faber.

C. Gebler (1995) *The Cure*. London: Abacus.

S. Heaney (1966) *Death of a Naturalist*. London: Faber and

Faber.

S. Heaney (1980) *Preoccupations: Selected Prose, 1968–1978*. London: Faber and Faber.

S. Heaney (2002) 'Seamus Heaney', in J. Brown (ed.) *In the Chair: Interviews with Poets from the North of Ireland*. Cliffs of Moher, Co. Clare: Salmon Publishing.

S. Heaney (2006) *District and Circle*. London: Faber and Faber.

S. Heaney (2011) *Human Chain*. London: Faber and Faber.

S. Howe (2000) *Ireland and Empire: Colonial Legacies in Irish History and Culture*. Oxford: Oxford University Press.

P. Kavanagh (1943) 'The Twelfth of July', in *Patrick Kavanagh, Uncollected Poems: City Commentary*. Available at: www.jstor.org/stable/282723?seq=1#page_scan_tab_cont ents (Accessed 26 July 2015).

P. Kavanagh (1964; rpt 1973) *Patrick Kavanagh: Collected Poems*. New York: Devain-Adair; New York: Norton.

M. Longley (2007) *Collected Poems*. London: Jonathan Cape.

L. MacNeice (1966; 1979) 'Autumn Journal', in *Louis MacNeice: Collected Poems*. London: Faber and Faber, rpt in F. Ormbsy (ed.) *Poets from the North of Ireland*. Belfast: Blackstaff Press.

C. McCann (1998) *This Side of Brightness*. New York: Picador.

J. Montague (1972; rpt 1991) 'A Lost Tradition', in *The Rough Field*. Dublin: Dolmen Press; in S. Deane (ed.) *The Field Day Anthology of Irish Literature*, vol. 1. Derry: Field Day Publications, p. 1354.

P. Muldoon (1986) 'The Big House', in *Paul Muldoon, Selected Poems, 1968–1983*. London: Faber, 1986, pp. 22–3.

P. Murphy (2010) 'Tom Murphy and the Syntax of History', in C Murray (ed.) *'Alive in Time': The Enduring Drama of Tom Murphy. New Essays*. Dublin: Carysfort Press, pp. 57–

72.

S. Mustafa (2002) 'Demythologizing Ireland: Revisionism and the Irish Colonial Experience', in G. Hopper and C. Graham *Irish and Postcolonial Writing*. Basingstoke, Hampshire: Palgrave Macmillan, pp. 66–86.

M. Na gCopaleen (1941; rpt 1978) *An Béal Bocht*. Dublin: An Preas Naisunta. Translated from the Irish by P. Power *The Poor Mouth*. London: Hart-Davis, MacGibbon.

F. O'Brien (1939; rpt 1975) *At Swim-Two-Birds*. London: Longmans; Harmondsworth, Middlesex: Penguin.

J. O'Connor (2011) *Ghost Light*. London: Vintage.

B. O'Donoghue (2015) 'Distraction as Inspiration'(The Heaney O'Driscoll Memorial Lecture). Unpublished lecture, John Hewitt Summer School, Armagh, 27 July 2015.

C. Tóibín (2009) *Brooklyn*. New York: Scribner.